Python API Development Fundamentals

Develop a full-stack web application with Python and Flask

Jack Chan

Ray Chung

Jack Huang

Python API Development Fundamentals

Authors: Jack Chan, Ray Chung, and Jack Huang

Technical Reviewer: Amritansh

Managing Editor: Aditya Shah

Acquisitions Editors: Kunal Sawant and Anindya Sil

Production Editor: Salma Patel

Editorial Board: Shubhopriya Banerjee, Bharat Botle, Ewan Buckingham, Megan Carlisle, Mahesh Dhyani, Manasa Kumar, Alex Mazonowicz, Bridget Neale, Dominic Pereira, Shiny Poojary, Abhisekh Rane, Erol Staveley, Ankita Thakur, Nitesh Thakur, and Jonathan Wray.

First Published: November 2019

Production Reference: 1211119

ISBN: 978-1-83898-399-4

Published by Packt Publishing Ltd.

Livery Place, 35 Livery Street

Birmingham B3 2PB, UK

Table of Contents

Summary

Chapter 2: Starting to Build Our Project   35

Chapter 5: Object Serialization with marshmallow   125

Chapter 6: Email Confirmation   161

Chapter 7: Working with Images   181

Chapter 9: Building More Features 227

Chapter 10: Deployment 249

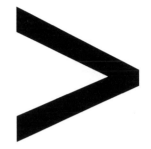

Preface

About

This section briefly introduces the authors, the coverage of this book, the technical skills you'll need to get started, and the hardware and software requirements required to complete all of the included activities and exercises.

About the Book

Python is a flexible language that can be used for much more than just script development. By knowing how the Python RESTful APIs work, you can build a powerful backend for web applications and mobile applications using Python.

You'll take your first steps by building a simple API and learning how the frontend web interface can communicate with the backend. You'll also learn how to serialize and deserialize objects using the marshmallow library. Then, you'll learn how to authenticate and authorize users using Flask-JWT. Apart from all this, you'll also learn how to enhance your APIs by adding useful features, such as email, image upload, searching, and pagination. You'll wrap up the whole book by deploying the APIs to the cloud.

By the end of this book, you'll have the confidence and skill to leverage the power of RESTful APIs and Python to build efficient web applications.

About the Authors

Jack Chan started programming at the age of 10. He was an active participant in worldwide programming contests at university. Since graduation, he has been working in the finance and IT industries for more than 10 years, building systems that analyze millions of transactions and positions to spot suspicious activity. He has leveraged the powerful analytical Python libraries to perform data analysis and performance optimization for a trading system that works at a microsecond level. He has an in-depth knowledge of the modern software development life cycle, which uses automated testing, continuous integration, and agile methodologies. Among all programming languages, he found Python to be the most expressive and powerful. He has created courses and taught students all over the world, using Python as the teaching language. Inspiring aspiring developers to take on the software engineering career path has always been Jack's goal.

Ray Chung is a developer and an instructor. He loves helping students learn to code and master software development. He is now self-employed and develops web applications, network applications, and chatbots using Python. The first program he sold was a network application that helped clients to configure, maintain and test thousands of multi-vendor network devices. He's experienced with big projects such as a Marathon's online registration system, rental car management systems, and more. He has worked extensively with Google App Engine, PostgreSQL, and advanced system architecture design. He has been a self-taught developer for many years and knows the most efficient ways to learn a new skill.

Jack Huang is a programmer with more than 7 years of experience in developing web applications in Python, Javascript, and .NET. He is skilled in web frameworks such as Flask, Django, and Vue, as well as in PostgreSQL, DynamoDB, MongoDB, RabbitMQ, Redis, Elasticsearch, RESTful API design, payment processing, system architecture design, database design, and Unix systems. He has written applications for an accessories shop platform, an ERP system, a divination web application, a podcast platform, a job search service, a blog system, a salon reservation system, an e-commerce service, and more. He also has experience in handling large amounts of data and optimizing payment processing. He is an expert web application developer who loves coding and is constantly following the newest technology.

Learning Objectives

By the end of this book, you will be able to:

- Understand the concept of a RESTful API
- Build a RESTful API using Flask and the Flask-Restful extension
- Manipulate a database using Flask-SQLAlchemy and Flask-Migrate
- Send out plaintext and HTML format emails using the Mailgun API
- Implement a pagination function using Flask-SQLAlchemy
- Use caching to improve API performance and efficiently obtain the latest information
- Deploy an application to Heroku and test it using Postman

Audience

This book is ideal for aspiring software developers who have a basic-to-intermediate knowledge of Python programming and who want to develop web applications using Python. Knowledge of how web applications work will be beneficial, but is not essential.

Approach

This book takes the learning-by-doing approach to explain concepts to you. You'll build a real-life web application by implementing each concept that you learn in theory. This way, you'll reinforce your new skill.

Hardware Requirements

For the optimal experience, we recommend the following hardware configuration:

- Processor: Intel Core i5 or equivalent

- Memory: 4 GB RAM (8 GB preferred)

- Storage: 35 GB available space

Software Requirements

We also recommend that you have the following software installed in advance:

- OS: Windows 7 SP1 64-bit, Windows 8.1 64-bit or Windows 10 64-bit, Ubuntu Linux, or the latest version of OS X

- Browser: Google Chrome/Mozilla Firefox (the latest version)

- Python 3.4+ (the latest version is Python 3.8: from `https://python.org`)

- Pycharm

- Postman

- Postgres Database

Conventions

Code words in the text, database table names, folder names, filenames, file extensions, pathnames, dummy URLs, user input, and Twitter handles are shown as follows:

"Next, we will work on the **create_recipe** function, which creates a recipe in memory. Use the **/recipes** route to trigger the **create_recipe** function and the **methods = [POST]** argument to specify that the route decorator will only respond to POST requests."

New terms and important words are shown in bold. Words that you see on screen, for example, in menus or dialog boxes, appear in the text like this: " Then, select **Definition** and set the password. Click **Save**".

A block of code is set as follows:

```
if not recipe:
        return jsonify({'message': 'recipe not found'}), HTTPStatus.NOT_
FOUND
```

Installation and Setup

Before we can do awesome things with data, we need to be prepared with the most productive environment. In this short section, we will see how to do that.

Installing Python

Go to https://www.python.org/downloads/ and follow the instructions specific to your platform.

Installing Pycharm Community Edition

Go to https://www.jetbrains.com/pycharm/download/ and follow the instructions specific to your platform.

Installing Postman

Go to https://www.getpostman.com/downloads/ and follow the instructions specific to your platform.

Installing Postgres Database

We are going to install Postgres on our local machine:

1. Go to http://www.postgresql.org and click **Download** for the download page.

2. Select macOS or Windows, depending on your operation system.

3. Under **Interactive installer by EnterpriseDB**, download the latest version of the installer. The installer contains PostgreSQL as well as pgAdmin, which is a graphical tool for managing and developing your databases.

4. Install Postgres version 11.4. Follow the on-screen instructions to install Postgres and set the password.

5. Once you are done with the installation, you will be brought to pgAdmin. Please set up a pgAdmin password.

Additional Resources

The code bundle for this book is also hosted on GitHub at https://github.com/TrainingByPackt/Python-API-Development-Fundamentals. We also have other code bundles from our rich catalog of courses and videos available at https://github.com/PacktPublishing/. Check them out!

Your First Step

Learning Objectives

By the end of this chapter, you will be able to:

- Replicate the concepts of RESTful API
- Describe the meaning of different HTTP methods and statuses
- Get hands-on experience on PyCharm IDE
- Build a RESTful API and execute CRUD using Flask
- Use JSON messages to communicate with the APIs
- Test API endpoints using Postman and httpie/curl command-line tools

This chapter introduces API and explains the concepts of web services, API and REST.

Introduction

We are in the internet era, a world where everything is connected. Data flows seamlessly from one place to another. We can get all the information in the world with a few clicks on a website. Take Skyscanner as an example, we just need to put in the date and location of our trips, and it can find us the cheapest flight in a split second; the hero behind the scenes that provides this data is API.

In this chapter, you will learn what a web service, an API, and REST are. We will start by teaching the fundamental concepts of APIs. Then we will look at real-life examples of how different web services (Google, Facebook, and so on) use the REST API.

Finally, we will develop our first simple Python RESTful API using Python. Python is a popular and powerful programming language. Apart from its extensive use in the realm of artificial intelligence, it is also widely used in web application development, big data analysis, web scraping, and process automation. What makes Python excel in so many areas is the extensive number of frameworks available. The frameworks do all the heavy lifting jobs and that allows the developers to focus on the actual application design and development.

In this chapter, you will see how data is encoded and communicated between the frontend and the backend. You will learn technical details about the JSON format, the HTTP protocol, HTTP status codes, and so on. All the development work will be verified and tested using Postman and httpie/curl. We will take you through the whole process of web application development. Not only will you learn the essential aspects of developing a RESTful API, but you will also learn about the thinking process, design, development, testing, and even deployment. This is a journey of learning the complete software development life cycle. Let's embark on our exciting journey now!

Understanding API

API stands for application programming interface; it is an interface for the website (or mobile application) to communicate with the backend logic. Simply put, it is like a messenger that takes a request from the users and sends the request to the backend system. Once the backend system responds, it will then pass that response to the users. A metaphor for this is a waiter/waitress, who can understand different customers' orders. They will then act as a middleman between the customers and the chefs in the kitchen.

If you were the boss of the restaurant, the key benefit of having a waiter/waitress here between your customer and the kitchen is that the customers will be shielded from seeing your business secrets. They don't need to know how the meal is prepared. They just need to send an order through the waiter/waitress, and they will get the meal they ordered. In this scenario, the waiter acts like the API. The following figure helps illustrate the analogy.

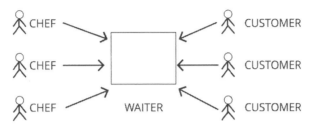

Figure 1.1: The waiter acting as the API for the customer

Similarly, in computer science, one of the key benefits of having API is encapsulation. We encapsulate the logic so that people outside won't be able to see it. With this arrangement, big companies with sensitive information are willing to provide services to the world through APIs, confident that their internal information won't be revealed. Take Skyscanner again as an example. The company is comfortable with using an API to allow customers to book their flights, but at the same time, personal data from other customers that are stored in their internal database won't leak.

An API is also a standard interface that can communicate with different types of frontend Terminals, they can be mobile applications or websites. As long as the frontend is sending the same request to the API, it will get the same result back. If we go back to our metaphor, the waiter/waitress will serve all kinds of customers, regardless of their gender, age, language, and so on.

Now, imagine you are a software engineer at Skyscanner who is responsible for developing an API. What will your job be? Let me tell you. Your job will be to write a program that can take booking requests (date and location) from customers through the website, and then look up matching flights in the Skyscanner database and return the flight details to the customers. Throughout this book, you will be our API engineering intern. We will guide you, step by step, through the process of developing a RESTful API project that can serve the users of your system.

RESTful API

REST stands for Representational State Transfer. It was first defined in Dr. Roy Fielding's dissertation (Architectural Styles and the Design of Network-Based Software Architectures) back in 2000. This dissertation is considered to be the bible in the web domain. REST is not a standard or protocol; it is more like a software architectural style. Many engineers follow this architectural style to build their applications, such as eBay, Facebook, and Google Maps. These web applications serve huge amounts of traffic every second, so you can see that REST really is a scalable architecture style. And when we say RESTful API, we are referring to an API that conforms to the REST constraints/ principles.

REST Constraints/Principles

There are five important constraints/principles for the REST architecture style:

- Client-server: There is an interface between the client and the server. The client and server communicate through this interface and are independent of each other. Either side can be replaced as long as the interface stays the same. Requests always come from the client-side.

- Stateless: There is no concept of state for a request. Every request is considered to be independent and complete. There is no dependence on the previous request nor dependence on a session to maintain the connection status.

- Cacheable: Things are cacheable on the server or client-side to improve performance.

- Layered system: There can be multiple layers in the system, and the goal here is to hide the actual logic/resources. These layers can perform different functions, such as caching and encryption.

- Uniform interface: The interface stays the same. This helps to decouple the client and server logic.

HTTP Protocol

To better understand what REST is and make sure we are implementing the REST style, we can simply talk about the HTTP protocol. HTTP is an implementation of the REST architecture style. It is short for HyperText Transfer Protocol and is the standard protocol used on the worldwide web. We use it every day to browse different websites. That's why all the websites we visit are prefixed with http.

In the HTTP protocol, there are different types of service request methods. Each service request method has a special definition that is specific to it. When the frontend interface interacts with the backend API through a URL, they need to, at the same time, define the HTTP method for this request. Different HTTP methods are like different service counters. For example, reading and creating data are completely different services, so they should be handled by different service counters, meaning different HTTP methods.

- **GET**: For reading data
- **POST**: For creating data
- **PUT**: For updating data by completely replacing data with new content
- **PATCH**: For updating data, but by partially modifying a few attributes
- **DELETE**: For deleting data

Simply put, different HTTP methods are like the verbs for REST API. They are used for performing different actions on the same set of data.

HTTP Methods and CRUD

We can easily build a RESTful API by leveraging what has already been provided by the HTTP protocol. Let's take a look at the HTTP methods that we can use to communicate with the server.

In this book, we will build a recipe sharing platform with a RESTful API as the backend. This platform will allow users to create and share their own recipes. At the same time, users will also be able to read recipes shared by other users. Using this recipe sharing platform as an example, to achieve these functionalities, we will need our API to be able to perform different actions on the recipes. We can leverage different HTTP methods here. For example, we can use the **GET** method to request **http://localhost:5000/recipes** for all the recipes. We can use the **POST** method to request **http://localhost:5000/recipes** to create a new recipe. We can also use the **DELETE** method to request **http://localhost:5000/recipes/20** to delete a recipe with **ID = 20**. Please refer to the following table for details.

HTTP Method	CRUD	Description	Example
GET	Read/Retrieve	Getting a resource	Getting all recipes back http://localhost:5000/recipes
GET	Read /Retrieve	Getting a resource	Getting a recipe with ID = 20 http://localhost:5000/recipes/20
POST	Create	Creating a resource	Adding a recipe http://localhost:5000/recipes
PUT	Update	Updating a resource	Updating a recipe with ID = 20 http://localhost:5000/recipes/20
DELETE	Delete	Deleting a resource	Deleting a recipe with ID = 20 http://localhost:5000/recipes/20

Figure 1.2: HTTP methods

We can see that asking the backend API to work for us is simple. We can simply use the HTTP protocol to communicate our request.

In fact, with this recipe sharing platform, you can see the majority of the actions we require will revolve around CREATE, READ, UPDATE, and DELETE. This is generally true for all other web applications as well. In the developer community, we call this CRUD in short. In a nutshell, CRUD models the life cycle of database record management.

Modeling our web applications this way can help us easily construct a functioning web system, as these actions are related to the HTTP methods. Constructing our application with this architecture is simple, powerful, and highly readable.

As you can probably imagine, we will need to send information to the backend server. For example, you may want to store a recipe in the backend database. You send the recipe over HTTP with a pre-agreed format with the backend. A pre-agreed format can be understood as a language used to communicate with the waiter/waitress in our previous metaphor. In real life, we have different languages, such as English, German, Chinese, and so on. We need to speak the right language for the other side to understand. In the web API domain, there are two prevalent standards, JSON and XML. We will mainly talk about JSON here because it is more readable and widely adopted.

The JSON Format

JavaScript Object Notation (**JSON**) is a simple plaintext format that is capable of representing complex data structures. We can use this format to represent strings, numbers, arrays, and even objects. Once we have the information "JSONified," we can use this widely adopted format to communicate with the API.

We are going to show you what a JSON format file looks like. In the following example, you will see that we are representing two recipes in JSON format. A JSON document is a plaintext document; there is no encryption here. It is so readable that I am sure you can already tell (without further explanation) that there are two recipes here, each with an ID, name, and description.

Here are a few notes on JSON syntax:

- Arrays are enclosed by **[]**
- Objects can be represented by **{}**
- Names/values always exist in pairs, and are delimited by ":"
- Strings are enclosed by ""

Following is a sample code file with JSON syntax:

```
{
  "recipes":[
    {
      "id":1,
      "name":"Egg Salad",
      "description":"Place an egg in a saucepan and..."
    },
    {
      "id":2,
      "name":"Tomato Pasta",
      "description":"Bring a large pot of lightly salted water to a boil..."
    }
  ]
}
```

HTTP Status Codes

An HTTP status code is a code that is returned in the HTTP protocol. It is usually hidden from users, so you probably didn't realize it exists. In fact, every HTTP response from the server contains a status code. And as we construct our RESTful API, we need to comply with the HTTP protocol. The status code helps the frontend client understand the status of their request, that is, whether it is a success or failure. For example, there could be a client request about creating a record in the backend database. In that case, once the database record has been successfully created, the server should return an HTTP status code 201 (Created). If there is an error (such as a syntax error in the JSON document), the server should return an HTTP status code 400 (Bad Request) instead.

Commonly used HTTP Status Codes

Let's discuss some commonly used status codes. They are as follows:

- 200 OK means the request has been successful. The request could be a GET, PUT, or PATCH.

- 201 Created means the POST request has been successful and a record has been created.

- 204 No Content means the DELETE request has been successful.

- 400 Bad Request means there is something wrong with the client request. For example, there is a syntax error in the JSON format.

- 401 Unauthorized means the client request is missing authentication details.

- 403 Forbidden means the requested resource is forbidden.

- 404 Not Found means the requested resource doesn't exist.

Open API

Open API is a third-party API that is open to use. There are plenty of them available out there. Companies are eager to open their APIs to expand their user base but at the same time keep their source code proprietary. These APIs can be accessible by us as well. Let's take a look at some of the APIs from Facebook.

For example, we can use the HTTP GET method to access **https://graph.facebook.com/ {page_id}/feed**, which will give us the feeds on the Facebook page with **ID** = **{page_id}**. We can send an HTTP request using the **POST** method to **https://graph.facebook.com/ {page_id}/feed**, and then we can create a post on the Facebook page with **ID** = **{page_ id}**.

> **Note**
>
> The Facebook fans page API details can be found at https://developers.facebook. com/docs/pages/publishing.

Now, let's look at another internet giant, Google. Google also provides some Gmail APIs that we can use to manage the email labels in our mailbox. Here is a screenshot from the Gmail API documentation:

Method	HTTP request	Description
URIs relative to https://www.googleapis.com/gmail/v1/users, unless otherwise noted		
create	POST /userId/labels	Creates a new label.
delete	DELETE /userId/labels/id	Immediately and permanently deletes the specified label and removes it from any messages and threads that it is applied to.
get	GET /userId/labels/id	Gets the specified label.
list	GET /userId/labels	Lists all labels in the user's mailbox.
patch	PATCH /userId/labels/id	Updates the specified label. This method supports patch semantics.
update	PUT /userId/labels/id	Updates the specified label.

Figure 1.3: Gmail API documentation

> **Note**
>
> The Gmail Label API is available at https://developers.google.com/gmail/api/v1/ reference/.

The Flask Web Framework

Flask is a web framework that we can use to easily build a web application. Web applications usually need some core functionalities, such as interacting with client requests, routing URLs to resources, rendering web pages, and interacting with backend databases. A web application framework such as Flask provides the necessary packages, modules that do the heavy lifting. So, as a developer, we only need to focus on the actual application logic.

There are, of course, other available web frameworks available on the market. One strong competitor of Flask is Django. It is also a Python web framework. The reason why we choose Flask in this book is that Flask is minimalistic. It is regarded as a micro-web-framework that only provides the absolutely essential packages for developers to start with. Because of that, it is easy to learn and is great for beginners.

And later, if we want to build further functions, there is a vast number of Flask extensions. You will see the power of Flask as we progress in this book.

Building a Simple Recipe Management Application

Let's do some simple exercises to test your knowledge. We are going to build a recipe-sharing platform throughout this book, and the API is the interface we expose to the public. We will first define what functions we want to provide and the corresponding URLs. These are the basic functions that we will probably need:

HTTP Methods	Functions	URL examples
GET	Get all the recipes	http://localhost:5000/recipes
GET	Get one particular recipe	http://localhost:5000/recipes/20
POST	Create a recipe	http://localhost:5000/recipes
PUT	Update a recipe	http://localhost:5000/recipes/20
DELETE	Delete a recipe	http://localhost:5000/recipes/20

Figure 1.4: HTTP methods and functions

A typical recipe should have the following attributes

- **ID**: The unique identifier for the recipe
- **Name**: The name of the recipe
- **Description**: The description of the recipe

We are going to build an API that lists all the recipes stored in our system. The API will be designed to return different results with different URLs. For example, **http://localhost:5000/recipes** is going to give us all the recipes stored in our system, while **http://localhost:5000/recipes/20** will give us the recipe with **ID = 20**. Upon successful recipe retrieval, we will also see the HTTP status is set to 200 (OK). This indicates that our request has been successful.

When we create a new recipe, we use the HTTP POST method to query **http://localhost:5000/recipes** with all the necessary parameters to describe our recipe in JSON format. The JSON format is simply a key/value pair. If our request is successful, the recipe will be created in the backend and will return HTTP status 201 (Created). Together with the HTTP status, it will also send the recipe that has just been created in JSON format.

When we update a recipe, we use the HTTP PUT method to send the data to **http://localhost:5000/recipes/20** with all the necessary parameters for the updated recipe in JSON format. If our request is successful, the recipe will be updated in the backend and it will return HTTP status 200 (OK). Together with the HTTP status, it will also send the updated recipe in JSON format.

When we delete a recipe, we can use the HTTP Delete method to send the data to **http://localhost:5000/recipes/20**. This will remove the recipe with **ID = 20**.

Now you know where we are heading to, let's roll up our sleeves and get our hands dirty!

Virtual Environment

It is always recommended for developers to develop their application inside a virtual environment instead of directly on their local environment.

The reason is that virtual environments are independent application development environments. We can create multiple virtual environments on a local machine, and these virtual environments can have their own version of Python, their own packages, their own environment variables, and so on. These virtual environments won't interfere with each other even though they are built on the same local machine.

In the following exercise, we will create a development project in the PyCharm IDE. We will show you how to set up a virtual environment for this project in PyCharm.

Exercise 1: Building Our First Flask Application

We are going to build our first Flask application in this exercise. You will realize how simple it is to build an application along the way. PyCharm is a great **integrated development environment** (**IDE**) with a nice GUI that will make our development process easier. We will learn about the workflow of application development, including the creation of the application project and installing the necessary Python packages:

1. Create a new project in PyCharm with **File > New Project**. Name our project **basic-api**. PyCharm will automatically help us to create a virtual environment for this new project.

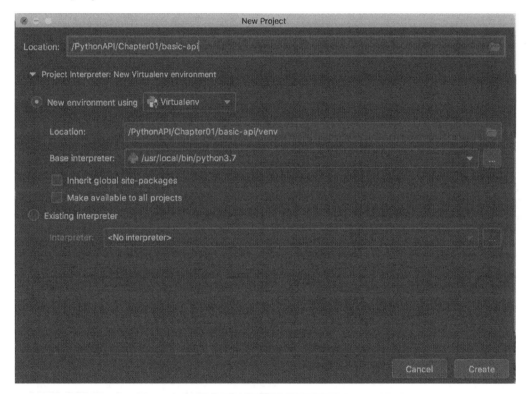

Figure 1.5: Creating a new project

It's a good practice for projects to run on their own assigned independent virtual environments, so these projects can run on different packages and they won't affect each other.

2. Install the necessary packages in our virtual environment. To do that, we can create a file named **requirements.txt** in our project and type in the following text. We want to install **Flask** (version **1.0.3**) and **httpie** (version **1.0.2**):

```
Flask==1.0.3
httpie==1.0.2
```

Following screenshot shows the installation of Flask and httpie in **requirements. txt**:

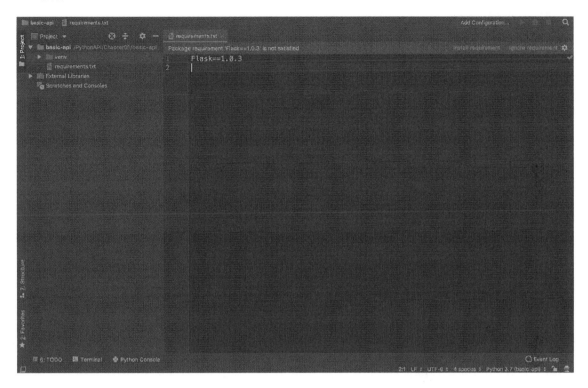

Figure 1.6: Installing Flask and httpie in requirements.txt

PyCharm is going to prompt us on the missing package, as shown in the screenshot. Clicking on **Install requirement** will let PyCharm take care of the installation for us in the virtual environment. Once the installation is done, we can create our first Python file, called **app.py**.

> **Note**
>
> To install the Python packages, we can also run the **pip install -r requirements.txt** command in Terminal. It will yield the same result.
>
> The Flask package that we are installing is a web micro-framework. It is extremely lightweight and allows us to build a web service with just a few lines of code.

3. Let's type in the following code in **app.py**, then *right-click* on the filename of **app.py** in the left panel, and select **run app** to execute our first web service in Flask:

```python
from flask import Flask

app = Flask(__name__)

@app.route("/")
def hello():
    return "Hello World!"

if __name__ == "__main__":
    app.run()
```

What this does is it first imports the Flask package in **app.py**, then it instantiates a **Flask** object, and finally, it assigns it to the **app** variable. We have created the main function as the entry point for our startup script. This subsequently brings up the Flask web server. After that, we have defined our first API function, **hello**, which returns a "**Hello World**" response. Using the Flask decorator, we can route the GET request URL to this function.

4. Now open the browser and type **http://localhost:5000**, You will see the string **Hello World!**. No special format, just plaintext. This means your first web service passed the test, it works!

Figure 1.7: Browser showing Hello World in plaintext

This is a very good start! Though this web service merely returns the plain text string, we can build a lot of stuff on top of that.

I hope you can see how simple it is to build a web service using Flask; it is literally just a few lines of code. In fact, there are more Flask extensions out there that can help us build fancy functions. And be patient, we will talk about that in the subsequent chapters. For now, let's stay simple and get ourselves familiar with Flask first.

For production-grade applications, data is usually stored in a database. We haven't looked at how to interact with the database yet, so for now, we are going to simply store them in memory. Since we are building a recipe sharing platform, we will be creating two recipes in our next exercise, and we'll let them live in the memory.

Exercise 2: Managing Recipes with Flask

In this exercise, we are going to work on our recipe management application with Flask. We will implement functionality to get recipes, to create recipes, and to update recipes. Without further ado, let's get started:

> **Note**
>
> For the complete code, please refer to https://github.com/TrainingByPackt/Python-API-Development-Fundamentals/tree/master/Lesson01/Exercise02.

1. First, clean up **app.py** and start everything all over again, import the packages that we need for this web service from the preceding code:

   ```
   from flask import Flask, jsonify, request
   ```

   The jsonify package here is to convert our Python objects (such as a list) to JSON format. It will also change the content type in our HTTP response to application/json. Simply put, it takes care of the heavy lifting of converting to JSON format for us.

2. Then we import the **HTTPStatus** enum, which includes different HTTP statuses:

   ```
   from http import HTTPStatus
   ```

   For instance, we will have **HTTPStatus.CREATED (201)** and **HTTPStatus.NOT_FOUND (404)**.

3. Create an instance of the **Flask** class

   ```
   app = Flask(__name__)
   ```

4. Define the recipes list. We store two recipes in the list. They are stored in the memory

   ```
   recipes = [
       {
           'id': 1,
           'name': 'Egg Salad',
           'description': 'This is a lovely egg salad recipe.'
       },
       {
           'id': 2, 'name': 'Tomato Pasta',
           'description': 'This is a lovely tomato pasta recipe.'
       }
   ]
   ```

5. Use the route decorator to tell Flask that the **/recipes** route will route to the **get_recipes** function, and the **methods = ['GET']** argument to specify that the route decorator will only respond to GET requests:

```
@app.route('/recipes', methods=['GET'])
def get_recipes():
```

> **Note**
>
> Please note that if we don't specify methods argument, the default will still be only responding to GET requests.

6. After that, use the **jsonify** function to convert the list of recipes to JSON format and respond to the client:

```
return jsonify({'data': recipes})
```

7. After getting a specific recipe, if you only want to retrieve one specific recipe, then use the **/recipes/<int:recipe_id>** route to trigger the **get_recipe(recipe_id)** function.

```
@app.route('/recipes/<int:recipe_id>', methods=['GET'])
```

The syntax **<int:recipe_id>** syntax means the value in the route will be assigned to the integer variable id integer variable and can be used in the function. Our function **get_recipe(recipe_id)** function will then loop through the whole "**recipes**" list and locate the recipe that has the id that we are looking for. If that recipe exists, then we will return it.

8. Take a closer look at our **get_recipe** function. Get the next recipe in the loop by using **recipe = next((recipe for recipe in recipes if recipe['id'] == recipe_id), None)**. Here, the line **for recipe in recipes** iterates through all the recipes in our recipe collection and finds out the recipe with **id = recipe_id**. Once we have found it, we store it in the iterator and retrieve it using the next function. If there is no such recipe with that ID, **None** will be returned:

```
def get_recipe(recipe_id):
    recipe = next((recipe for recipe in recipes if recipe['id'] == recipe_id), None)

    if recipe:
        return jsonify(recipe)

    return jsonify({'message': 'recipe not found'}), HTTPStatus.NOT_FOUND
```

9. Next, we will work on the **create_recipe** function, which creates a recipe in memory. Use the **/recipes** route to the **create_recipe** function and the "**methods = [POST]**" argument to specify that the route decorator will only respond to POST requests:

```
@app.route('/recipes', methods=['POST'])
```

10. After that, use the **request.get_json** method to get the name and description from the client POST request. These two values together with a self-incremented id that we generate will be stored in the recipe (dictionary object) and then appended to our recipes list. At this point in time, the recipe is created and stored:

```
def create_recipe():
    data = request.get_json()

    name = data.get('name')
    description = data.get('description')

    recipe = {
        'id': len(recipes) + 1,
        'name': name,
        'description': description
    }

    recipes.append(recipe)
```

11. Finally, return the recipe that has just been created in JSON format, together with an **HTTP 201 (CREATED)** status. The following code highlights this:

```
    return jsonify(recipe), HTTPStatus.CREATED
```

12. The next part of code is about updating recipes. Again, use the same line of code here, **recipe = next((recipe for recipe in recipes if recipe['id'] == recipe_id), None)** to get the recipe with a specific ID:

```
@app.route('/recipes/<int:recipe_id>', methods=['PUT'])
def update_recipe(recipe_id):
    recipe = next((recipe for recipe in recipes if recipe['id'] == recipe_id), None)
```

13. The next few lines of code say that if we can't find the recipe, we will return a **recipe not found** message in JSON format, together with a **HTTP NOT_FOUND** status:

```
if not recipe:
    return jsonify({'message': 'recipe not found'}), HTTPStatus.NOT_
FOUND
```

14. If we found the recipe, then perform the **recipe.update** function, and put in the new name and description you get from the client request:

```
data = request.get_json()

recipe.update(
    {
        'name': data.get('name'),
        'description': data.get('description')
    }
)
```

15. Finally, we convert the updated recipe to JSON format using the **jsonify** function and return together with a default HTTP status **200 (OK)**. The following code highlights this:

```
return jsonify(recipe)
```

16. The last few lines of code in our program is for starting up the Flask server:

```
if __name__ == '__main__':
    app.run()
```

17. Once the code is done, *right-click* on the **app.py** file and click **run** to start the application. The Flask server will be started up and our application is ready to be tested. The full code looks like this:

```
from flask import Flask, jsonify, request
from http import HTTPStatus

app = Flask(__name__)

recipes = [
    {
        'id': 1,
        'name': 'Egg Salad',
        'description': 'This is a lovely egg salad recipe.'
    },
    {
```

```python
            'id': 2, 'name': 'Tomato Pasta',
            'description': 'This is a lovely tomato pasta recipe.'
    }
]

@app.route('/recipes/', methods=['GET'])
def get_recipes():
    return jsonify({'data': recipes})

@app.route('/recipes/<int:recipe_id>', methods=['GET'])
def get_recipe(recipe_id):
    recipe = next((recipe for recipe in recipes if recipe['id'] == recipe_
id), None)

    if recipe:
        return jsonify(recipe)

    return jsonify({'message': 'recipe not found'}), HTTPStatus.NOT_FOUND

@app.route('/recipes', methods=['POST'])
def create_recipe():
    data = request.get_json()

    name = data.get('name')
    description = data.get('description')

    recipe = {
        'id': len(recipes) + 1,
        'name': name,
        'description': description
    }

    recipes.append(recipe)

    return jsonify(recipe), HTTPStatus.CREATED

@app.route('/recipes/<int:recipe_id>', methods=['PUT'])
def update_recipe(recipe_id):
    recipe = next((recipe for recipe in recipes if recipe['id'] == recipe_
id), None)

    if not recipe:
```

```
            return jsonify({'message': 'recipe not found'}), HTTPStatus.NOT_
    FOUND

        data = request.get_json()

        recipe.update(
            {
                'name': data.get('name'),
                'description': data.get('description')
            }
        )

        return jsonify(recipe)

if __name__ == '__main__':
    app.run()
```

The output is shown in the following screenshot:

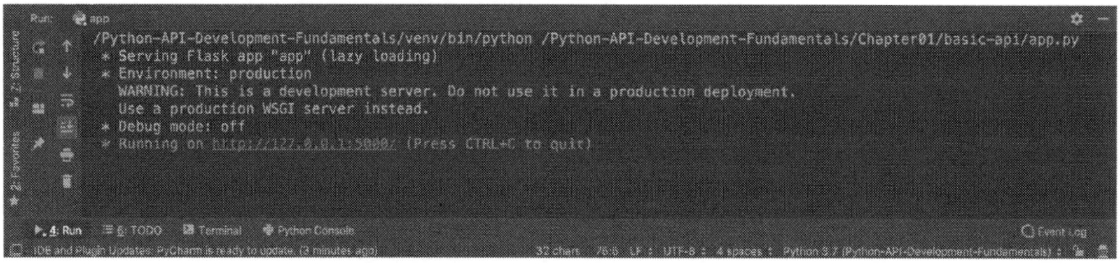

Figure 1.8: The final Flask server

In the following sections, we will show you how to test your web service using curl/ httpie or Postman.

Using curl or httpie to Test All the Endpoints

In this section, we will go through ways to test the API service endpoints in our recipe management application using Command Prompt. Testing is a very important step in application development. This is to ensure the functions we developed are working as expected. We can use curl or httpie, depending on your personal preference. In the subsequent exercise, we will show you both tools.

Curl (or cURL) is a command-line tool that can transfer data using URLs. We can use this tool to send requests to our API endpoints and examine the response. If you are running on macOS, you don't need to install curl. It is pre-installed in the system and you can find it in Terminal. You can also run it in the Terminal in PyCharm. However, if you are running on Windows, you need to download and install it for free from http:// curl.haxx.se/download.html.

Httpie (aych-tee-tee-pie) is another command-line client that does a similar thing. It was built with the goal to improve the communication between the CLI (command-line interface) and the web. It is pretty user-friendly. For more details about httpie, please refer to https://httpie.org/.

We added **httpie==1.0.2** in our requirements.txt previously, so PyCharm should have already installed it for us. The main benefit of having httpie is it will beautifully format the JSON document, making it more readable. And believe me, that will save us a lot of time when we move on to verifying the HTTP response from the server.

Exercise 3: Testing Our API Endpoints with httpie and curl

In this exercise, we are going to use httpie and curl to test our API endpoints. We will test the functions of getting all the recipes back from the server, and also creating/ updating the recipes:

1. We will first open the Terminal in PyCharm. It is located at the bottom of the application. It will look as shown in the following screenshot:

Figure 1.9: PyCharm Terminal

2. Type in the following httpie command to get the recipes from our API endpoint, **http://localhost:5000/recipes**; we will be using the HTTP GET method here:

```
http GET localhost:5000/recipes
```

3. If you prefer to do it the curl way, use the following command instead. Note that we have different parameters here: **-i** is for showing the header in the response and **-X** is for specifying the HTTP method. We will be using **GET** here:

```
curl -i -X GET localhost:5000/recipes
```

> **Note**
>
> The http GET and curl-i -X GET commands basically do the same thing, which is using the HTTP **GET** method to send a request to **http://localhost:5000/ recipes**. If the code that we put in on the server-side is working properly, the request will go through the **/recipes** route and the **get_recipes** function will be invoked. This will then get us all the recipes in JSON format.

Take a look at the response we get. The first few lines in the response are the header. It has the HTTP status **200 OK** and a **Content-Length** of **175** bytes. The **Content-Type** is **application/json** and, in the end, we have the response body in JSON format:

```
HTTP/1.0 200 OK
Content-Length: 175
Content-Type: application/json
Date: Mon, 15 Jul 2019 12:40:44 GMT
Server: Werkzeug/0.15.4 Python/3.7.0

{
    "data": [
        {
            "description": "This is a lovely egg salad recipe.",
            "id": 1,
            "name": "Egg Salad"
        },
        {
            "description": "This is a lovely tomato pasta recipe.",
            "id": 2,
            "name": "Tomato Pasta"
        }
    ]
}
```

4. After that, let's create a recipe. This time, use the HTTP **POST** method, as we have lots of information that cannot be encoded in the URL. Please take a look at the following httpie command:

```
http POST localhost:5000/recipes name="Cheese Pizza" description="This is
a lovely cheese pizza"
```

5. And then following is the curl command. The -H here is to specify the header in the request. Put in **Content-Type: application/json**, as we are going to send over the details of the new recipe in JSON format. The **-d** here is to specify the HTTP **POST** data, which is our new recipe:

```
curl -i -X POST localhost:5000/recipes -H "Content-Type: application/
json" -d '{"name":"Cheese Pizza", "description":"This is a lovely cheese
pizza"}'
```

6. The **@app.route('/recipes', methods=['POST'])** in the backend to catch this client request and invoke the **create_recipe** function. It will get the recipe details from the client request and save it to a list in the application memory. Once the recipe is successfully stored in the memory, it will return an HTTP status of **201 CREATED**, and the new recipe will also be returned in the HTTP response for us to verify:

```
HTTP/1.0 201 CREATED
Content-Length: 77
Content-Type: application/json
Date: Mon, 15 Jul 2019 14:26:11 GMT
Server: Werkzeug/0.15.4 Python/3.7.0

{
    "description": "This is a lovely cheese pizza",
    "id": 3,
    "name": "Cheese Pizza"
}
```

7. Now, get all the recipes again to verify if our previous recipe was really created successfully. We expect to receive three recipes in the response now:

```
http GET localhost:5000/recipes
curl -i -X GET localhost:5000/recipes
```

8. Use either one of the preceding commands. They do the same thing, which is to trigger the `get_recipes` function and get us all the recipes currently stored in the application memory in JSON format.

   In the following response, we can see that the HTTP header is saying OK, and the Content-Length is now slightly longer than our previous response, that is, **252** bytes. This makes sense because we are expecting to see one more recipe in the response. The Content-Type is again **application/json**, with the body storing the recipes in JSON format. Now we can see our new recipe with ID **3**:

```
HTTP/1.0 200 OK
Content-Length: 252
Content-Type: application/json
Date: Tue, 16 Jul 2019 01:55:30 GMT
Server: Werkzeug/0.15.4 Python/3.7.0


{
    "data": [
        {
            "description": "This is a lovely egg salad recipe.",
            "id": 1,
            "name": "Egg Salad"
        },
        {
            "description": "This is a lovely tomato pasta recipe.",
            "id": 2,
            "name": "Tomato Pasta"
        },
        {
            "description": "This is a lovely cheese pizza",
            "id": 3,
            "name": "Cheese Pizza"
        }
    ]
}
```

9. Cool! So far, we are in pretty good shape. Now, test our application by trying to modify the recipe with ID 3. Use the HTTP **PUT** method and send over the modified name and description of the recipe to **localhost:5000/recipes/3**:

```
http PUT localhost:5000/recipes/3 name="Lovely Cheese Pizza"
description="This is a lovely cheese pizza recipe."
```

The following is the curl command. Again, **-H** is to specify the header in the HTTP request, and we are setting that to **"Content-Type: application/json"**; **-d** is to specify that our data should be in JSON format:

```
curl -i -X PUT localhost:5000/recipes/3 -H "Content-Type: application/
json" -d '{"name":"Lovely Cheese Pizza", "description":"This is a lovely
cheese pizza recipe."}'
```

10. If things are working properly, then the client request will be caught by the **@app. route('/recipes/<int:recipe_id>', methods=['PUT'])** route. It will then invoke the **update_recipe(recipe_id)** function to look for the recipe with the passed-in **recipe_id**, update it, and return it. Together with the updated recipe in JSON format, we will also receive the HTTP status of **OK (200)**:

```
HTTP/1.0 200 OK
Content-Length: 92
Content-Type: application/json
Date: Tue, 16 Jul 2019 02:04:57 GMT
Server: Werkzeug/0.15.4 Python/3.7.0

{
    "description": "This is a lovely cheese pizza recipe.",
    "id": 3,
    "name": "Lovely Cheese Pizza"
}
```

11. Alright, all good so far. Now, go on and see if we can get a particular recipe. To do this, send a request to **localhost:5000/recipes/3** to get the recipe with ID **3**, and confirm whether our previous update was successful:

    ```
    http GET localhost:5000/recipes/3
    ```

    We can also use a **curl** command:

    ```
    curl -i -X GET localhost:5000/recipes/3
    ```

12. The application will look for the recipe with the **recipe_id** and return it in JSON format, together with an HTTP status of **200 OK**:

    ```
    HTTP/1.0 200 OK
    Content-Length: 92
    Content-Type: application/json
    Date: Tue, 16 Jul 2019 06:10:49 GMT
    Server: Werkzeug/0.15.4 Python/3.7.0


    {
        "description": "This is a lovely cheese pizza recipe.",
        "id": 3,
        "name": "Lovely Cheese Pizza"
    }
    ```

13. Now, what if we try a recipe ID that we know doesn't exist? How will the application behave? Test it out with the httpie command as follows:

    ```
    http GET localhost:5000/recipes/101
    ```

    Alternatively, use the following **curl** command, which will do the same thing as in the preceding code:

    ```
    curl -i -X GET localhost:5000/recipes/101
    ```

14. Similarly, `@app.route('/recipes/<int:recipe_id>', methods=['GET'])` in the application will catch this client request and try to look for the recipe with ID = 101. The application will return with an HTTP status of **404** and a `message: "recipe not found"` in JSON format:

```
HTTP/1.0 404 NOT FOUND
Content-Length: 31
Content-Type: application/json
Date: Tue, 16 Jul 2019 06:15:31 GMT
Server: Werkzeug/0.15.4 Python/3.7.0


{
    "message": "recipe not found"
}
```

If your application passed the test, congratulations! It is a pretty solid implementation. You can choose to perform more tests by yourself if you want to.

Postman

A Postman is a handy tool for API testing. It has a user-friendly GUI that we can send HTTP requests through. It allows us to send requests with different HTTP methods (that is, GET, POST, PUT, and DELETE) and we can check the response from the server. With this tool, we can easily test our API by sending a client request and checking the HTTP response. We can also save our test cases and group them into different collections.

The Postman GUI

We assume you should have already installed Postman by following the steps in the preface. When you open Postman, you should see the screen shown in the following screenshot. The left-hand side is a navigation panel for you to navigate through your historical or saved requests. In Postman, your requests are going to be organized into collections, which is like a folder in the filesystem. You can put relevant saved requests in the same collection.

The top panel is for you to compose your request. As you have learned from the command-line testing tool, we can have different HTTP verbs (such as GET and PUT). We also need to put in an API endpoint to send the request to. For some requests, you may also need to pass in additional parameters. These can all be done in Postman.

The bottom panel shows the server response:

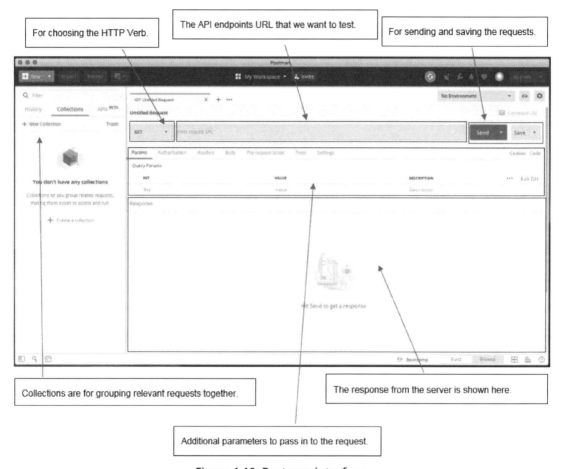

Figure 1.10: Postman interface

Sending a GET Request

Sending a GET request is simple; we just need to fill in the target URL:

1. Select **GET** as our HTTP method in the drop-down list.
2. Enter the request URL (such as **http://localhost:5000/API1**).
3. Click the **Send** button.

Sending a POST Request

Sending a POST request, however, will take a bit more work, because very often, we will put extra data in the request. For example, if you want to send some JSON data to an API endpoint, you can do the following:

1. Select **POST** as our HTTP method in the drop-down list.

2. Enter the request URL (such as **http://localhost:5000/API2**).

3. Select the **Body** Tab. Also, select the "**raw**" radio button.

4. Choose "**JSON (application/json)**" from the right drop-down menu. Put in the JSON data to the Body content area:

    ```
    {
        "key1": "value1",
        "key2": "value2"
    }
    ```

5. Click the **Send** button.

Saving a Request

Very often, you will want to save your request for later use. This saving feature in Postman is particularly useful during regression testing. To save your request, you just need to click the save button, follow the on-screen instructions, and save it in a collection. Then you will see your saved request in the left navigation panel.

> **Note**
>
> You may need to open an account in Postman before you can save the request. Please follow the on-screen instructions accordingly.
>
> If you want to learn more about Postman, click on the "Bootcamp" button at the bottom of Postman. You will see interactive tutorials showing you how to use Postman step-by-step on the screen.

Activity 1: Sending Requests to Our APIs Using Postman

Now that we have learned how to use Postman, we are going to test our application using Postman instead of the curl/httpie command-line testing tools. In this activity, we will be using this tool to test the CRUD functions in our web service:

1. Create a request in Postman and get all the recipes.

2. Use a **POST** request to create a recipe.

3. Create a request to get all the recipes.

4. Send an update request to modify the recipe that we have just created.

5. Send a request to get a specific recipe.

6. Send a request to search for a recipe that doesn't exist.

> **Note**
>
> The solution for this activity can be found on page 286.

If your application passed the test, congratulations! It is a pretty solid implementation.

Exercise 4: Automated Testing Using Postman

In this exercise, we would like to show you how we can use Postman as a powerful automatic testing tool. An automatic testing tool allows us to repeatedly send requests to the APIs, thus achieve testing automation. Postman allows us to do this. We can save historical requests in a collection so that you can reuse the same test cases next time:

1. Hover the cursor over the request; the **Save Request** button will appear:

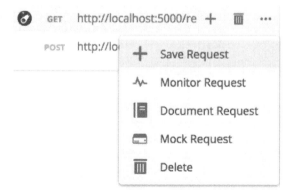

Figure 1.11: Saving the request

2. Click on the Save Request button, and you will see a dialog box popping up, asking for more information. Type in **Get all recipes** for the request name and click on **Create Collection** at the bottom. Then, type in **Basic API** as the collection name and tick to confirm. Click **Save to Basic API**:

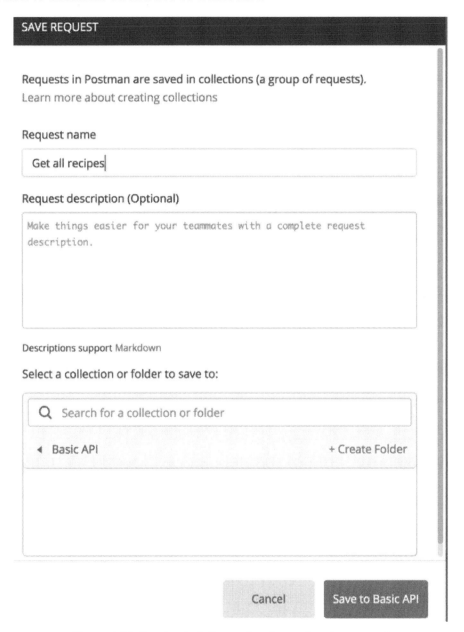

Figure 1.12: Putting in information for saving the request

3. The collection will then be created. Now, save our request to this collection for future use. We can also click on the **Collections** tab to see all the requests in that collection:

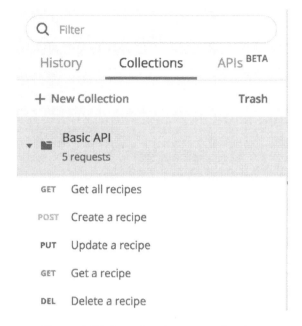

Figure 1.13: Creating the new collection

Now we have a bunch of saved requests in our collection. Next time, if we make any changes in our application, we can rerun these tests to make sure the previously developed APIs are still working fine. This is called regression testing in the developer community. And Postman is a simple yet powerful tool for us to perform such testing.

Activity 2: Implement and Test the delete_recipe Function

Now we have a basic understanding of how to implement the API. We have coded the create and update recipe functions. In this activity, you will implement the `delete_recipe` function yourself.

You have learned about both the command-line and GUI testing tools. You will test the application using these tools after the implementation. This is what you need to do:

1. Implement a **delete_recipe** function in **app.py** that can delete a specific recipe. Create the API endpoint accordingly.

2. Start the application, make it ready for testing.

3. Use httpie or curl to delete the recipe with **ID = 1**.

4. Use Postman to delete the recipe with **ID = 2**.

> **Note**
>
> The solution for this activity can be found on page 291.

Summary

In this chapter, we have built a basic RESTful API using Flask. We did CRUD (Create, Read, Update, Delete) operations on our recipes, and through this, you should have grasped the concepts and fundamentals of APIs. We have also talked about relevant concepts, such as HTTP methods, HTTP status codes, JSON, and routing. We wrapped up the chapter by showing you different ways (command prompt, GUI) to test the web services that we have built.

After laying a good foundation, in the next chapter, we will continue to develop our recipe sharing platform step by step. You will learn the whole process of RESTful API development. Just stay with us, the best is yet to come!

Starting to Build Our Project

Learning Objectives

By the end of this chapter, you will be able to:

- Build a Restful API service efficiently using the Flask-Restful package
- Build an extendable Flask project
- Perform CRUD operations using the model
- Test RESTful APIs using curl, httpie, and Postman

In this chapter, we will start to work on the food recipe-sharing platform and learn how to create a RESTful API application.

Introduction

Now that we've introduced APIs and learned a bit about HTTP and REST, we will work on building an application (the recipe-sharing app known as Smilecook). In this chapter, we aim to kick-start the actual project development. This is a recipe-sharing platform in which users can create accounts and share their own recipes with other users. As you can imagine, it will contain a lot of API endpoints for our users so that they can manage their recipes. We will be using the Flask-RESTful package to efficiently develop our RESTful API.

This chapter will talk about the **CRUD** (**Create, Read, Update, Delete**) of these recipes, as well as how to set the publish status of the recipe.

What is Flask-RESTful?

Flask-RESTful is a Flask extension that allows us to quickly develop RESTful APIs. Compared to the built-in wrapper, `@app.route('/')`, which we discussed in the previous chapter, Flask-RESTful allows us to maintain and structure the API endpoints in a much better and easier way.

In this chapter, we will develop our project using this Flask extension so that you will see how we can structure our endpoints.

Using Flask-RESTful to Develop Our Recipe-Sharing Platform, "Smilecook"

In this book, we are going to develop a recipe-sharing platform called **Smilecook**. Beginning with this chapter, we will start adding functions to it. We believe this approach will help you learn about the key concepts and skills you will need so that you can develop this application and help it reach its full potential, while at the same time helping you understand the entire development workflow.

First, we will build the basic CRUD functions of the recipes. The Flask-RESTful package allows us to structure our code in a more comprehensive way. We will define certain methods in a resource and link them to the endpoints. The flow of a GET request, for example, will be for the request to be sent to the endpoints (`http://localhost:5000/recipes`), which will then be handled by the `GET` method we are going to implement in the resource. This will result in the recipes being returned to us.

Apart from the basic CRUD functions, we will also implement the publish and unpublish functions on these recipes. This can be done through the **PUT** and **DELETE** methods, which can be found in the **RecipePublishResource** class. We will link these two methods to the **http://localhost:5000/recipes/1/publish** endpoint (for the recipe whose *ID = 1*). For details of our endpoint design, please refer to the following table:

HTTP Verb	Description	Methods to handle the request	URL
GET	Gets all the recipes	RecipeListResource.get	http://localhost:5000/recipes
POST	Creates a recipe	RecipeListResource.post	http://localhost:5000/recipes
GET	Gets a recipe	RecipeResource.get	http://localhost:5000/recipes/1
PUT	Updates a recipe	RecipeResource.put	http://localhost:5000/recipes/1
DELETE	Deletes a recipe	RecipeResource.delete	http://localhost:5000/recipes/1
PUT	Sets a recipe to published	RecipePublishResource.put	http://localhost:5000/recipes/1/publish
DELETE	Sets a recipe to draft	RecipePublishResource.delete	http://localhost:5000/recipes/1/publish

Figure 2.1: Details of our endpoint designs

Virtual Environment

PyCharm will help us create a virtual environment. We want to develop our project in its own virtual environment in order to keep it isolated. Due to this, we will have absolute control over the versions of the packages that we are going to use.

The best way to learn is through practice. Let's get our hands dirty now!

Exercise 5: Creating a Development Project in PyCharm

Before you start developing the Python application, you'll need to create a development project in PyCharm. PyCharm manages things using projects. In this exercise, you will learn how to create a new development project in PyCharm called Smilecook. You will also need to install the necessary packages for this project. Let's get started:

1. Create the project and name it **smilecook**:

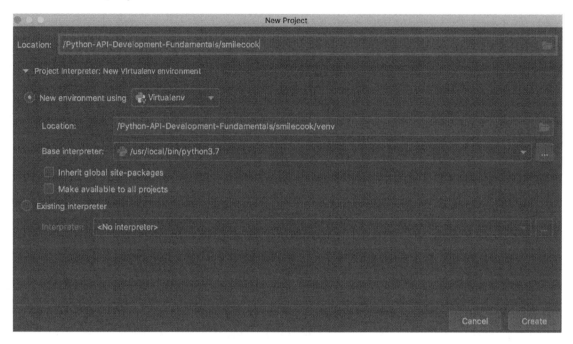

Figure 2.2: Creating a project

2. Check the project structure and ensure that the virtual environment has been created. Once the module has been created, we will be able to see the project's hierarchy on the left-hand side panel. We can see the **venv** folder under the project folder, which was created and activated by PyCharm. Now, when we write code under this project, it will be run in the virtual environment:

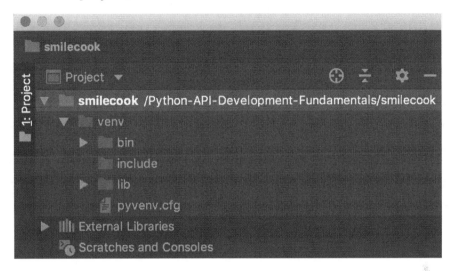

Figure 2.3: Checking the project structure and ensuring that the virtual environment has been created

3. Install the required packages for this chapter. To do this, create a file called `requirements.txt` under our project folder. Type in the following code to specify the packages you want to install:

```
Flask==1.0.3
Flask-RESTful==0.3.7
httpie==1.0.3
```

4. Use the `pip` command to install these packages. After that, in the **Terminal** tab, at the bottom of Pycharm, use the following `pip` command to install the packages that we specified in the `requirements.txt` file:

```
pip install -r requirements.txt
```

5. You should now see something similar in the following screenshot. Here, we can see that the packages are being installed on the virtual environment:

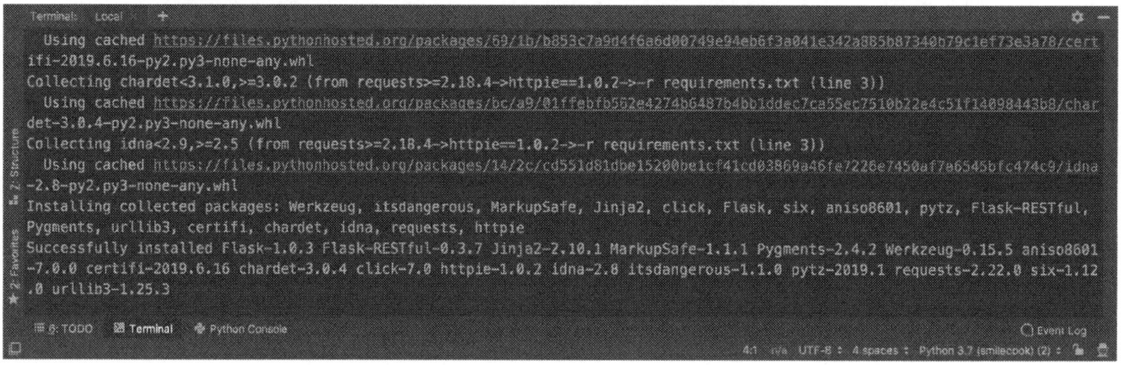

Figure 2.4: Installing the packages on the virtual environment

Congratulations! You have created a PyCharm project for our Smilecook application. This is the first step of you embarking on your journey as a developer!

Creating a Recipe Model

As you can imagine, a recipe may have several attributes. To save every detail of these attributes, we will model the recipe using a class. This recipe class is going to have several essential attributes.

Here is a brief description of the attributes that we will define in the recipe class:

- **name**: The name of the recipe.

- **description**: The description of the recipe.

- **num_of_servings**: The number of servings.

- **cook_time**: The cooking time required. This is an integer whose units are in seconds.

- **directions**: The directions.

- **is_publish**: The publish status of the recipe; the default is draft.

In the next exercise, we will show you how to code the recipe class so that it has these attributes.

Exercise 6: Creating the Recipe Model

In this exercise, we will code the recipe model, step by step. The **recipe** class will contain the attributes that we discussed previously. The code file for this exercise can be found in **Lesson2/Exercise06/models/recipe.py**.

Now, let's create the recipe class:

1. *Right-click* on the project name, that is, Smilecook, and create a **Python Package**. Name it **models**:

Figure 2.5: Creating a Python package and naming it models

2. Then, create a file called **recipe.py** under **models** and type in the following code:

```python
recipe_list = []


def get_last_id():
    if recipe_list:
        last_recipe = recipe_list[-1]
    else:
        return 1
    return last_recipe.id + 1
```

Let's pause for a while and examine the code here. First, we define **recipe_list = []** so that we can store the recipes in the application memory. Then, we define the **get_last_id** function to get the ID of our last recipe. Later, when we create a new recipe, we will use this method to evaluate the last ID in **recipe_list** so that we can come up with a new ID for the new recipe.

3. Define the recipe class using the following code. Type the following code into **recipe.py**, right after the **get_last_id** function that we implemented:

```python
class Recipe:

    def __init__(self, name, description, num_of_servings, cook_time,
    directions):
        self.id = get_last_id()
        self.name = name
        self.description = description
```

```
self.num_of_servings = num_of_servings
self.cook_time = cook_time
self.directions = directions
self.is_publish = False
```

The **Recipe** class has the **__init__** constructor method, which will take in parameters such as **name**, **description**, **num_of_servings**, **cook_time**, and **directions**, and create the recipe object based on that. The ID is self-incremented and **is_publish** is set to **false** by default. This means that, by default, the recipe will be set to draft (not published).

4. In the same **Recipe** class, define the **data** method for returning the data as a dictionary object. You will recall that, in Python, indentation matters. The following code is indented since it is under the **Recipe** class:

```
@property
def data(self):
    return {
        'id': self.id,
        'name': self.name,
        'description': self.description,
        'num_of_servings': self.num_of_servings,
        'cook_time': self.cook_time,
        'directions': self.directions
    }
```

Now that we have built the recipe model, we will go ahead and build the API endpoint using Flask-RESTful.

Resourceful Routing

The main building blocks in Flask-RESTful are resources. Resources are built on top of Flask's pluggable view. The concept of resourceful routing is that we want to structure all the client requests around resources. In our recipe-sharing platform, we are going to group the CRUD actions on a recipe under **RecipeResource**. For publish and unpublish actions, we will group them under a different **RecipePublishResource**. This provides a clear structure that other developers can follow.

The way in which we can implement these resources is simple: we just need to inherit from the **flask_restful.Resource** class and implement the methods that correspond to the HTTP verb inside it.

In the next exercise, we will define three subclasses: one for the collection of recipes, one for a single recipe, and one for publishing the recipe.

Exercise 7: Defining an API Endpoint for the Recipe Model

To build an API endpoint, we need to define a class that inherits from **flask_restful. Resource**. Then, we can declare the get and post methods inside the class. Let's get started:

1. Create a folder called **resources** under the project and then create a file called **recipe.py** under the **resources** folder.

> **Note**
>
> The code file for this can be found in the https://github.com/TrainingByPackt/ Python-API-Development-Fundamentals/tree/master/Lesson02/Exercise07/ resources.

2. Import the necessary packages, classes, and functions using the following code:

```
from flask import request
from flask_restful import Resource
from http import HTTPStatus

from models.recipe import Recipe, recipe_list
```

3. Right after the preceding code import, create the **RecipeListResource** class. This class has **GET** and **POST** methods, which are used to get and create the recipe's resources, respectively. We will finish the get method first:

```
class RecipeListResource(Resource):

    def get(self):

        data = []

        for recipe in recipe_list:
            if recipe.is_publish is True:
                data.append(recipe.data)

        return {'data': data}, HTTPStatus.OK
```

Here, we have created and implemented the **RecipeListResource** class, which inherits from **flask-restful.Resource**. The **get** method that we implemented is for getting all the public recipes back. It does this by declaring a **data** list and getting all the recipes with **is_publish** = **true** in **recipe_list**. These recipes are appended to our **data** list and returned to the users.

4. Add the **post** method. This is used to create the recipe:

```
def post(self):
    data = request.get_json()

    recipe = Recipe(name=data['name'],
                    description=data['description'],
                    num_of_servings=data['num_of_servings'],
                    cook_time=data['cook_time'],
                    directions=data['directions'])

    recipe_list.append(recipe)

    return recipe.data, HTTPStatus.CREATED
```

In this exercise, we have built two methods that handle the GET and POST client requests. The following table summarizes the methods that we have built in this exercise:

HTTP verb	Description	Class and Method	URL
GET	Gets all the recipes	RecipeListResource.get	http://localhost:5000/recipes
POST	Creates a recipe	RecipeListResource.post	http://localhost:5000/recipes

Figure 2.6: Client request methods that we used in this exercise

> **Note**
>
> We have skipped the step to jsonify the object before returning data to the client because Flask-RESTful has already done that for us behind the scenes.
>
> The **post** method that we built in this exercise is for creating a new recipe. It is a **POST** method. It does this by getting the JSON data back from the request using **request.get_json** and then creates the recipe object and stores that in **recipe_list**. Finally, it returns the recipe record with an HTTP status code **201 CREATED**.

Exercise 8: Defining the Recipe Resource

In this exercise, we will define the recipe resource. We are going to use two methods: the get method, for getting back a single recipe; and the put method, for updating the recipe. Let's get started:

1. Define the **RecipeResource** resource and implement the **get** method by using the following sample code:

```
class RecipeResource(Resource):

    def get(self, recipe_id):
        recipe = next((recipe for recipe in recipe_list if recipe.id ==
recipe_id and recipe.is_publish == True), None)

        if recipe is None:
            return {'message': 'recipe not found'}, HTTPStatus.NOT_FOUND

        return recipe.data, HTTPStatus.OK
```

Similarly, **RecipeResource** also inherits from **flask-restful.Resource**. The get method we are implementing here is getting back a single recipe. We do that by searching for **recipe_id** in **recipe_list**. We will only get back those recipes with **is_publish = true**. If no such recipe is found, we will return the message **recipe not found**. Otherwise, we will return the recipe, along with an HTTP status of **200 OK**.

2. Implement the **put** method with the following code:

```
    def put(self, recipe_id):
        data = request.get_json()

        recipe = next((recipe for recipe in recipe_list if recipe.id ==
recipe_id), None)

        if recipe is None:
            return {'message': 'recipe not found'}, HTTPStatus.NOT_FOUND

        recipe.name = data['name']
        recipe.description = data['description']
        recipe.num_of_servings = data['num_of_servings']
        recipe.cook_time = data['cook_time']
        recipe.directions = data['directions']

        return recipe.data, HTTPStatus.OK
```

The second method we've implemented here is **put**. It gets the recipe details from the client request using **request.get_json** and updates the recipe object. Then, it returns the HTTP status code **200 OK** if everything goes well.

Here, we have built two methods for the recipe resources. The **GET** and **PUT** methods are used to handle the corresponding client request. The following table shows the methods that we have built for the **RecipeResource** class in this exercise:

HTTP verb	Description	Class and Method	Example
GET	Gets a recipe	RecipeResource.get	http://localhost:5000/recipes/1
PUT	Updates a recipe	RecipeResource.put	http://localhost:5000/recipes/1

Figure 2.7: Methods that we have built for the RecipeResource class

Exercise 9: Publishing and Unpublishing the Recipes

In the previous exercises, we created the recipe resources and their associated methods. Now, our Smilecook application can read/write actions on recipes. However, at the beginning of this chapter, we said that the recipes can have two Statuses (unpublished and published). This allows the user to continue updating their unpublished recipes before publishing them to the world. In this exercise, we will define the resource for publishing and unpublishing a recipe. Let's get started:

1. Define the **RecipePublic** resource and implement the **put** method that will handle the HTTP PUT request:

```
class RecipePublishResource(Resource):

    def put(self, recipe_id):
        recipe = next((recipe for recipe in recipe_list if recipe.id ==
recipe_id), None)

        if recipe is None:
            return {'message': 'recipe not found'}, HTTPStatus.NOT_FOUND

        recipe.is_publish = True

        return {}, HTTPStatus.NO_CONTENT
```

RecipePublishResource inherits from **flask_restful.Resource**. The **put** method will locate the recipe with the passed-in **recipe_id** and update the **is_publish** status to true. Then, it will return **HTTPStatus.NO_CONTENT**, which shows us that the recipe has been published successfully.

2. Implement the **delete** method, which will handle the HTTP DELETE request:

```python
def delete(self, recipe_id):
    recipe = next((recipe for recipe in recipe_list if recipe.id ==
recipe_id), None)

    if recipe is None:
        return {'message': 'recipe not found'}, HTTPStatus.NOT_FOUND

    recipe.is_publish = False

    return {}, HTTPStatus.NO_CONTENT
```

The **delete** method is the opposite of the **put** method. Instead of setting **is_publish** to **true**, it sets it to **false** in order to unpublish the recipe.

You can also see that we are using these methods in a flexible manner; the **put** method is not necessarily for update, and the **delete** method is not necessarily for removal.

The following table shows all the methods that we have created in this exercise. Now that we have all three resources ready (**RecipeListResource**, **RecipeResource**, and **RecipePublishResource**), we will discuss endpoint configuration:

HTTP verb	Description	Class and Method	URL
PUT	Sets a recipe to published	RecipePublishResource.put	http://localhost:5000/recipes/1/publish
DELETE	Sets a recipe to draft	RecipePublishResource.delete	http://localhost:5000/recipes/1/publish

Figure 2.8: Methods that we used in this exercise

> **Note**
>
> If the client request is with an HTTP verb that has no corresponding handling method in the resource, Flask-RESTful will return the HTTP status code **405 Method Not Allowed**.

Configuring Endpoints

Now that we have defined all our resources, we will set up some endpoints so that users can send requests to them. These endpoints can be accessed by the users and are connected to specific resources. We will be using the **add_resource** method on the API object to specify the URL for these endpoints and route the client HTTP request to our resources.

For example, the **api.add_resource(RecipeListResource, '/recipes')** syntax is used to link the route (relative URL path) to **RecipeListResource** so that HTTP requests will be directed to this resource. Depending on the HTTP verb (for example, **GET**, and **POST**), the request will be handled by the corresponding methods in the resource accordingly.

Exercise 10: Creating the Main Application File

In this exercise, we will create our **app.py** file, which will be our main application file. We will set up Flask and initialize our **flask_restful.API** there. Finally, we will set up the endpoints so that users can send requests to our backend services. Let's get started:

1. Create the **app.py** file under the project folder.

2. Import the necessary classes using the following code:

    ```
    from flask import Flask
    from flask_restful import Api

    from resources.recipe import RecipeListResource, RecipeResource,
    RecipePublishResource
    ```

3. Set up Flask and initialize **flask_restful.API** with our Flask app:

    ```
    app = Flask(__name__)
    api = Api(app)
    ```

4. Add resource routing by passing in the URL so that it will route to our resources. Each resource will have its own HTTP method defined:

```python
api.add_resource(RecipeListResource, '/recipes')
api.add_resource(RecipeResource, '/recipes/<int:recipe_id>')
api.add_resource(RecipePublishResource, '/recipes/<int:recipe_id>/
publish')

if __name__ == '__main__':
    app.run(port=5000, debug=True)
```

> **Note**
>
> In **RecipeListResource**, we have defined the **get** and **post** methods. So, when there is a GET HTTP request to the "/recipes" URL route, it will invoke the **get** method under **RecipeListResource** and get back all the published recipes.

In the preceding code, you will notice that we have used **<int: recipe_id >** in the code. It is there as a placeholder for the recipe ID. When a GET HTTP request has been sent to the **route "/recipes/2"** URL, this will invoke the get method under **RecipeResource** with a parameter, that is, **recipe_id = 2**.

5. Save **app.py** and *right-click* on it to run the application. Flask will then start up and run on the localhost (**127.0.0.1**) at port **5000**:

Figure 2.9: Flask started and running on localhost

Congratulations! You have completed the API endpoint. Now, let's move on to testing. You can either test it in curl/httpie or Postman.

Making HTTP Requests to the Flask API using curl and httpie

Now, we are going to use the **httpie** and **curl** commands to test our API endpoints. We will test the functions for getting all the recipes back from the server and create/ update/delete, publish, and unpublish the recipes. The best way to learn this is to complete a hands-on exercise. Let's get started!

Exercise 11: Testing the Endpoints Using curl and httpie

In this exercise, we are going to use the httpie and curl commands to send requests to the endpoints so that we can create our first recipe. We want you to get comfortable using the httpie and curl command-line testing tool. Let's get started:

1. Open the Terminal in PyCharm and type in the following commands. You can use either the httpie or curl command. The following is the httpie command (**= is for string and := is for non-string**):

   ```
   http POST localhost:5000/recipes name="Cheese Pizza" description="This is
   a lovely cheese pizza" num_of_servings:=2 cook_time:=30 directions="This
   is how you make it"
   ```

   The following is the curl command. The **-H** argument is used to specify the header in the client request. We will set **Content-Type: application/json** as the header here. The **-d** argument is used for HTTP POST data, that is, the recipe in JSON format:

   ```
   curl -i -X POST localhost:5000/recipes -H "Content-Type: application/json"
   -d '{"name":"Cheese Pizza", "description":"This is a lovely cheese pizza",
   "num_of_servings":2, "cook_time":30, "directions":"This is how you make
   it" }'
   ```

2. Examine the response, you should see the following. Carefully examine it, it should be the same recipe as the one that was used in our request in *Step 1*:

   ```
   HTTP/1.0 201 CREATED
   Content-Type: application/json
   Content-Length: 188
   Server: Werkzeug/0.16.0 Python/3.7.0
   Date: Sun, 03 Nov 2019 03:19:00 GMT

   {
       "id": 1,
       "name": "Cheese Pizza",
       "description": "This is a lovely cheese pizza",
   ```

```
        "num_of_servings": 2,
        "cook_time": 30,
        "directions": "This is how you make it"
    }
```

> **Note**
>
> Once the client request has been sent to the server using the HTTP **POST** method, the **post** method in **RecipeResource** will pick up the request and save the recipe in the request to the application memory. The new recipe will be appended in **recipe_list**. Once everything is done, it will return HTTP **201 CREATED** and the newly created recipe in JSON format.

We have successfully created our first recipe on the platform. This recipe is stored on the server-side and we already have the API to retrieve it. Let's continue by creating our second recipe and retrieving all our recipes in one go.

Exercise 12: Testing the Auto-Incremented Recipe ID

Now that we have implemented the auto-incremented ID in our Smilecook application, let's see how it works in practice. In this exercise, we will create the second recipe using the httpie and curl commands. Note that the ID is auto- incremented for our second recipe. Let's get started:

1. Create a second recipe and note that the ID is automatically incremented. Send the following client request using httpie:

   ```
   http POST localhost:5000/recipes name="Tomato Pasta" description="This
   is a lovely tomato pasta recipe" num_of_servings:=3 cook_time:=20
   directions="This is how you make it"
   ```

   Alternatively, send the request using curl. Again, the **-H** argument is used to specify the header in the client request. We will set "**Content-Type: application/json**" as the header here. The **-d** argument is used for HTTP POST data, meaning that the recipe is in JSON format:

   ```
   curl -i -X POST localhost:5000/recipes -H "Content-Type: application/json"
   -d '{"name":"Tomato Pasta", "description":"This is a lovely tomato pasta
   recipe", "num_of_servings":3, "cook_time":20, "directions":"This is how
   you make it"}'
   ```

2. You should see the following response. Examine it carefully, it should be the same recipe as the one that was used in our request in *Step* 1:

```
HTTP/1.0 201 CREATED
Content-Type: application/json
Content-Length: 195
Server: Werkzeug/0.16.0 Python/3.7.0
Date: Sun, 03 Nov 2019 03:23:37 GMT


{
    "id": 2,
    "name": "Tomato Pasta",
    "description": "This is a lovely tomato pasta recipe",
    "num_of_servings": 3,
    "cook_time": 20,
    "directions": "This is how you make it"
}
```

Once the preceding client request has been sent to the server using the HTTP **POST** method, the **post** method in **RecipeResource** will pick up the request and save the recipe in the request to the application memory. The new recipe will be appended in **recipe_list**. This time, the ID will be automatically assigned to 2.

Exercise 13: Getting All the Recipes Back

In this exercise, we will be using the httpie and curl commands to get back all the recipes that we have created. We are doing this to ensure that our recipes are there in the backend server. Let's get started:

1. Retrieve all the recipes by sending the following client request using httpie:

```
http GET localhost:5000/recipes
```

Alternatively, send the following request using curl. The **-i** argument is used to state that we want to see the response header. **-X GET** means that we are sending the client request using the HTTP **GET** method:

```
curl -i -X GET localhost:5000/recipes
```

2. You should see the following response. Please examine it carefully:

```
HTTP/1.0 200 OK
Content-Length: 19
Content-Type: application/json
Date: Sun, 03 Nov 2019 03:24:53 GMT
Server: Werkzeug/0.16.0 Python/3.7.0


{
    "data": []
}
```

Once the preceding client request has been sent to the server using the HTTP GET method, the get method in **RecipeResource** will pick up the request and retrieve all the published recipes from **recipe_list** in the application memory.

> **Note**
>
> We should see an empty list in the HTTP response because all the recipes we have created in the previous steps are in draft form (not published).

Exercise 14: Testing the Recipe Resources

We have already tested the endpoints we built around the recipe resources. In this exercise, we will continue to use the httpie and curl commands to test the recipe publishing API. We can test it by sending requests asking to publish our recipes on the API endpoint. Let's get started:

1. Modify the publish status of the recipe with ID 1. We can send the following client request using the httpie command:

```
http PUT localhost:5000/recipes/1/publish
```

Alternatively, we can use the following curl command:

```
curl -i -X PUT localhost:5000/recipes/1/publish
```

> **Note**
>
> Once the preceding client request has been sent to the server using the HTTP PUT method, the **put** method in **RecipePublishResource** will pick up the request and assign **recipe_id** to be 1. The application will look for the recipe with **ID = 1** and update its publish status to **True**.

2. You should see the following response. Please examine it carefully:

```
HTTP/1.0 204 NO CONTENT
Content-Type: application/json
Date: Sun, 03 Nov 2019 03:25:48 GMT
Server: Werkzeug/0.16.0 Python/3.7.0
```

3. Now, retrieve all the published recipes and examine them. Then, send the following client request using httpie:

```
http GET localhost:5000/recipes
```

Alternatively, send the following request using curl. The **-i** argument is used to say that we want to see the response header. **-X GET** means that we are sending the client request using the HTTP GET method:

```
curl -i -X GET localhost:5000/recipes
```

4. You should see the following response. Please examine it carefully:

```
HTTP/1.0 200 OK
Content-Type: application/json
Content-Length: 276
Server: Werkzeug/0.16.0 Python/3.7.0
Date: Sun, 03 Nov 2019 03:26:43 GMT


{
    "data": [
        {
            "id": 1,
            "name": "Cheese Pizza",
            "description": "This is a lovely cheese pizza",
            "num_of_servings": 2,
            "cook_time": 30,
            "directions": "This is how you make it"
        }
    ]
}
```

Once the preceding client request has been sent to the server using the HTTP **GET** method, the get method in **RecipeResource** will pick up the request and retrieve all the published recipes from **recipe_list** in the application memory. This time, because the recipe with ID 1 has been set to publish, we shall see it in the HTTP response.

Exercise 15: Negative Testing

In the previous exercise, we successfully published our recipe. This is good because it shows us that the APIs that we've developed work. But the whole point of testing is to discover potential issues if any. We can perform so-called negative testing here. This is the process of deliberately testing the scenario with unwanted input. This exercise is going to test a request with an HTTP VERB that has no corresponding method defined in the resource. Let's get started:

1. Send the following request to the server-side. This HTTP method has not been defined; let's see what happens:

    ```
    http DELETE localhost:5000/recipes
    ```

    The following is the curl command, which does the same thing:

    ```
    curl -i -X DELETE localhost:5000/recipes
    ```

2. You should see the following response. Please examine it carefully:

    ```
    HTTP/1.0 405 METHOD NOT ALLOWED
    Content-Type: application/json
    Content-Length: 70
    Allow: POST, GET, HEAD, OPTIONS
    Server: Werkzeug/0.16.0 Python/3.7.0
    Date: Sun, 03 Nov 2019 03:27:37 GMT

    {
        "message": "The method is not allowed for the requested URL."
    }
    ```

    We should see a response with an HTTP status of **405**, which means that the method is not allowed for the requested URL. This makes sense because we have not defined a delete method in **RecipeListResource**.

Negative testing is important. We always want our testing to be more complete and covers more scenarios.

Exercise 16: Modifying the Recipes

In our Smilecook application, authors are allowed to update their recipes. It is like a blogging platform, where the authors can take their time to perfect their work, even after it has been published. Since we have already built the API, we would like to test it using Postman. Let's get started:

1. Use the PUT method to send the request to **localhost:5000/recipes/1**, along with the new recipe details:

   ```
   http PUT localhost:5000/recipes/1 name="Lovely Cheese Pizza"
   description="This is a lovely cheese pizza recipe" num_of_servings:=3
   cook_time:=60 directions="This is how you make it"
   ```

   Alternatively, send the following request using curl. The **-H** argument is used to specify the header in the client request. We will set "**Content-Type: application/json**" as the header here. The **-d** argument is used for HTTP POST data, meaning that the recipe will be in JSON format:

   ```
   curl -i -X PUT localhost:5000/recipes/1 -H "Content-Type: application/
   json" -d '{"name":"Lovely Cheese Pizza", "description":"This is a
   lovely cheese pizza recipe", "num_of_servings":3, "cook_time":60,
   "directions":"This is how you make it"}'
   ```

2. You should see the following response. Please examine it carefully:

   ```
   HTTP/1.0 200 OK
   Content-Type: application/json
   Content-Length: 202
   Server: Werkzeug/0.16.0 Python/3.7.0
   Date: Sun, 03 Nov 2019 03:28:57 GMT

   {
       "id": 1,
       "name": "Lovely Cheese Pizza",
       "description": "This is a lovely cheese pizza recipe",
       "num_of_servings": 3,
       "cook_time": 60,
       "directions": "This is how you make it"
   }
   ```

   Once the preceding client request has been sent to the server using the HTTP PUT method, the **put** method in **RecipeResource** will pick up the request and assign **recipe_id** to be 1. The application will look for the recipe with **id = 1** and update its details with those in the client request. The preceding response shows that the recipe with ID 1 is modified.

We just finished testing another important feature. You have been doing great. Let's keep going!

Exercise 17: Getting Back Specific Recipes with a Certain ID

So far, we have tested getting all the recipes back. But in the real world, a user will want to only get the recipes that they want to see. They can do this by using the recipe ID. This exercise will show you how to get a particular recipe with a certain ID. Let's get started:

1. Send the following client request using httpie:

   ```
   http GET localhost:5000/recipes/1
   ```

   Alternatively, use the following curl command, which does the same thing:

   ```
   curl -i -X GET localhost:5000/recipes/1
   You should see the following response. Please examine it carefully:
   HTTP/1.0 200 OK
   Content-Type: application/json
   Content-Length: 202
   Server: Werkzeug/0.16.0 Python/3.7.0
   Date: Sun, 03 Nov 2019 03:29:59 GMT


   {
       "id": 1,
       "name": "Lovely Cheese Pizza",
       "description": "This is a lovely cheese pizza recipe",
       "num_of_servings": 3,
       "cook_time": 60,
       "directions": "This is how you make it"
   }
   ```

   Once the preceding client request has been sent to the server using the HTTP **GET** method, the get method in **RecipeResource** will pick up the request and assign **recipe_id** to be 1. It will retrieve all the published recipes from **recipe_list** in the application memory with an HTTP status of HTTP **200**.

We have just tested our Smilecook application and confirmed that it can give us back the recipe we want.

Activity 3: Testing the APIs Using Postman

We added quite a few functions in the previous exercise. Now, we need to make sure that they work properly before we move on and develop other functions. In this activity, instead of using httpie/curl, we will be testing our API using Postman. Please follow these high-level steps:

1. Create the first recipe using Postman.

2. Create the second recipe using Postman.

3. Retrieve all the recipes using Postman.

4. Set the recipes to published using Postman.

5. Retrieve all the recipes using Postman again.

6. Modify the recipe using Postman.

7. Get a specific recipe back using Postman.

> **Note**
>
> The solution to this activity can be found on page 293.

Activity 4: Implementing the Delete Recipe Function

In this activity, you will implement the delete recipe function in the Smilecook application yourself. Do this by adding a delete function to **RecipeResource**, similar to what we did in the previous exercises. Then, we will follow the standard software development life cycle flow, which is used to test our implementation, using Postman. Follow these steps to complete this activity:

1. Add the delete function to **RecipeResource**.

2. Start up the Flask server for testing.

3. Create the first recipe using Postman.

4. Delete the recipe using Postman.

> **Note**
>
> The solution to this activity can be found on page 299.

Summary

In this chapter, we built the RESTful API using the Flask-RESTful package. By doing this, you have seen how simple and easy it is to perform such tasks. We are building our project in a structural manner, which allows us to easily extend the project in the subsequent chapters. In this chapter, we created the models and resources folder; we will be developing more models and resources later in this book. So far, our food recipe-sharing platform, Smilecook, is capable of performing CRUD, as well as setting the publish status of the recipe. We have also tested the application to make sure it is working properly. Finally, you started to realize the power of Postman, which greatly automates the whole testing process. In the next chapter, we will learn about how to perform data validation.

3

Manipulating a Database with SQLAlchemy

Learning Objectives

By the end of this chapter, you will be able to:

- Use the pgAdmin tool to manage a database
- Manipulate a database using SQLAlchemy
- Create database tables using Flask-Migrate
- Persist data into a database
- Hash confidential password data

This chapter covers using SQLAlchemy to access a database, including building a model, encrypting the password, ensuring each email is unique, and then saving the recipe data in the database.

Introduction

In the previous chapter, we were only storing our data in application memory. While it is easy to code that way, the data will be gone once the server restarts. That is obviously not ideal because we would expect the data to be persisted even after a server restart or application migration and suchlike. Therefore, in this chapter, we will talk about persisting data in a database. We will begin by installing the Postgres database on our local machine. Then, we will create a database using pgAdmin and interact with it using the **ORM** (**Object Relational Mapping**) package, SQLAlchemy. ORM allows us to interact with a database by means of an object instead of an SQL query. After that, we will define the user and recipe models, link them up, and use Flask-Migrate to create the corresponding tables in the database. Once that part is complete, we will go through exercises to understand the utilization of SQLAlchemy in the Python console. Lastly, we will add the resource for users so that new users can be created through an API.

Databases

You have probably heard of the term database before. It is basically a data storage system. But why do we need a system to store data? Why can't we just store everything in a text file and save that in the folder system? Apparently, a database does more than just storing data. It classifies and organizes data and helps to store it with less redundancy. It also makes data easier to maintain, making it more it secure and consistent. A database is usually managed by a **database management system** (**DBMS**)

Database Management System

A DBMS is an application that maneuvers and manages a database. It facilitates communication between the users and the database. Users can create, use, and maintain the database using this application.

A DBMS is crucial for data security and integrity. Popular database software and DBMSs include PostgreSQL, MySQL, Microsoft SQL Server, MariaDB, and Oracle Database. Most DBMSs use **structured query language** (**SQL**) to insert and extract data.

In this book, we will be using PostgreSQL as our backend database system. And we will also use pgAdmin, which is a tool for managing PostgreSQL. PostgreSQL is a powerful, open-source object-relational database management system with a 15-year history. It is well recognized as a result of its stability and data integrity.

SQL

SQL is a language that was specifically invented to manage and maneuver data. It can be classified further into the following types:

- **Data Query Language** (**DQL**) for extracting data. With the syntax like `SELECT column1, column2 FROM table WHERE conditions`, it can query against the table and extracts data (`column1, column2`) that satisfies a certain condition.

- **Data Manipulation Language** (**DML**) for manipulating data. It includes statements such as `INSERT`, `UPDATE`, and `DELETE`.

- **Data Control Language** (**DCL**) for controlling data access.

Although we have introduced a number of different languages here, the good thing is that we don't need to learn all of them. In fact, we are not going to query our database using SQL. We will just need to code in Python, and the ORM package will convert our Python code to SQL behind the scenes. It's a whole lot easier to work with databases nowadays.

ORM

Object Relational Mapping (**ORM**) is a programming technique that allows the developer to map objects in the programming language to the data model in a database. There is no longer any need to use SQL to interact with a database. The benefit of this is that developers can code in their own programming language and it will work on different types of databases.

The mapping works along the following lines:

- Class in Python = the table schema in the database

- Attributes in a class = fields in the table schema

- Objects = rows of data in the table

SQLAlchemy is the most popular ORM in the Python community. Next, let's delves further by attempting to create a database.

Exercise 18: Setting Up a Smilecook Database

Most applications nowadays require a database to store and manage data. Our application, Smilecook, is no exception. It is a recipe-sharing platform and is open to the public. Obviously, it will have to store the user data and recipe data. In this exercise, we will create the database administrator and set up the database for our Smilecook application:

1. To start with, we will create a role. A role is simply a concept that PostgreSQL uses to manage access. We can consider that as a user here. *Right-click* on **PostgreSQL 11** under **Servers**, select **Create**, and then **Login/Group Role...**:

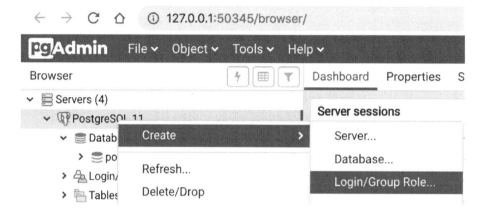

Figure 3.1: Selecting Login/Group Role...

2. Fill in the login name, which will be used later for connecting to the database:

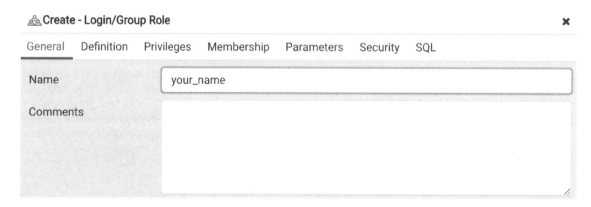

Figure 3.2: Filling in the login name

3. Then, select **Definition** and set the password. Click **Save**:

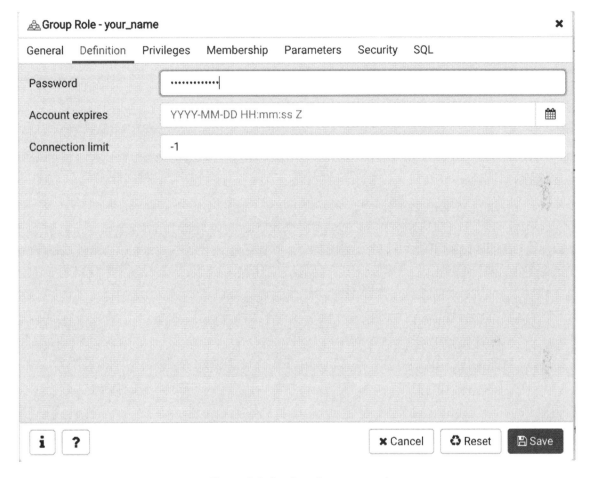

Figure 3.3: Setting the password

4. Now, go to **Privileges**, and select **Yes** for **Can login?**. This will allow us to log in to the database using this account:

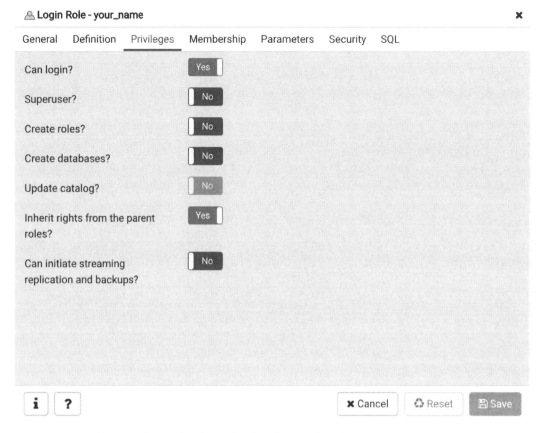

Figure 3.4: Logging in to the database using the account created

5. *Right-click* on **Databases**, and create a database from there:

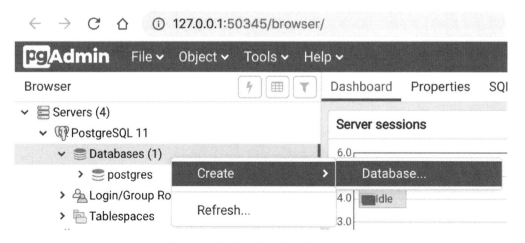

Figure 3.5: Creating the database

6. Name the database **smilecook**, and set the role that we have just created to **Owner**. Click **Save**:

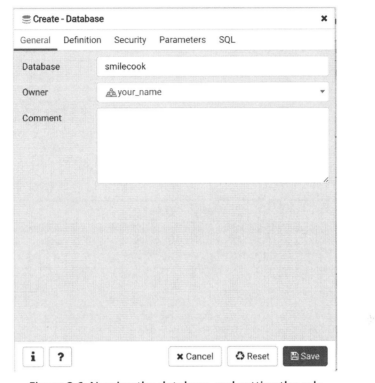

Figure 3.6: Naming the database and setting the role

Now we have created the Smilecook database, but it is empty at the moment. In the next exercise, we will use Flask-SQLAlchemy and Flask-Migrate to create our database tables. You will notice that there is no SQL query involved.

Defining Our Models

Before we go into the implementation, we need to first define and understand the fields that we will be working with. We will cover two essential models: **User** and **Recipe**. Models are like schemas in the database. A model is a class and can be instantiated. It contains attributes that correspond to fields in database schemas.

The user model

The user model will be mapped to the user table in the database. The fields and methods we defined for our user model are as follows:

- `id`: The identity of a user.

- `username`: The username of the user. The maximum length allowed is 80 characters. It can't be null and is a unique field.

- `email`: The user's email. The maximum length allowed is 200. It can't be blank and is a unique field.

- `password`: The user's password. The maximum length allowed is 200.

- `is_active`: This is to indicate whether the account is activated by email. It is a Boolean field with a default value of **False**.

- `recipes`: This doesn't create a field in the database table. This is just to define the relationship with the recipe model. So, subsequently, we can get all recipes using `user.recipes`.

- `created_at`: The creation time of the user.

- `updated_at`: The last update time of the user.

We are also going to define three methods in the user model:

- `get_by_username`: This method is used for searching the user by username.

- `get_by_email`: This method is used for searching the user by email.

- `save`: This is to persist the data to the database.

The recipe model

The recipe model will be mapped to the user table in the database. The fields we defined for our recipe model are as follows:

- `id`: The identity of a recipe.

- `name`: The name of the recipe. The maximum length allowed is 100 characters. It can't be null.

- `description`: The description of the recipe. The maximum length allowed is 200.

- `num_of_servings`: The number of servings. This needs to be an integer.

- **cook_time**: The cooking time in minutes. This field only accepts an integer.
- **directions**: The directions of the recipe. This can have a maximum length of 1,000.
- **is_publish**: This is to indicate whether the recipe has been published. It is set to **False** by default.
- **created_at**: The creation time of the recipe.
- **updated_at**: The last update time of the recipe.

With the model designs in our mind, we are now ready to use these models in our next exercise. Before that, let's also just briefly understand some of the key packages that we will be using. These are as follows:

- Flask-SQLAlchemy: This is a very popular ORM package that allows us to access objects rather than database tables for data. With ORM, we do not need to rely on SQL anymore.
- Flask-Migrate: This is a package for database migration; it works on top of Alembic.
- Psycopg2-binary: This is the adapter for the Postgres database.
- Passlib: This is a password hashing library for Python.

Exercise 19: Installing Packages and Defining Models

This exercise is designed to install the necessary packages and define the user and recipe models. The user and recipe models are going to be Python classes; there will not be any SQL coding in this exercise. We want to show you how we can interact with the database by simply coding in Python:

1. We will add the required packages in the **requirements.txt** file. If you remember, by putting the package name and version in **requirements.txt**, we can install them in the Python virtual environment by using a single **pip** command:

    ```
    Flask-SQLAlchemy==2.4.0
    Flask-Migrate==2.5.2
    psycopg2-binary==2.8.3
    passlib==1.7.1
    ```

2. We can run the following **pip install** command to install the necessary packages:

```
pip install -r requirements.txt
```

The installation result will be shown onscreen:

```
Installing collected packages: SQLAlchemy, Flask-SQLAlchemy, alembic,
Flask-Migrate, psycopg2-binary, passlib
  Running setup.py install for SQLAlchemy ... done
  Running setup.py install for alembic ... done
Successfully installed Flask-Migrate-2.5.2 Flask-SQLAlchemy-2.4.0
SQLAlchemy-1.3.6 alembic-1.0.11 passlib-1.7.1 psycopg2-binary-2.8.3
```

3. Create a **Config.py** file and type in the following code:

```
class Config:
    DEBUG = True

    SQLALCHEMY_DATABASE_URI = 'postgresql+psycopg2://{your_name}:{your_
password}@localhost/{db_name}
    SQLALCHEMY_TRACK_MODIFICATIONS = False
```

We can set **DEBUG = True** here for debugging purposes. As regards **SQLALCHEMY_DATABASE_URI**, this is the path of the database. Please replace the username and password with the one we created for the **Role** in **pgAdmin**. Also, replace the database name as well.

4. Now, create **extensions.py** under the Smilecook project and type in the following code:

```
from flask_sqlalchemy import SQLAlchemy

db = SQLAlchemy()
```

5. Create **user.py** under the folder models and type in the following code:

```
from extensions import db

class User(db.Model):
    __tablename__ = 'user'

    id = db.Column(db.Integer, primary_key=True)
    username = db.Column(db.String(80), nullable=False, unique=True)
    email = db.Column(db.String(200), nullable=False, unique=True)
    password = db.Column(db.String(200))
```

```
    is_active = db.Column(db.Boolean(), default=False)
    created_at = db.Column(db.DateTime(), nullable=False, server_
default=db.func.now())
    updated_at = db.Column(db.DateTime(), nullable=False, server_
default=db.func.now(), onupdate=db.func.now())

    recipes = db.relationship('Recipe', backref='user')

    @classmethod
    def get_by_username(cls, username):
        return cls.query.filter_by(username=username).first()

    @classmethod
    def get_by_email(cls, email):
        return cls.query.filter_by(email=email).first()

    def save(self):
        db.session.add(self)
        db.session.commit()
```

6. Replace **recipe.py** with the following code. We are adding the import **db** statement here and have also modified the **Recipe** class. The code related to **recipe_list** is still valid here, so we are retaining that part of the code:

```
from extensions import db


recipe_list = []


def get_last_id():
    if recipe_list:
        last_recipe = recipe_list[-1]
    else:
        return 1
    return last_recipe.id + 1


class Recipe(db.Model):
    __tablename__ = 'recipe'

    id = db.Column(db.Integer, primary_key=True)
```

```
        name = db.Column(db.String(100), nullable=False)
        description = db.Column(db.String(200))
        num_of_servings = db.Column(db.Integer)
        cook_time = db.Column(db.Integer)
        directions = db.Column(db.String(1000))
        is_publish = db.Column(db.Boolean(), default=False)
        created_at = db.Column(db.DateTime(), nullable=False, server_
default=db.func.now())
        updated_at = db.Column(db.DateTime(), nullable=False, server_
default=db.func.now(), onupdate=db.func.now())

        user_id = db.Column(db.Integer(), db.ForeignKey("user.id"))
```

7. Now, rewrite **app.py** with the following code. We are structuring our code in a more proper way, making it more readable and maintainable. First, import the required packages at the beginning of the code file.

> **Note**
>
> You're also importing the user model because SQLAlchemy needs the user model to create the corresponding table in the database.

For the recipe model, we don't need to include this here because that has already been done in **resources.recipe**, and we are already importing **resources.recipe** here:

```
from flask import Flask
from flask_migrate import Migrate
from flask_restful import Api

from config import Config
from extensions import db
from models.user import User
from resources.recipe import RecipeListResource, RecipeResource,
RecipePublishResource
```

8. Use the **create_app()** function to create the Flask app. This will invoke **register_ extensions(app)** to initialize SQLAlchemy and set up Flask-Migrate. It will then invoke **register_resources(app)** to set up resource routing:

```
def create_app():
    app = Flask(__name__)
    app.config.from_object(Config)

    register_extensions(app)
    register_resources(app)

    return app


def register_extensions(app):
    db.init_app(app)
    migrate = Migrate(app, db)


def register_resources(app):
    api = Api(app)

    api.add_resource(RecipeListResource, '/recipes')
    api.add_resource(RecipeResource, '/recipes/<int:recipe_id>')
    api.add_resource(RecipePublishResource, '/recipes/<int:recipe_id>/
publish')
```

9. Finally, use **app = create_app()** to create the Flask app, and use **app.run()** to start the application:

```
if __name__ == '__main__':
    app = create_app()
    app.run()
```

10. Save **app.py** and *right-click* on it to run the application. Flask will then be started up and run on the localhost (**127.0.0.1**) on port 5000:

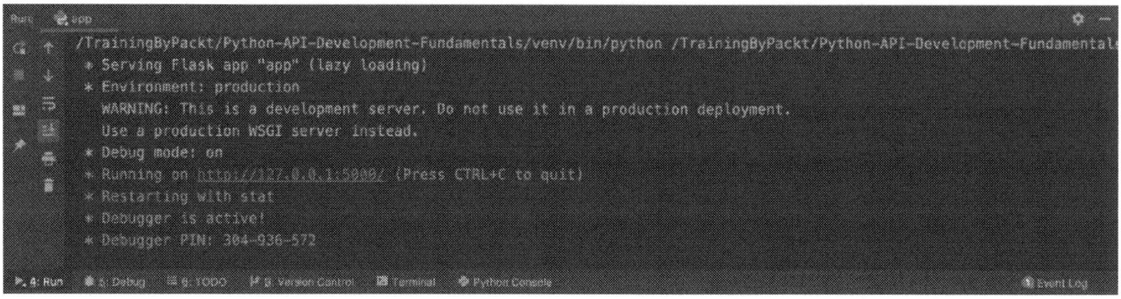

Figure 3.7: Flask started on localhost

We have successfully installed the necessary ORM-related packages, and defined the user and recipe models. Having first installed the packages, we ran the installation in our virtual environment. We created **config.py**, **extensions.py**, and **user.py** files and replaced **app.py**. Finally, we restructured our Flask app and saw how well it runs.

Exercise 20: Using Flask-Migrate to Build a Database Upgrade Script

Having successfully understood how to work with our two main models, user and recipe, we have now built the perfect foundation. The next step is execution. We will use Flask-Migrate to build a script to create the user and recipe tables:

1. Use the following command in the Terminal to initialize our database. This will create a migration repository:

```
flask db init
```

You should see the following onscreen:

```
Creating directory /Python-API-Development-Fundamentals/smilecook/
migrations ... done
Creating directory /Python-API-Development-Fundamentals/smilecook/
migrations/versions ... done
Generating /Python-API-Development-Fundamentals/smilecook/migrations/
script.py.mako ... done
Generating /Python-API-Development-Fundamentals/smilecook/migrations/env.
py ... done
Generating /Python-API-Development-Fundamentals/smilecook/migrations/
README ... done
```

```
Generating /Python-API-Development-Fundamentals/smilecook/migrations/
alembic.ini ... done
Please edit configuration/connection/logging settings in '/Python-API-
Development-
Fundamentals/smilecook/migrations/alembic.ini' before proceeding.
```

You should now see the following new files in PyCharm:

Figure 3.8: New folders in PyCharm

2. Now, run the **flask db migrate** command to create the database and tables. There is no need for us to use SQL here:

```
flask db migrate
```

Flask-Migrate detected two objects (**user** and **recipe**) and created two corresponding tables for them:

```
INFO  [alembic.runtime.migration] Context impl PostgresqlImpl.
INFO  [alembic.runtime.migration] Will assume transactional DDL.
INFO  [alembic.autogenerate.compare] Detected added table 'user'
INFO  [alembic.autogenerate.compare] Detected added table 'recipe'
  Generating /Python-API-Development-Fundamentals/smilecook/migrations/
versions/a6d248ab7b23_.py ... done
```

3. Now, please check **/migrations/versions/a6d248ab7b23_.py** under the **versions** folder. This file is created by Flask-Migrate. Note that you may get a different revision ID here. Please review the file before you run the flask **db** upgrade command. That's because, sometimes, it may not detect every change you make to your models:

```
"""empty message

Revision ID: a6d248ab7b23
Revises:
Create Date: 2019-07-22 16:10:41.644737

"""
from alembic import op
import sqlalchemy as sa


# revision identifiers, used by Alembic.
revision = 'a6d248ab7b23'
down_revision = None
branch_labels = None
depends_on = None


def upgrade():
    # ### commands auto generated by Alembic - please adjust! ###
    op.create_table('user',
    sa.Column('id', sa.Integer(), nullable=False),
    sa.Column('username', sa.String(length=80), nullable=False),
    sa.Column('email', sa.String(length=200), nullable=False),
    sa.Column('password', sa.String(), nullable=True),
    sa.Column('is_active', sa.Boolean(), nullable=True),
    sa.Column('created_at', sa.DateTime(), server_default=sa.
text('now()'), nullable=False),
    sa.Column('updated_at', sa.DateTime(), server_default=sa.
text('now()'), nullable=False),
    sa.PrimaryKeyConstraint('id'),
    sa.UniqueConstraint('email')
    )
    op.create_table('recipe',
    sa.Column('id', sa.Integer(), nullable=False),
    sa.Column('name', sa.String(length=100), nullable=False),
```

```
        sa.Column('description', sa.String(length=500), nullable=True),
        sa.Column('num_of_servings', sa.Integer(), nullable=True),
        sa.Column('cook_time', sa.Integer(), nullable=True),
        sa.Column('directions', sa.String(), nullable=True),
        sa.Column('is_publish', sa.Boolean(), nullable=True),
        sa.Column('created_at', sa.DateTime(), server_default=sa.
    text('now()'), nullable=False),
        sa.Column('updated_at', sa.DateTime(), server_default=sa.
    text('now()'), nullable=False),
        sa.Column('user_id', sa.Integer(), nullable=True),
        sa.ForeignKeyConstraint(['user_id'], ['user.id'], ),
        sa.PrimaryKeyConstraint('id')
        )
        # ### end Alembic commands ###



    def downgrade():
        # ### commands auto generated by Alembic - please adjust! ###
        op.drop_table('recipe')
        op.drop_table('user')
        # ### end Alembic commands ###
```

There are two functions in this autogenerated file; one is upgraded, and this is to add the new recipe and user to the table, while the other one is downgraded, which is to go back to the previous version.

4. We will then execute the **flask db upgrade** command, which will upgrade our database to conform with the latest specification in our models:

```
flask db upgrade
```

This command will invoke **upgrade()** to upgrade the database:

```
INFO  [alembic.runtime.migration] Context impl PostgresqlImpl.
INFO  [alembic.runtime.migration] Will assume transactional DDL.
INFO  [alembic.runtime.migration] Running upgrade  -> a6d248ab7b23, empty
message
```

> **Note**
>
> In the future, whenever we need to upgrade the database, we can just call **flask db migrate** and **flask db upgrade**.

5. Check the database tables in **pgAdmin**. Now, we can see whether the tables have been created in the database. Go to **smilecook** >> **Schemas** >> **Tables to verify**:

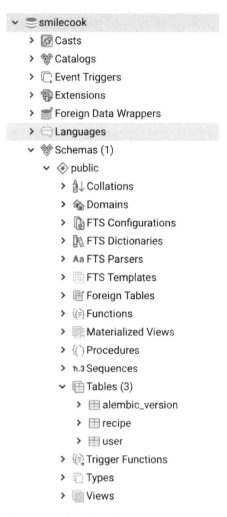

Figure 3.9: Checking the database tables

If you see the recipe and user tables in our **Smilecook** database, this means you have successfully created them in Python without any SQL. Isn't that cool?!

Next, we will try our hand at database insertion. Let's look at the following exercise.

Exercise 21: Applying Database Insertion

This exercise is designed for us to test database insertion. We will first create a user, and then create two recipes under that user:

1. Import modules in the Python console. Open the Python console at the bottom of PyCharm and type in the following code to import the necessary classes:

    ```
    from app import *
    from models.user import User
    from models.recipe import Recipe
    app = create_app()
    ```

2. Create our first **user** object and save that to the database by typing in the following code in the Python console:

    ```
    user = User(username='jack', email='jack@gmail.com', password='WkQa')
    db.session.add(user)
    db.session.commit()
    ```

3. Now, check the **user** details. Please note that the ID of the user has already been assigned to **1**:

    ```
    >>>user.username
    'jack'
    >>>user.id
    1
    >>>user.email
    'jack@gmail.com'
    ```

4. Since the user is persisted in the database, we will verify that there:

Figure 3.10: Verifying the user in the database

5. We can see a record there in the **user** table:

id	username	email	password	is_active	created_at	updated_at
[PK] integer	character varying (80)	character varying (200)	character varying (200)	boolean	timestamp without time zone	timestamp without time zone
1	1 jack	jack@gmail.com	WkQa	false	2019-10-08 11:53:35.786042	2019-10-08 11:53:35.786042

Data Output   Explain   Messages   Notifications

Figure 3.11: Record in the user table

7. Next, we will create two recipes using the following code. One thing to note is that the **user_id** attribute of the recipe is set to **user.id**. This is to indicate that the recipe was created by the user **Jack**:

```
pizza = Recipe(name='Cheese Pizza', description='This is a lovely cheese
pizza recipe', num_of_servings=2, cook_time=30, directions='This is how
you make it', user_id=user.id)
db.session.add(pizza)
db.session.commit()


pasta = Recipe(name='Tomato Pasta', description='This is a lovely tomato
pasta recipe', num_of_servings=3, cook_time=20, directions='This is how
you make it', user_id=user.id)
db.session.add(pasta)
db.session.commit()
```

8. We will then check whether the two recipes have been created in the database:

Data Output   Explain   Messages   Notifications

id	name	description	num_of_servings	cook_time	directions	is_publish	created_at	updated_at	user_id
[PK] integer	character varying (100)	character varying (200)	integer	integer	character varying (1000)	boolean	timestamp wi	timestamp wi	integer
1	1 Cheese Pizza	This is a lovely chees...	2	30	This is how you make it	false	2019-10-08...	2019-10-08...	1
2	2 Tomato Pasta	This is a lovely tomat...	3	20	This is how you make it	false	2019-10-08...	2019-10-08...	1

Figure 3.12: Checking whether the two recipes have been created

9. We will search for the user with the username **jack** in the database and get all the recipes created by that user in their object attribute, **recipes**:

```
>>> user = User.query.filter_by(username='jack').first()
>>> user.recipes
```

We will get a list of two recipes:

```
[<Recipe 1>, <Recipe 2>]
```

10. We can display the details of the recipes using the **for** loop. We get the recipe name using **recipe.name**, while we get the user's name using **recipe.user.username**:

```
>>> for recipe in user.recipes:
    print('{} recipe made by {} can serve {} people.'.format(recipe.name,
recipe.user.username, recipe.num_of_servings))
```

You should see the following result on the screen:

```
Cheese Pizza recipe made by jack can serve 2 people.
Tomato Pasta recipe made by jack can serve 3 people.
```

You have just learned how to command your application using the Python console. You have just created the user and recipe models and saved them in the database. The entire process is SQL-free, as you can see. Let's do an activity to reinforce your knowledge.

Activity 5: Creating a User and a Recipe

In this activity, we will test our APIs by running a few more test cases. We want to create a new user, **Peter**, and create two recipes under him in the database. Let's see if you know how to write the code for that in the Python interactive console:

1. Import the **User** and **Recipe** classes and create the Flask app using the Python console.

2. Create a new user, **Peter**.

3. Create two recipes and assign **Peter** as the author.

> **Note**
>
> The solution for this activity can be found on page 302.

If you can see that the data has successfully been created in the database, congratulations – you already know how to use Python console to interact with the database! Next, we will implement a user registration feature.

Password Hashing

Hashing is a one-way mathematical function. It requires little computing power to convert a plaintext string to its hash value (hashes). However, it will require a huge amount of computing power to retrieve the original string from the hash value (it's almost impossible). Therefore, we call it a one-way function:

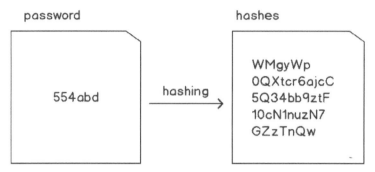

Figure 3.13: Workings of the hash function

With this property, a hash function is perfect for a hashing password. We will hash the user's password into hashes before we save it to the database so that it is unrecognizable and irreversible. And next time, when the user logs in, what the platform does is to convert the input the password to its hash value, and then compare that with the hash value stored in the database. That way, we can perform a password comparison without leaking the sensitive password information to others.

Exercise 22: Implement the User Registration Feature and Hash the User's Password

In this exercise, we will work on the user registration feature. We will also implement two functions for hashing the user's password:

1. Create **utils.py** under the application project folder and type in the following code. The code is to hash the password. We do not want to store plaintext passwords in our database on account of security concerns. Therefore, we will use the **passlib** modules for hashing. We defined two methods here:

   ```
   from passlib.hash import pbkdf2_sha256


   def hash_password(password):
   ```

```
        return pbkdf2_sha256.hash(password)



    def check_password(password, hashed):
        return pbkdf2_sha256.verify(password, hashed)
```

The **hash_password(password)** function is for password hashing and **check_password(password, hashed)** is for user authentication. It hashes the user-input password and compares that with the one we saved in the database.

2. Create **user.py** in the **resources** folder, and then type in the following code. We will first import the necessary modules and implement the **Post** method in **UserListResource**:

```
from flask import request
from flask_restful import Resource
from http import HTTPStatus

from utils import hash_password
from models.user import User


class UserListResource(Resource):
    def post(self):
        json_data = request.get_json()

        username = json_data.get('username')
        email = json_data.get('email')
        non_hash_password = json_data.get('password')
```

When there is a client request hitting **http://localhost/users** with the HTTP **POST** method, the application will get the JSON formatted data in the request. There should be a username, email, and password.

3. Check whether the user already exists in the database by means of **User.get_by_user(username)**. If such an entry is found, that means the user has already registered and we will simply return an error message. We will also perform the same check on **email** as well:

```
if User.get_by_username(username):
        return {'message': 'username already used'}, HTTPStatus.BAD_
REQUEST


if User.get_by_email(email):
        return {'message': 'email already used'}, HTTPStatus.BAD_
REQUEST
```

4. Once all the validations are passed, go ahead and create the user in the database. The password will be hashed, and the user object will be created. The user object will then be saved to the database using **user.save()**. Finally, the user details are returned in JSON format, with an **HTTP** status code of **201**:

```
password = hash_password(non_hash_password)

user = User(
        username=username,
        email=email,
        password=password
)

user.save()

data = {
        'id': user.id,
        'username': user.username,
        'email': user.email
}

return data, HTTPStatus.CREATED
```

5. Add user resource routing to **app.py**:

```
from extensions import db

from resources.user import UserListResource
from resources.recipe import RecipeListResource, RecipeResource,
RecipePublishResource


def register_resources(app):
    api = Api(app)

    api.add_resource(UserListResource, '/users')
    api.add_resource(RecipeListResource, '/recipes')
```

Replace **from models.user import User** in **app.py** with **from resources.user import UserListResource**. The user model is already imported in **resources.user**, so there is no need to reimport that again. Please add **api.add_resource(UserListResource, '/users')** to the code as well.

Run the application. Flask will then be started up and run on localhost (**127.0.0.1**) on port **5000**:

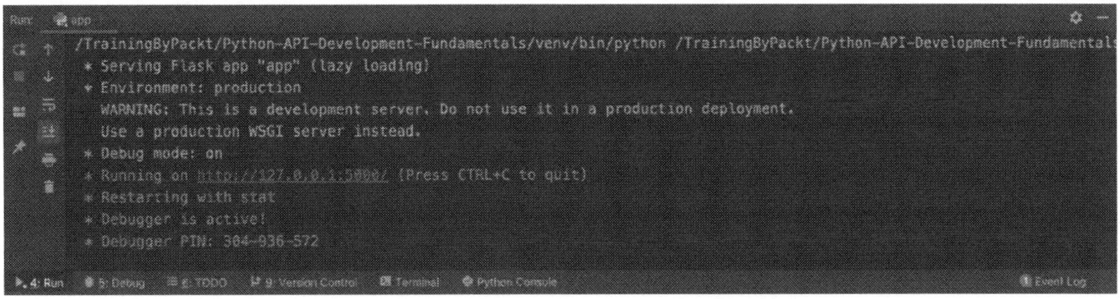

Figure 3.14: Flask started on localhost

So, we have just finished the password hashing exercise. From now on, whenever there is a new user registered in our Smilecook application, their password will be hashed and stored safely in the database. Let's test and see whether that is the case in our next exercise.

> **Note**
>
> The reason why we are not discussing the recipe resource here is that there will be an author ID in the recipe. The author ID will be a foreign key that links to the user model. We will talk about the user login function in our next chapter. Only after that can we get the user ID and finish the recipe resource.

Exercise 23: Testing the Application in Postman

In this exercise, we are going to test the application in Postman. We will first register a user account and make sure the user data is stored in the database. We also need to verify that the password is hashed. Having created a user, now let's test our API endpoint here:

1. Click on the **Collections** tab in Postman.

2. Create a new collection, and name it `User`.

3. Create a new request, `UserList`, under that collection. You can do this by clicking on the **...** next to the **User** collection.

4. Edit the **UserList** request, and then set the HTTP method to `POST`.

5. Type in `http://localhost:5000/users` in the URL field.

6. Go to the **Body** Tab, select **raw** as the datatype, and then select **JSON (application/json)** as the data format.

7. Insert the following user details and then save.:

```
{
    "username": "jack",
    "email": "jack@gmail.com",
    "password": "WkQa"
}
```

8. Click **Send**. The result can be seen in the following screenshot:

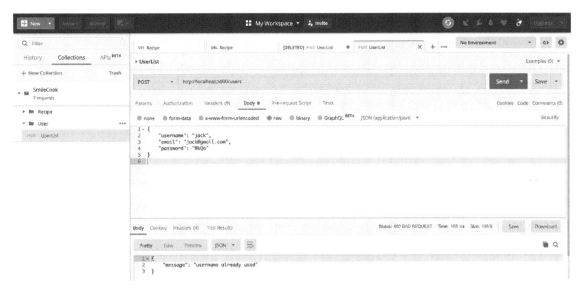

Figure 3.15: Creating a user with an existing username

You will then see the following data returned; the HTTP status is **400 BAD REQUEST**. We can also see the error message in the **Body** field showing that the username has been registered.

9. Create another user with the details shown in the following code:

```
{
    "username": "ray",
    "email": "ray@gmail.com",
    "password": "WkQa"
}
```

The result can be seen in the following screenshot:

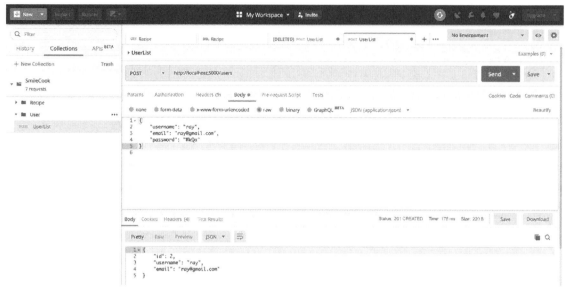

Figure 3.16: Creating another user

Now, the second account has been successfully created.

10. Check the data in the database as follows:

Id [PK] integer	username character varying (80)	email character varying (200)	password character varying	is_active boolean
1	1 jack	jack@gmail.com	WkQa	false
2	2 ray	ray@gmail.com	$pbkdf2-sha256$29000$ZMzZ25uztjbmPKc0xhhDKA$11y...	false

Figure 3.17: Checking the data in the database

Now, we can see a new user record created in the database table. And you can see that the password is hashed.

By doing this testing exercise, we can be assured that our user registration workflow is functioning well. And, most importantly, user passwords are kept as the hash value in the database. That is a much safer way to store a password, as even the database administrator can't see it.

Activity 6: Upgrading and Downgrading a Database

1. In this activity, we will upgrade and downgrade our database to simulate a scenario where we need to add an attribute under the **user** class, but later we change our mind and need to remove it. The following are the high-level steps that we need to perform in order to complete this activity:

2. Add a new attribute to the **user** class. This attribute should be called **bio** and will be a string that represents information about the user.

3. Run the **flask db migrate** command to create the database and tables.

4. Now, check **/migrations/versions/6971bd62ec60_.py** under the **versions** folder. This file is created by Flask-Migrate.

5. Execute the **flask db upgrade** command to upgrade our database to conform with the latest specification in our models.

6. Check whether the new field is created in the database.

7. Run the **downgrade** command to remove the new field.

8. Check whether the field has been removed.

> **Note**
>
> The solution for this activity can be found on page 303.

If you see that the new field has been removed, that means you have successfully downgraded the database in Python without writing any SQL. And don't forget to delete the user model's bio attribute in models/user.py, also delete the script that we created which is **a6d248ab7b23.py** in migrations/versions folder. You have just learned a very useful skill that you will probably need frequently in the future. One tip for you is that you should back up your database prior to any database schema update. This is to ensure the data won't get lost.

Summary

In this chapter, we built the Postgres database locally and learned how to use the pgAdmin tool to manage it. Then, through the SQLAlchemy module, we developed an object library to manipulate the database. This is much easier than using SQL syntax directly. And, as long as we define the relationship between models, we can easily get the information we want. This results in higher code readability, fewer lines of code, and the elimination of repetitive SQL. We then use Flask-Migrate to build all the data tables. Then, when we migrate the database in the future, we simply need two commands – `flask db migrate` and `flask db upgrade`; it's simple and easy. Although Flask-Migrate can help us to set up and migrate a database more easily, in a production environment, performing this kind of migration still requires extra due diligence. We should always back up the database to safeguard our precious data.

During development, we should frequently test our code to make sure it is behaving as expected. We shouldn't wait till the end to perform big-bang testing. We can unit test our functions and API endpoints, once they are complete. Using the Python console to perform this kind of simple test is recommended. Iteratively testing our application can also foster the best programming practice. This forces us to think about how we can structure our code in an elegant manner and avoid technical debt accumulation.

Finally, we created an API for user registration. In the next chapter, we will work on user login and recipe creation for authenticated users.

Authentication Services and Security with JWT

Learning Objectives

By the end of this chapter, you will be able to:

- Apply your knowledge of JWT
- Create an access token using Flask-JWT-Extended
- Develop a membership login system
- Implement an access control system (authentication and permissions)
- Work with a refresh token
- Restrict access using a blacklist

This chapter covers how to develop a user login/logout function using JWT.

Introduction

In the previous chapter, we completed the database setup and configuration and linked the database to the code using ORM. We then implemented the user registration API on top of that. This chapter is divided into four parts. The first part is about authenticating the user and allowing them to log in to their own private profile page. The second part completes the recipe sharing system, allowing users to publish or unpublish their recipes. The third part shows how to refresh the security token and implement the logout feature. And finally, we will talk about how we can use the **blacklist** function to force the user to log out.

User authentication is important in modern systems, especially if they are deployed on the internet. Thousands of users visit the same website, using the same web application. Without user authentication and access control, everything would be shared. Look at your Facebook/Instagram account – there are also user authentication and access controls implemented in the system. Only you can log in to your account and manage your posts and photos. For our Smilecook application, we will need the same feature.

We will start by discussing JWT.

JWT

JWT is used for user authentication and is passed between the user and the server. The full definition of the acronym is **JSON Web Token**. The way they work is to encode the user identity and sign it digitally, making it an unforgeable token that identifies the user, and the application can later control access for the user based on their identity.

A JWT is a string composed of the header, payload, and signature. Those three parts are separated by a .. Here is an example:

```
eyJ0eXAiOiJKV1QiLCJhbGciOiJIUzI1NiJ9.eyJpYXQiOjE1NjQ5ODI5OTcs
Im5iZiI6MTU2NDk4Mjk5NywianRpIjoiMGIzOTVlODQtNjFjMy00NjM3LTkwMzYtZjgyZDgy
YTllNzc5IiwiZXhwIjoxNTY0OTgzODk3LCJpZGVudGl0eSI6MywiZnJlc2giOmZhbHNlLCJ
0eXBlIjoiYWNjZXNzIn0.t6F3cnAmbUXY_PwLnnBkKD3Z6aJNvIDQ6khMJWj9xZM
```

The header of the **JWT** contains the encryption type, **"alg": "HS256"**, and the encryption algorithm, **"typ": "JWT"**. We can see this clearly if we **base64** decode the header string:

```
>>> import base64
>>> header = 'eyJ0eXAiOiJKV1QiLCJhbGciOiJIUzI1NiJ9'
>>> base64.b64decode(header)


b'{"typ":"JWT","alg":"HS256"}'
```

The content of the **payload** part is arbitrary. It can be anything the developer likes. We can put in it the user ID, nickname, and so on. When the application server receives this token, it can **base64** decode it and obtain the information inside. One important thing to note is that this information is not encrypted, therefore it is not recommended to store credit card details or passwords here:

```
>>> import base64
>>> payload = 'eyJpYXQiOjE1NjQ5ODI5OTcsIm5iZiI6MTU2NDk4Mjk5NywianRpI
joiMGIzOTVlODQtNjFjMy00NjM3LTkwMzYtZjgyZDgyYTllNzc5IiwiZXhwIjoxNTY0
OTgzODk3LCJpZGVudGl0eSI6MywiZnJlc2giOmZhbHNlLCJ0eXBlIjoiYWNjZXNzIn0'
>>> base64.b64decode(payload + '==')


b'{"iat":1564982997,"nbf":1564982997,"jti":"0b395e84-61c3-4637-9036-f82d82a9
e779","exp":1564983897,"identity":3,"fresh":false,"type":"access"}'
```

The **secret** part here is a signature created by the **HS256** algorithm. The algorithm is encrypting the encoded header and payload data with a secret key that is known by the application server only. While anyone can modify the JWT content, that would result in a different signature, thus the data integrity is protected.

We can make use of the free service at https://jwt.io/ to have a better view of the structure and content in the JWT token:

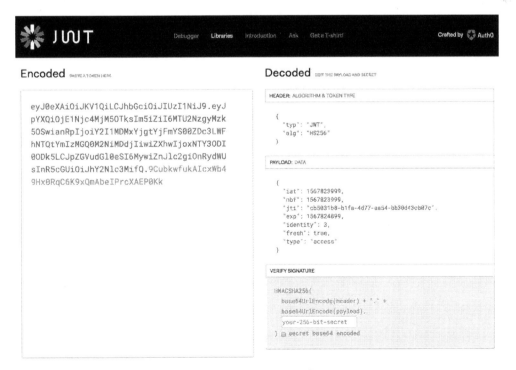

Figure 4.1: The JWT website

With a simple structure, `header.payload.secret`, we have a JWT, which will be used in this project for user authentication. Based on the user's identity, we can then apply access controls or other kinds of logic.

Flask-JWT-Extended

Flask-JWT-Extended is a user authentication package that provides the `create_access_token` function for making new access JWTs. It also provides the `jwt_required` decorator for protecting the API endpoints (for checking whether users have logged in). Also, the `get_jwt_identity()` function is provided to get the identity of a JWT in a protected endpoint. This allows us to know who the authenticated users are. This is an extremely useful package for user authentication.

Before we dive into the coming exercise, let's first discuss two very important key configurations that we will be using. They are as follows:

- **SECRET_KEY**: This is the key for encrypting the message and generating the signature. We recommend that you use a complex string.

- **JWT_ERROR_MESSAGE_KEY**: This is the key for the error message whenever there is an error. The default value is `msg`, but we are setting that to the `message` here.

We will work on the user login function together in the next exercise. You will learn how user login works and how we can tell who the authenticated user is.

> **Note**
>
> For more information on Flask-JWT-Extended, you can refer to this link: https://flask-jwt-extended.readthedocs.io/en/latest/options.html.

Exercise 24: Implementing a User Login Function

In this exercise, we will build the user login function. We will use the Flask-JWT-Extended package. Through this exercise, you will learn how we can generate JWTs in Flask. Users will enter their credentials in **http://localhost:5000/token** and they will get a token. They can then use that token to access **http://localhost:5000/users/{username}** and check their personal information registered in the system. If they don't have the token, they will only see their own ID and username. This is the access control function of our Smilecook application:

1. Install the **Flask-JWT-Extended** package by adding the following lines in **requirements.txt**:

   ```
   Flask-JWT-Extended==3.20.0
   ```

2. Run the following command to install all of the necessary packages:

   ```
   pip install -r requirements.txt
   ```

   You should see the following installation result on the screen:

   ```
   Installing collected packages: PyJWT, Flask-JWT-Extended
      Running setup.py install for Flask-JWT-Extended ... done
   Successfully installed Flask-JWT-Extended-3.20.0 PyJWT-1.7.1
   ```

3. Configure **Flask-JWT-Extended** by adding the following settings to the **Config** class in the **config.py** file:

   ```
   SECRET_KEY = 'super-secret-key'
   JWT_ERROR_MESSAGE_KEY = 'message'
   ```

4. Put the following code in **extension.py**:

   ```
   from flask_jwt_extended import JWTManager

   jwt = JWTManager()
   ```

   Here, we are trying to create an instance of **Flask-JWT-Extended**. We first import the **JWTManager** class from **flask_jwt_extended**, then we instantiate a **Flask-JWT-Extended** instance by calling **JWTManager()**, and assign it to the **jwt** variable.

5. Type the following code in **app.py**:

```
from extensions import db, jwt

def register_extensions(app):
    db.init_app(app)
    migrate = Migrate(app, db)
    jwt.init_app(app)
```

We first imported **jwt** from **extensions**, and then we initialized **jwt** with **jwt.init_app(app)** in **register_extensions(app)**.

6. Now we will create the resource for the login. We will first create the **token.py** file in the **resources** folder and type in the following code. We first import all the necessary modules, functions, and classes:

```
from http import HTTPStatus
from flask import request
from flask_restful import Resource
from flask_jwt_extended import create_access_token

from utils import check_password
from models.user import User
```

7. Then, define a class called **TokenResource**. This class inherits from **flask_restful.Resource**:

```
class TokenResource(Resource):
```

8. Inside the class, we create a **post** method. When a user logs in, this method will be invoked and it will take the **email** and **password** from the client JSON request. It will use the **get_by_email** method to verify the correctness of the user's credentials:

```
def post(self):

    json_data = request.get_json()
    email = json_data.get('email')
    password = json_data.get('password')

    user = User.get_by_email(email=email)

    if not user or not check_password(password, user.password):
```

```
            return {'message': 'email or password is incorrect'},
HTTPStatus.UNAUTHORIZED

        access_token = create_access_token(identity=user.id)

        return {'access_token': access_token}, HTTPStatus.OK
```

If they are invalid, the method will stop there and return **401 UNAUTHORIZED**, with an email message saying **email or password is incorrect**. Otherwise, it will create an access token with the user id as the identity to the user.

> **Note**
>
> The way the **check_password** function works is by hashing the password the client passes in and comparing that hash value with the one stored in the database, using the **pbkdf2_sha256.verify(password, hashed)** function. There is no plaintext password comparison here.

9. We will then create a new resource, which is for getting user details. If the user is not authenticated, they can only see their ID and username. Otherwise, they will see their personal email as well. We can add the following code to **resources/user. py**.

    We first import the necessary modules, functions, and classes:

    ```
    from flask_jwt_extended import jwt_optional, get_jwt_identity
    ```

10. Then, we define a **UserResource** class that inherits from **flask_restful.Resource**:

    ```
    class UserResource(Resource):
    ```

11. In this class, we define a **get** method and wrap it with a **jwt_optional** decorator. This implies that the endpoint is accessible regardless of the procession of the token:

    ```
    @jwt_optional
    def get(self, username):
    ```

12. We then perform a similar routine to the previous step and check whether the **username** can be found in the database:

```
user = User.get_by_username(username=username)

if user is None:
    return {'message': 'user not found'}, HTTPStatus.NOT_FOUND
```

13. If it is found in the database, we will further check whether it matches the identity of the user ID in the JWT:

```
current_user = get_jwt_identity()
```

14. Depending on the result in the previous step, we apply access control and output different information:

```
if current_user == user.id:
    data = {
        'id': user.id,
        'username': user.username,
        'email': user.email,
    }

else:
    data = {
        'id': user.id,
        'username': user.username,
    }

return data, HTTPStatus.OK
```

15. Finally, we will import the resources we created in the previous steps and add them to the **api** in **app.py**:

```
from resources.user import UserListResource, UserResource
from resources.token import TokenResource

def register_resources(app):
    api = Api(app)

    api.add_resource(UserListResource, '/users')
    api.add_resource(UserResource, '/users/<string:username>')

    api.add_resource(TokenResource, '/token')
```

16. Right-click on it to run the application. **Flask** will then be started up and run on localhost (**127.0.0.1**) at port **5000**:

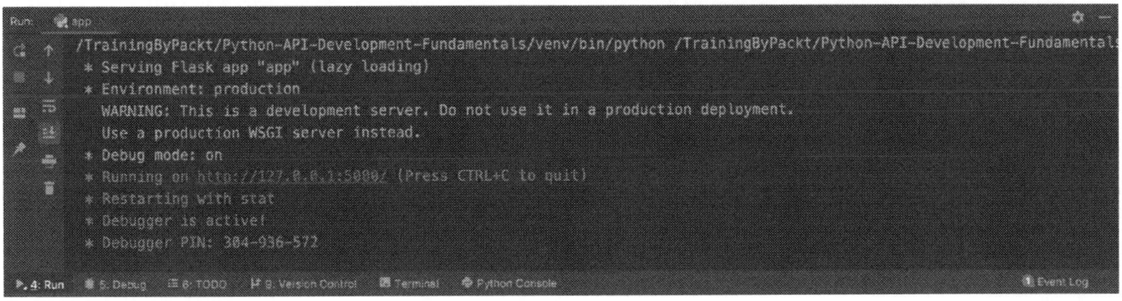

Figure 4.2: Run the application to start and run Flask on localhost

So, we have completed the user login function. This will allow users to visit the access-controlled APIs after login. Let's test it in our next exercise!

Exercise 25: Testing the User Login Function

In this exercise, we will test the login function and verify the user information stored in the database. We will also test that the user information obtained from the **http://localhost:5000/users/{username}** API is different before and after user login:

1. The first thing to do is to create a user. Click on the **Collections** tab and choose **POST UserList**.

2. Select the **Body** tab, select the **raw** radio button, and choose **JSON (application/json)** from the drop-down list. Put in the following user details (JSON format) in the **Body** field:

```
{
    "username": "james",
    "email": "james@gmail.com",
    "password": "WkQad19"
}
```

3. Click **Send** to register. The result is shown in the following screenshot:

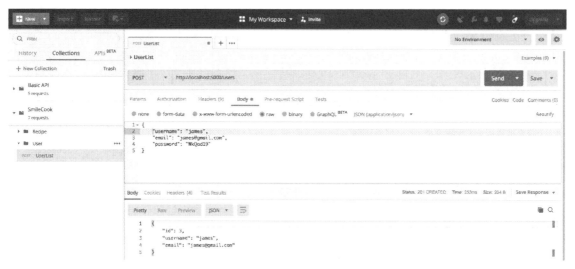

Figure 4.3: Creating a user

You will then see the response. The HTTP status is **201 CREATED**, meaning that the user registration has been successful. And we can see the user details in the response body. **"id": 3** here means that the user is the third successfully registered user.

4. We will then try to check the user information without logging in. Let's see what information we can get. Click on the **Collections** tab, create a new request with the name **User**, and save it under the **User** folder.

5. Edit the request and put **http://localhost:5000/users/james** in the URL field. **Save** the request so that it can be reused later.

6. Click **Send** to get the user details. The result is shown in the following screenshot:

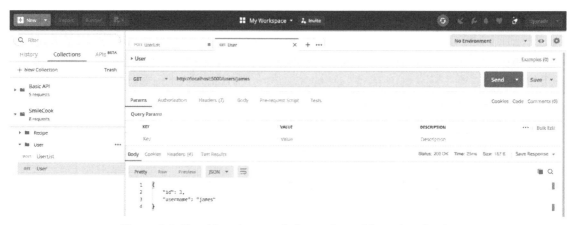

Figure 4.4: Checking the user information without logging in

You will then see the response. The HTTP Status is **200 OK**, meaning the request has been successful. We can see the ID and username in the response body. However, we can't see the email address here because it is private information and is only visible to the authenticated user.

7. Now, log in through the API. Click on the **Collections** tab. Create a new folder called **Token** and create a new request called **Token** inside it.

8. Edit the request, change the method to **POST**, and put `http://localhost:5000/token` in the URL field.

9. Click the **Body** tab, check the **raw** radio button, and select **JSON (application/json)** in the drop-down menu. Type in the following JSON content in the **Body** field and click **Save**:

```
{
    "email": "james@gmail.com",
    "password": "WkQad19"
}
```

10. Click **Send** to log in. The result is shown in the following screenshot:

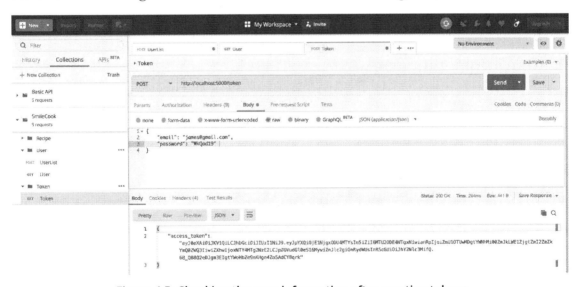

Figure 4.5: Checking the user information after creating tokens

You will then see the response. The HTTP status code **200** means the login has been successful. We can see the access token in the response body. We will rely on this token to show that the user has logged in.

11. Now check the user information again after we have logged in. Click the **Collections** tab and select the **GET User** request.

12. Select the **Headers** tab, select **Authorization** in the **KEY** field, type `Bearer {token}` in the **VALUE** field, where the token is what we obtained in step 10.

13. Click **Send** to get the user details. The result is shown in the following screenshot:

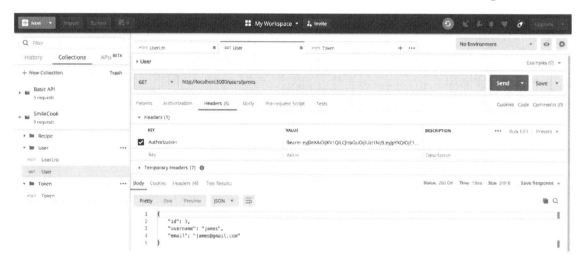

Figure 4.6: Checking the user information after logging in

You will then see the response, the HTTP status code **200** means the request is successful. And in the response body, we can see information including **id**, **username**, and **email**.

In this exercise, we can see how access control really works. We can see the difference in the HTTP response before and after the user is authenticated. This is very important for our Smilecook application because we want to protect our users' privacy. There is information that only certain authenticated users can see.

Exercise 26: Creating the me Endpoint

In this exercise, we will create a special endpoint, **/users/me**. That will allow us to get the authenticated user information back by using **access_token**. We will first create a new **resource** class under the **user** model. There will be a **get** method in it, and we will finally associate this with the new API endpoint:

1. Add the **get_by_id** method in **models/user.py**. For convenience's sake, we will use this method to get the user object by ID:

   ```python
   @classmethod
   def get_by_id(cls, id):
           return cls.query.filter_by(id=id).first()
   ```

2. In **resources/user.py**, import **jwt_required** and create a **MeResource** class:

   ```python
   from flask_jwt_extended import jwt_optional, get_jwt_identity, jwt_required


   class MeResource(Resource):

       @jwt_required
       def get(self):

           user = User.get_by_id(id=get_jwt_identity())

           data = {
                   'id': user.id,
                   'username': user.username,
                   'email': user.email,
           }

           return data, HTTPStatus.OK
   ```

The **get** method here will get the user information by the ID in the JWT.

3. In **app.py**, import the **MeResource** class. Add the **/me** endpoint:

```
from resources.user import UserListResource, UserResource, MeResource

api.add_resource(MeResource, '/me')
```

4. Right-click on it to run the application. **Flask** will then be started up and run on localhost (**127.0.0.1**) at port **5000**:

```
Run:    app
        /TrainingByPackt/Python-API-Development-Fundamentals/venv/bin/python /TrainingByPackt/Python-API-Development-Fundamental
        * Serving Flask app "app" (lazy loading)
        * Environment: production
          WARNING: This is a development server. Do not use it in a production deployment.
          Use a production WSGI server instead.
        * Debug mode: on
        * Running on http://127.0.0.1:5000/ (Press CTRL+C to quit)
        * Restarting with stat
        * Debugger is active!
        * Debugger PIN: 304-936-572

4: Run    5: Debug    6: TODO    9: Version Control    Terminal    Python Console                    Event Log
```

Figure 4.7: Run the application to start and run the Flask on localhost

5. Now check the user information again after we have logged in using the users/me endpoint. Click on the **Collections** tab and create a new request called **Me** in the **User** folder.

6. Put **http://localhost:5000/me** in the URL field.

7. Select the **Headers** tab, select **Authorization** in the **KEY** field and type in **Bearer {token}** in the **VALUE** field, where the token is what we obtained in the previous exercise.

8. Click **Send** to get the user details. The result is shown in the following screenshot:

Figure 4.8: Checking the user information after we have logged in

This new API endpoint allows us to get the authenticated user information just by using the access token. This means that whenever the user is in the authenticated state, we can get their information. Now that we have pretty much figured out the users, let's work on the recipes.

Designing the Methods in the Recipe Model

Now, we have finished the user registration and login feature, we will work on the recipe management features of our Smilecook application. That will need a few methods in the **Recipe** class to do the work. In our design, we will have the following five methods:

- **data**: This is used to return the data in a dictionary format.
- **get_all_published**: This method gets all the published recipes.
- **get_by_id**: This method gets the recipes by ID.
- **save**: This method persists data to the database.
- **delete**: This method deletes data from the database.

These five methods cover pretty much all the necessary recipe management functions. In the next exercise, we will work on implementing these methods in our Smilecook application.

Exercise 27: Implementing Access-Controlled Recipe Management Functions

The aim of this exercise is to implement different recipe management functions on our platform so that users can manage their own recipes in our Smilecook application. We will also have to modify **RecipeListResource** and **RecipeResource** to restrict access to certain methods there:

1. In **models/recipe.py**, add the **data**, **get_all_published**, **get_by_id**, **save**, and **delete** methods to the **Recipe** class:

```python
def data(self):
    return {
        'id': self.id,
        'name': self.name,
        'description': self.description,
        'num_of_servings': self.num_of_servings,
        'cook_time': self.cook_time,
        'directions': self.directions,
        'user_id': self.user_id
    }
```

```python
    @classmethod
    def get_all_published(cls):
        return cls.query.filter_by(is_publish=True).all()

    @classmethod
    def get_by_id(cls, recipe_id):
        return cls.query.filter_by(id=recipe_id).first()

    def save(self):
        db.session.add(self)
        db.session.commit()

    def delete(self):
        db.session.delete(self)
        db.session.commit()
```

2. Delete the following code in **models/recipe.py**:

```python
recipe_list = []

def get_last_id():
    if recipe_list:
        last_recipe = recipe_list[-1]
    else:
        return 1
    return last_recipe.id + 1
```

3. In **resources/recipe.py**, import **get_jwt_identity**, **jwt_required**, and **jwt_optional**:

```python
from flask_jwt_extended import get_jwt_identity, jwt_required, jwt_optional
```

4. Remove import **recipe_list**

```python
from models.recipe import Recipe
```

5. We will then modify the **get** method in the **RecipeListResource** class. We will get all the published recipes by triggering **Recipe.get_all_published()**.Then, in the **for** loop, it iterates through the recipe list, converts each recipe into a dictionary object, and returns the dictionary list:

```python
class RecipeListResource(Resource):

    def get(self):

        recipes = Recipe.get_all_published()
```

```
data = []

for recipe in recipes:
    data.append(recipe.data())

return {'data': data}, HTTPStatus.OK
```

6. We then continue to modify the **post** method in the **RecipeListResource** class. The **@jwt_required** decorator here says that the method can only be invoked after the user has logged in. Inside the method, it gets all the recipe details from the client requests and saves them in the database. Finally, it will return the data with an HTTP status code of **201 CREATED**:

```
@jwt_required
def post(self):

    json_data = request.get_json()
    current_user = get_jwt_identity()
    recipe = Recipe(name= json_data['name'],
                    description= json_data['description'],
                    num_of_servings= json_data['num_of_servings'],
                    cook_time= json_data['cook_time'],
                    directions= json_data['directions'],
                    user_id=current_user)

    recipe.save()

    return recipe.data(), HTTPStatus.CREATED
```

7. We will modify the **get** method in **RecipeResource** to get a specific recipe. The **@jwt_optional** decorator specifies that the JWT is optional. Inside the method, we use **Recipe.get_by_id(recipe_id=recipe_id)** to get the recipe. If the specific recipe is not found, we will return **404 NOT_FOUND**. If it is found, we will then change the user who owns the recipe and the status. There is access control here, so it will return **403 FORBIDDEN** or **200 OK** depending on the situation:

```
class RecipeResource(Resource):

    @jwt_optional
    def get(self, recipe_id):

        recipe = Recipe.get_by_id(recipe_id=recipe_id)

        if recipe is None:
```

```
            return {'message': 'Recipe not found'}, HTTPStatus.NOT_FOUND

        current_user = get_jwt_identity()

        if recipe.is_publish == False and recipe.user_id != current_user:
            return {'message': 'Access is not allowed'}, HTTPStatus.
    FORBIDDEN

        return recipe.data(), HTTPStatus.OK
```

8. We will modify the **put** method in **RecipeResource** to get a specific recipe. This **put** method is to update the recipe details. It will first check whether the recipe exists and whether the user has update privileges. If everything is okay, it will go ahead to update the recipe details and save it to the database:

```
@jwt_required
def put(self, recipe_id):

    json_data = request.get_json()

    recipe = Recipe.get_by_id(recipe_id=recipe_id)

    if recipe is None:
        return {'message': 'Recipe not found'}, HTTPStatus.NOT_FOUND

    current_user = get_jwt_identity()

    if current_user != recipe.user_id:
        return {'message': 'Access is not allowed'}, HTTPStatus.
    FORBIDDEN

        recipe.name = json_data['name']
        recipe.description = json_data['description']
        recipe.num_of_servings = json_data['num_of_servings']
        recipe.cook_time = json_data['cook_time']
        recipe.directions = json_data['directions']

        recipe.save()

        return recipe.data(), HTTPStatus.OK
```

9. We will modify the **delete** method in **RecipeResource** to get a specific recipe. This is for deleting a recipe. The **@jwt_required** decorator implies that the JWT is required. When the user has logged in, they can access this path and delete the specified recipe if it exists:

```
@jwt_required
def delete(self, recipe_id):

    recipe = Recipe.get_by_id(recipe_id=recipe_id)

    if recipe is None:
        return {'message': 'Recipe not found'}, HTTPStatus.NOT_FOUND

    current_user = get_jwt_identity()

    if current_user != recipe.user_id:
        return {'message': 'Access is not allowed'}, HTTPStatus.
FORBIDDEN

    recipe.delete()

    return {}, HTTPStatus.NO_CONTENT
```

So, in this exercise, we have implemented the recipe management functions and added access control to the resources. Now, only authorized users are allowed to manage their recipes. Let's test whether this is really the case in our next exercise.

Exercise 28: Testing the Recipe Management Functions

The aim of this exercise is to test all the recipe management functions using Postman. We registered an account in our previous exercise and logged in. We will use the same authenticated user to test adding, updating, and deleting recipes:

1. Create a recipe through our API. Click on the **Collections** tab and select the **POST RecipeList** request that we created previously.

2. Go to the **Headers** tab, select **Authorization** in the **KEY** field and `Bearer {token}` in the **VALUE** field, where the token is the JWT token we got in our previous exercise. The result is shown in the following screenshot:

Figure 4.9: Creating a recipe through the API

3. Go to the **Body** tab and type in the following recipe details:

```
{
    "name": "Cheese Pizza",
    "description": "This is a lovely cheese pizza",
    "num_of_servings": 2,
    "cook_time": 30,
    "directions": "This is how you make it"
}
```

4. Click **Send** to create a new recipe. The result is shown in the following screenshot:

Figure 4.10: New recipe created

You will then see the response. The HTTP status code **201** here means the recipe is created successfully. And we can see the details in the HTTP response body. We can see from the response that the **user_id** is **3**, which is the user ID of the currently authenticated user.

5. Get the recipe with **id = 3** in the state that the user has logged in. Click on the **Collections** tab and select the **GET** recipe request that we created previously.

6. Go to the **Headers** tab, select **Authorization** in the **KEY** field and **Bearer {token}** in the **VALUE** field, where the token is the JWT token we got in the previous exercise.

7. Click **Send** to check the recipe. The result is shown in the following screenshot:

Figure 4.11: Recipe with ID 3 after the user is logged in

You will then see the response. We can see the recipe details in the body. That is because the user is authenticated.

8. Get the recipe with **id = 3** in the state that the user has *not* logged in. The expected result is that we won't be able to see the unpublished recipe. Click on the **Collections** tab and select the **GET Recipe** request that we created previously.

9. Go to the **Headers** tab and uncheck **Authorization**, meaning that we are not going to put in the JWT token. Click **Send** to check the recipe. The result is shown in the following screenshot:

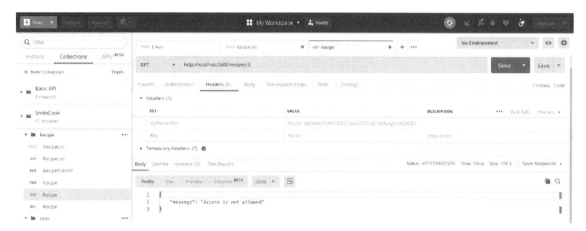

Figure 4.12: Recipe with ID 3 and the user not logged in

You will then see the response; the HTTP status code is **403 FORBIDDEN**. This is because the recipe is unpublished and we have implemented access control on our API so that only authenticated users can see their own recipes in the draft. We see the message **Access is not allowed** because we have not logged in yet. The unpublished recipe is not available to the public.

So, we have tested the access control recipe management functions. We can see how these can be used in real-world scenarios. Next, we will discuss refresh tokens, which are for keeping our users in the logged-in state.

Refresh Tokens

For the sake of security, we often set an expiration time for our tokens (`flask-jwt-extended` defaults that to 15 minutes). Because a token will expire, we need a function to refresh it without users putting in their credentials again.

Flask-JWT-Extended provides refresh-token-related functions. A refresh token is a long-lived token that can be used to generate new access tokens. Please don't mix up refresh tokens and access tokens. A refresh token can only be used to obtain a new access token; it cannot be used as an access token to access restricted endpoints. For example, endpoints that have the `jwt_required()` or `jwt_optional()` decorators need an access token.

Here's a brief explanation of the refresh-token-related functions in Flask-JWT-Extended:

- **create_access_token**: This function creates a new access token.

- **create_refresh_token**: This function creates a refresh token.

- **jwt_refresh_token_required**: This is a decorator specifying that the refresh token is required.

- **get_jwt_identity**: This function gets the user that holds the current access token.

You will learn more about these functions in the next exercise. We will also add a **fresh** attribute to our token. This **fresh** attribute will only be set to **True** when users get the token by putting in their credentials. When they simply refresh the token, they will get a token with **fresh = false**. The reason for a refresh token is that we would like to avoid users having to put their credentials in again and again. However, for some critical functions, for example, changing passwords, we will still require them to have a fresh token.

Exercise 29: Adding a Refresh Token Function

In this exercise, we will be adding a refresh token feature to our Smilecook application so that when the user's access token expires, they can use the refresh token to obtain a new access token:

1. In **resources/token.py**, import the necessary functions from **flask_jwt_extended**:

```
from flask_jwt_extended import (
    create_access_token,
    create_refresh_token,
    jwt_refresh_token_required,
    get_jwt_identity
)
```

2. Modify the **post** method under **TokenResource** to generate a **token** and a **refresh_token** for the user:

```
def post(self):
    data = request.get_json()
    email = data.get('email')
    password = data.get('password')
    user = User.get_by_email(email=email)
    if not user or not check_password(password, user.password):
        return {'message': 'username or password is incorrect'},
HTTPStatus.UNAUTHORIZED
```

```
access_token = create_access_token(identity=user.id, fresh=True)
refresh_token = create_refresh_token(identity=user.id)
return {'access_token': access_token, 'refresh_token': refresh_
token}, HTTPStatus.OK
```

We pass in the **fresh=True** parameter to the **create_access_token** function. We then invoke the **create_refresh_token** function to generate a **refresh** token.

3. Add the **RefreshResource** class to **token.py**. Please add the following code:

```
class RefreshResource(Resource):

    @jwt_refresh_token_required
    def post(self):
        current_user = get_jwt_identity()

        access_token = create_access_token(identity=current_user,
fresh=False)

        return {access_token: access_token}, HTTPStatus.OK
```

The **@jwt_refresh_token_required** decorator specifies that this endpoint will require a **refresh** token. In this method, we are generating a token for the user with **fresh=false**.

4. Finally, add the route for **RefreshResource**:

```
from resources.token import TokenResource, RefreshResource

def register_resources(app):

    api.add_resource(RefreshResource, '/refresh')
```

5. Save **app.py** and right-click on it to run the application. **Flask** will then be started up and run on localhost (**127.0.0.1**) at port **5000**:

Figure 4.13: Run the application to start and run Flask on localhost

Congratulations! We have just added the refresh token function. Let's move on to the testing part.

Exercise 30: Obtaining a New Access Token Using a Refresh Token

In this exercise, we will be using Postman to log in to the user account and get the access token and refresh token. Later on, we will obtain a new access token by using the refresh token. This is to simulate a real-life scenario in which we want to keep the user logged in:

1. We will test logging first. Click on the **Collections** tab. Select the **POST Token** request that we created previously.

2. Check the **raw** radio button and select **JSON (application/json)** from the drop-down menu.

3. Add the following JSON content in the **Body** field:

   ```
   {
       "email": "james@gmail.com",
       "password": "WkQad19"
   }
   ```

4. Click **Send** to login to the account. The result is shown in the following screenshot:

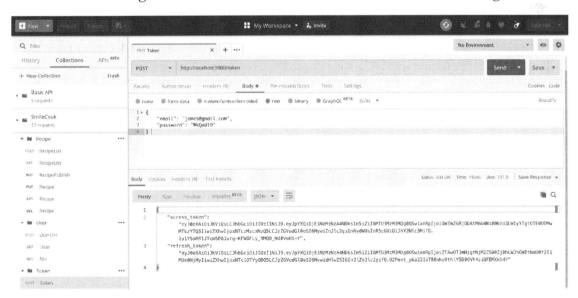

Figure 4.14: Testing the login

We can see that the HTTP status code is **200 OK**, meaning the login has been successful. We can also see the access token and refresh token in the body.

5. Next, we will get the **access** token by using the **refresh** token. Click on the **Collections** tab. Create a new request, name it **Refresh**, and save it in the **Token** folder.

6. Select this new request and choose **POST** as the method. Put `http://localhost:5000/refresh` in the **URL** field.

7. Go to the **Headers** tab and select **Authorization** in the **KEY** field and `Bearer {token}` in the **VALUE** field, where the token is the **JWT** we got in step 4.

8. Click **Send** to refresh the token. The result is shown in the following screenshot:

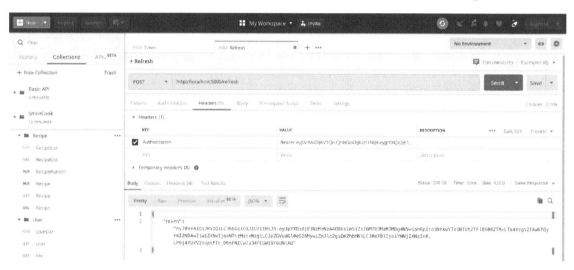

Figure 4.15: Accessing the token using the refresh token

We can see HTTP status **200 OK**, which means the request has been successful. And we can see the new access token in the response body. If the access token expires in the future, we can use a refresh token to obtain a new access token.

The User Logout Mechanism

The Flask-JWT-Extended package supports the logout function. The way it works is to put the token into a blacklist when the user is logged out. A **blacklist** is basically a blocklist; it is an access control mechanism. Things (for example, emails, tokens, IDs, and so on) on the list will be denied access. With the blacklist in place, the application can use `token_in_blacklist_loader` to verify whether the user has logged out or not:

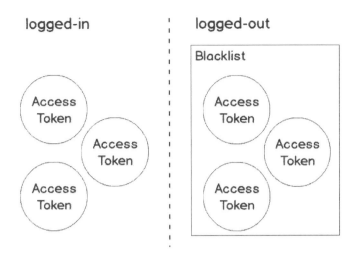

Figure 4.16: The user logout mechanism using a blacklist

In the next exercise, we want you to try implementing this logout function. It will test your understanding of the login and logout flow.

Exercise 31: Implementing the Logout Function

In this exercise, we will implement the logout function. We will first declare a **black_list** to store all the **logged-out** access tokens. Later, when the user wants to visit the access-controlled API endpoints, we will first check whether the access token is still valid using the blacklist:

1. Import **get_raw_jwt**. In **resources/token.py**, we will import **jwt_required** and **get_raw_jwt** from **flask_jwt_extended**:

    ```
    from flask_jwt_extended import (
        create_access_token,
        create_refresh_token,
        jwt_refresh_token_required,
        get_jwt_identity,
        jwt_required,
        get_raw_jwt
    )
    ```

2. In **resources/token.py**, assign **set()** to **black_list**:

    ```
    black_list = set()
    ```

3. Create the **RevokeResource** class and define the **post** method. We will apply the **@ jwt_required** decorator here to control the access to this endpoint. In this method, we get the token using **get_raw_jwt()['jti']** and put it in the blacklist:

```
class RevokeResource(Resource):

    @jwt_required
    def post(self):
        jti = get_raw_jwt()['jti']

        black_list.add(jti)

        return {'message': 'Successfully logged out'}, HTTPStatus.OK
```

4. We will then add the following code in **config.py**. As you can tell, we are enabling the blacklist feature and also telling the application to check both the **access** and **refresh** token:

```
class Config:
    JWT_BLACKLIST_ENABLED = True
    JWT_BLACKLIST_TOKEN_CHECKS = ['access', 'refresh']
```

5. We will then import **RevokeResource** and **black_list** in **app.py**:

```
from resources.token import TokenResource, RefreshResource,
RevokeResource, black_list
```

6. Then, inside **register_extensions(app)**, we will add the following lines of code. This is to check whether the token is on the blacklist:

```
def register_extensions(app):
    db.app = app
    db.init_app(app)
    migrate = Migrate(app, db)
    jwt.init_app(app)

    @jwt.token_in_blacklist_loader
    def check_if_token_in_blacklist(decrypted_token):
        jti = decrypted_token['jti']
        return jti in black_list
```

7. Finally, add the route in **register_resources**:

```
def register_resources(app):

    api.add_resource(TokenResource, '/token')
    api.add_resource(RefreshResource, '/refresh')
    api.add_resource(RevokeResource, '/revoke')
```

8. Save **app.py** and right-click on it to run the application. **Flask** will then be started up and run on localhost (**127.0.0.1**) at port **5000**:

Figure 4.17: Run the application to start Flask

Once the server is started, that means we are ready to test our refresh token API.

Exercise 32: Testing the Logout Function

In this exercise, we are going to test the logout function that we have just implemented in the previous exercise. Once we have logged out, we will try accessing an access-controlled endpoint and make sure we no longer have access to it:

1. We will log out from our application. Click on the **Collections** tab and create a new request, name it **Revoke**, and save it in the **Token** folder.

2. Select this new request and choose **POST** as the method. Put **http://localhost:5000/revoke** in the URL field.

3. Go to the **Headers** tab. Select **Authorization** in the **KEY** field and **Bearer {token}** in the **VALUE** field, where the token is the JWT we got in the previous exercise.

4. Click **Send** to log out. The result is shown in the following screenshot:

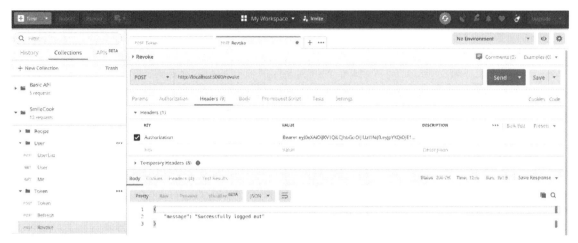

Figure 4.18: Logging out from the application

You will then see the response, HTTP status **200 OK**, meaning that the user has logged out successfully. Besides this, we can also see the message saying that the user has **successfully logged out**.

5. Log out again and see what happens. Click **Send** again, and you will then see the following response:

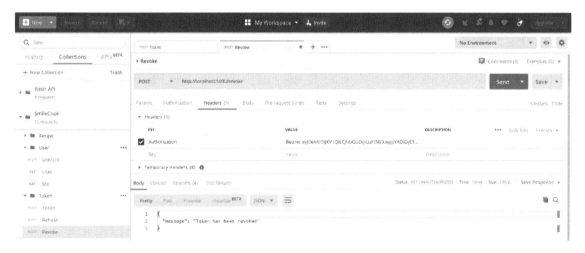

Figure 4.19: Logging out again

We can see HTTP status **401 UNAUTHORIZED**, meaning the user doesn't have access to this endpoint because the original access token has already been placed on the blacklist. In the response body, we can see the message **Token has been revoked**, meaning the user has successfully logged out.

Activity 7: Implementing Access Control on the publish/unpublish Recipe Function

In this activity, we will implement access control on the **publish/unpublish** recipe API endpoint so that only authenticated users can **publish/unpublish** their own recipe. Follow these steps to complete the activity:

1. Modify the **put** method in **RecipePublishResource** to restrict access to authenticated users.

2. Modify the **delete** method in **RecipePublishResource**.

3. Log in to the user account and get the access token.

4. Publish the recipe with **id** = **3** in the state that the user has logged in.

5. Unpublish a recipe **id** = **3** in the state that the user has logged in

> **Note**
>
> The solution for this activity can be found on page 307.

If you got everything right, congratulations! That means you have added access control to the publish and unpublish recipe function. Now, recipes are protected in the Smilecook application. Only the authors of the recipes can manage their own recipes now.

Summary

In this chapter, we learned how to use Flask-JWT-Extended for access control. This is an important and fundamental feature that almost all online platforms will require. At the end of the chapter, we touched on the topic of maintaining the liveliness of a token. This is advanced but applicable knowledge that you will use in developing real-life RESTful APIs. In the next chapter, we will start to talk about data verification.

5

Object Serialization with marshmallow

Learning Objectives

By the end of this chapter, you will be able to:

- Create a schema for serialization/deserialization
- Validate the data in a client request
- Perform data filtering before displaying the data to the client
- Use the HTTP PATCH method to partially update data

This chapter covers serialization and deserialization, as well as data filtering and validation with marshmallow.

Introduction

In this era of information explosion, the correctness of data is crucially important. We need to ensure that the data passed in by the client is in the format we expect. For example, we expect the `cooking time` variable to be a data type integer with a value of 30, but the client could pass in a string data type, with `value = "thirty minutes"`. They mean the same thing, and both are understandable to human beings but the system won't be able to interpret them. In this chapter, we will learn about data validation, making sure the system only takes valid data. The marshmallow package not only helps us to verify the client's data but also to verify the data that we send back. This ensures data integrity in both directions, which will greatly improve the quality of the system.

In this chapter, we will focus on doing three essential things: first, we will modify the `User` class and add in the API verification. This is mainly to show the basic functions of marshmallow. We'll then modify the `Recipe` class, add a custom authentication method, and optimize the code. Finally, a new feature will be added, which allows us to query all the recipes of a specific user and filter the recipes with different publish statuses by the visibility parameter. With this in mind, let's move on to the first topic: **Serialization** versus **Deserialization**.

Serialization versus Deserialization

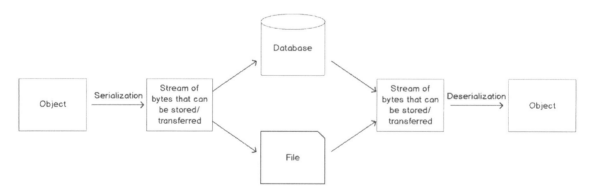

Figure 5.1: Serialization versus deserialization

An object is something that lives in the application memory. We can invoke its method or access its attributes in our application. However, when we want to transfer or store an object, we will have to convert it into a storable or transferrable format, and that format will be a stream of bytes. It can then be stored in a text file, in a database, or be transmitted over the internet. The process of converting an object to a stream of bytes is called serialization. This stream of bytes persists the state of the object so that it can be recreated later. The recreation of the object from a stream of bytes is called deserialization.

Serialization/deserialization is an essential part of RESTful API development. During actual development, the data validation related to business logic will often be included in the serialization and deserialization implementation processes as well.

marshmallow

marshmallow itself is an excellent package for serialization and deserialization in Python, as well as providing validation features. It allows developers to define schemas, which can be used to represent a field in various ways (required and validation), and automatically perform validation during deserialization. We will start by implementing a data validation function in this chapter. We will implement it using the marshmallow package to ensure that the information the user entered is correct. We will work with you through various exercises and activities to test serialization and deserialization afterward with Postman.

A Simple Schema

We will be using the `Schema` class from marshmallow to specify the fields for the objects that we want to serialize/deserialize. Without knowing the schema of the objects and how we want to serialize the fields, we can't perform serialization or deserialization. In the following example, you can see we have a simple `SimpleSchema` class, which extends `marshmallow.Schema`, and there are two fields defined there, **id** and **username**:

```
from marshmallow import Schema, fields


class SimpleSchema(Schema):


    id = fields.Int()
    username = fields.String()
```

The data type of the fields are defined using the `marshmallow` fields. From the preceding example, the **id** field is an **integer**, while the **username** field is a **string**. There are a number of different data types in marshmallow, including **Str**, **Int**, **Bool**, **Float**, **DateTime**, **Email**, **Nested**, and so on.

With the schema specified, we can start doing object serialization and deserialization. We can serialize objects in our application and return them in the HTTP response. Or, the other way round, we can take in a request from users and deserialize that into an object so that it can be used in our application.

Field Validation

We can also add field-level validation during serialization/deserialization. Again, this can be done in the schema definition. For example, if we want to specify a field as mandatory, we can add in the **required=True** argument. Using the same **SimpleSchema** example, we can specify the **username** field as mandatory as follows:

```
class SimpleSchema(Schema):


    id = fields.Int()

    username = fields.String(required=True)
```

If this **SimpleSchema** is used to deserialize the JSON request from the user and the **username** field is not filled in there, there will be an error message, **Validation errors**, and the HTTP status code will be **400 Bad Request**:

```
{
    "message": "Validation errors",
    "errors": {
        "username": [
            "Missing data for the required field."
        ]
    }
}
```

Now we will learn how to customize deserialization methods.

Customizing Deserialization Methods

We can also customize the way we want to deserialize certain fields. We can do so by using **Method** fields in marshmallow. A **Method** field receives an optional **deserialize** argument, which defines how the field should be deserialized.

From the following **SimpleSchema** example, we can define a custom method to deserialize the **password** field. We just need to pass in the **deserialize='load_password'** argument. It will invoke the **load_password** method to deserialize the **password** field:

```
class SimpleSchema(Schema):
    id = fields.Int()
    username = fields.String(required=True)
```

```
password = fields.Method(required=True, deserialize='load_password')
def load_password(self, value):
    return hash_password(value)
```

In the next section, we will learn how to use the **UserSchema** design.

UserSchema Design

Now we have learned why we need to use **Schema** and how we can define a schema, we will start to work on that in our **Smilecook** application. In the case of user registration, we will expect the user to fill in their information on a web form, and then send the details in JSON format to the server. Our **Smilecook** application will then deserialize it to be a **User** object, which can be worked on in our application.

We will, therefore, need to define a **UserSchema** class to specify the expected attributes in the JSON request coming from the frontend. We will need the following fields:

- **id**: Use **fields.Int()** to represent an integer. In addition, **dump_only=True** means that this property is only available for serialization, not deserialization. This is because **id** is autogenerated, not passed in by the user.

- **username**: Use **fields.String()** to represent a string and apply **required=True** to indicate that this property is mandatory. When the client sends JSON data without the username, there will be a validation error.

- **email**: Use **fields.Email()** to indicate that **email** format is needed, and apply **required=True** to indicate that this property is mandatory.

- **password:fields.Method()** is a **Method** field. The **Method** field here receives an optional **deserialize** argument, which defines how the field should be deserialized. We use **deserialize='load_password'** to indicate that the **load_password(self, value)** method will be invoked when using **load()** deserialization. Please note that this **load_password(self, value)** method will only be invoked during **load()** deserialization.

- **created_at:fields.DateTime()** represents the time format, and **dump_only=True** means that this property will only be available in serialization.

- **updated_at:fields.DateTime()** represents the time format, and **dump_only=True** means that this property will only be available in serialization.

In our next exercise, we will install the marshmallow package in our **Smilecook** project. Then, we will define the **UserSchema** and use it in **UserListResource** and **UserResource**.

Exercise 33: Using marshmallow to Validate the User Data

Firstly, we will perform data verification using marshmallow. We will install the **marshmallow** package and build **UserSchema**, and then use it in **UserListResource** to transmit the **User** object:

1. We will first install the marshmallow package. Please enter the following in **requirements.txt**:

   ```
   marshmallow==2.19.5
   ```

2. Run the **pip install** command:

   ```
   pip install -r requirements.txt
   ```

   You should see the result that follows:

   ```
   Installing collected packages: marshmallow
   Successfully installed marshmallow-2.19.5
   ```

3. Create a folder under the **Smilecook** project and name it **schemas**. We will store all our schema files here.

4. Create a **user.py** file under that and enter the following code. Use a schema to define the basic structure of the content of our expected client request. The following code creates **UserSchema** to define the attributes we will receive in the client request:

   ```python
   from marshmallow import Schema, fields

   from utils import hash_password

   class UserSchema(Schema):
       class Meta:
           ordered = True

       id = fields.Int(dump_only=True)
       username = fields.String(required=True)
       email = fields.Email(required=True)
       password = fields.Method(required=True, deserialize='load_password')

       created_at = fields.DateTime(dump_only=True)
       updated_at = fields.DateTime(dump_only=True)

       def load_password(self, value):
           return hash_password(value)
   ```

Before defining **UserSchema**, we need to first import **Schema** and **fields** from marshmallow. All self-defined marshmallow schemas must inherit **marshmallow. Schema**. Then, we import **hash_password**, and we define four attributes: **id**, **username**, **email**, and **password** in **UserSchema**.

5. Add the following code in **resources/user.py**. We will first import the **UserSchema** class from the previous step and instantiate two **UserSchema** objects here. One of them is for use in public, and we can see that the email is excluded:

```
from schemas.user import UserSchema

user_schema = UserSchema()
user_public_schema = UserSchema(exclude=('email', ))
```

For our **user** resource, when the authenticated user accesses its **users/<username>** endpoint, they can get **id**, **username**, and **email**. But if they are not authenticated or are accessing other people's **/users/<username>** endpoint, the email address will be hidden.

6. We will then modify **UserListResource** to the following to validate the data in the user's request:

```
class UserListResource(Resource):
    def post(self):
        json_data = request.get_json()

        data, errors = user_schema.load(data=json_data)

        if errors:
            return {'message': 'Validation errors', 'errors': errors},
HTTPStatus.BAD_REQUEST
```

7. In the same **UserListResource.post**, we will proceed if there is no error. It will then check whether **username** and **email** exist, and if everything is fine, we will use **User(**data)** to create a user instance, the ****data** will give us keyword arguments for the **User** class, then we use **user.save()** to store things in the database:

```
        if User.get_by_username(data.get('username')):
            return {'message': 'username already used'}, HTTPStatus.BAD_
REQUEST

        if User.get_by_email(data.get('email')):
            return {'message': 'email already used'}, HTTPStatus.BAD_
REQUEST
```

```
user = User(**data)
user.save()
```

8. Finally, also in **UsersLitResource.post**, we use **user_schema.dump(user).data** to return the successfully registered user data. It will contain **id**, **username**, **created_at**, **updated_at**, and **email**:

```
return user_schema.dump(user).data, HTTPStatus.CREATED
```

9. Next, we will modify **UserResource**. We will see the difference between with and without filtering email using **user_schema** and **user_public_schema** here:

```
class UserResource(Resource):

    @jwt_optional
    def get(self, username):

        user = User.get_by_username(username=username)

        if user is None:
            return {'message': 'user not found'}, HTTPStatus.NOT_FOUND

        current_user = get_jwt_identity()

        if current_user == user.id:
            data = user_schema.dump(user).data

        else:
            data = user_public_schema.dump(user).data

        return data, HTTPStatus.OK
```

When a user sends a request to **/users/<username/**, we will get their username. If a user can't be found, we will get **404 Not Found** error. If the user is found, we will check whether this user is the one currently logged in. If so, the user information will be serialized using **user_schema.dump(user).data**, which contains all the information. Otherwise, **user_public_schema.dump(user).data** will be used, which excludes the email information. Finally, it returns data with the HTTP status code **200 OK**.

10. Next, we will modify **MeResource**. It will be serialized using **user_schema.dump(user). data**, which contains all the information of the user:

```
class MeResource(Resource):

    @ jwt_required
    def get(self):
        user = User.get_by_id(id=get_jwt_identity())
        return user_schema.dump(user).data, HTTPStatus.OK
```

11. Save **app.py** and right-click on it to run the application. Flask will then be started up and run on the localhost (**127.0.0.1**) at port **5000**:

Figure 5.2: Run the application and then run Flask on the localhost

So, we have finished adding marshmallow to the picture. From now onward, when we transfer the **User** object between the frontend and backend, it will first be serialized/ deserialized. In the process, we can leverage the data validation functions provided by marshmallow to make our API endpoints even more secure.

Exercise 34: Testing the User Endpoint before and after Authentication

We implemented different user schemas in the previous exercise one for private viewing and one for public viewing. In this exercise, we are going to test whether they work as expected. We will check the data in the HTTP response and verify whether we get different user information before and after authentication. We want to hide the user's email address from the public, to protect user privacy.

We will do the whole test using Postman. Let's get started!

1. Check the **user** details before the user has logged in. We shouldn't see the user's email address in the result. Click on the **Collections** tab.

2. Select the **GET User** request.

3. Enter **http://localhost:5000/users/james** in the URL field. You can replace the username **James** with any username that is appropriate.

4. Click **Send** to check the user details for James. The result is shown in the following screenshot:

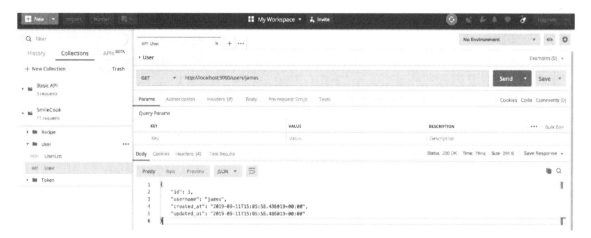

Figure 5.3: Checking the user details for James

You will then see the return response. We can see that the HTTP status code is **200 OK**, meaning we successfully get back **user** details. And in the response body, we can see the user details for James. We can see the **username**, **created_at**, **updated_at**, and **id**, but not the email address.

5. Now, let's login using Postman. Select the **POST Token** request. Click **Send** to log in. The result is shown in the following screenshot:

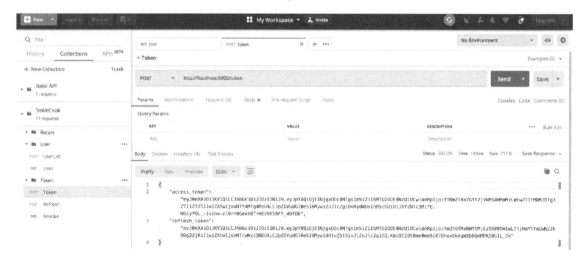

Figure 5.4: Log in and select the POST Token request

You will then see the response body for the access token and the refresh token.

7. Check the **user** details after the user has logged in. You should see the user's email address in the result. Click on the **Collections** tab. Choose to **GET User**. Select the **Headers** tab.

8. Enter `Authorization` in the **KEY** field and `Bearer {token}` in the **VALUE** field, where the token is the **JWT** token we got in *step 5*.

9. Click **Send** to check the user details for James. The result is shown in the following screenshot:

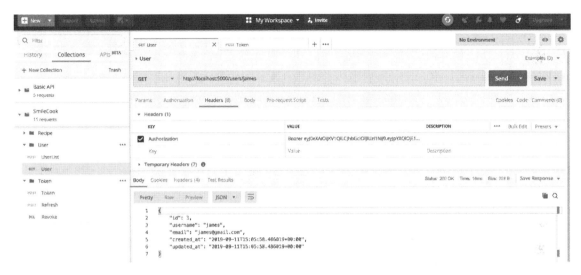

Figure 5.5: Checking the details after the user has logged in

You will then see the return response. In the response body, we can see the user details for James. We can see all his information, including his email address.

So, by using the **exclude** parameter in the user schema, we can easily exclude certain sensitive fields from showing up in the HTTP response. Apart from the **exclude** parameter, marshmallow also has the **include** parameter, which you can explore more yourself if you are interested.

RecipeSchema Design

So, we have done the serialization/deserialization for the **User** object. Now we are going to design the schema for the **Recipe** object. In the case of the **Recipe** update, we will expect the user to fill in updated recipe details on a web form, and then send the details in JSON format to the server. Our **Smilecook** application will then deserialize it to be a **Recipe** object, which can be worked on in our application.

RecipeSchema should inherit `marshmallow.Schema` and contains the following attributes:

- **id**: Use `fields.Int()` to represent an integer, and apply `dump_only=True` to specify that this property is only available for serialization.

- **name**: Use `fields.String()` to represent a string and apply `required=True` to indicate that this attribute is required.

- **description**: Use `fields.String()` to represent a string.

- **num_of_servings**: Use `fields.Int()` to represent an integer.

- **cook_time**: Use `fields.Int()` to represent an integer.

- **directions**: Use `fields.String()` to represent a string.

- **is_publish**: Use `fields.Boolean()` to represent a Boolean, and apply `dump_only=True` to specify that this attribute is only available for serialization.

- **author**: This attribute is used to display the author of the recipe.

- **created_at**: Use `fields.DateTime` to represent the format of the time, and `dump_only=True` means that this attribute is only available for serialization.

- **updated_at**: Use `fields.DateTime` to represent the format of the time, and `dump_only=True` means that this attribute is only available for serialization.

Exercise 35: Implementing RecipeSchema

Now we have the **RecipeSchema** design in mind. In this exercise, we will learn more about marshmallow by implementing **RecipeSchema**. Not only can we just validate the data type of **fields**, but we can also build our own validation function. Let's get started:

1. First, we import **schema**, **fields**, **post_dump**, **validate**, **validates**, and **ValidationError** and create the **recipe schema** by entering the following code in `schemas/recipe.py`:

```
from marshmallow import Schema, fields, post_dump, validate, validates,
ValidationError

class RecipeSchema(Schema):
    class Meta:
        ordered = True

    id = fields.Integer(dump_only=True)
    name = fields.String(required=True, validate=[validate.
Length(max=100)])
```

```
description = fields.String(validate=[validate.Length(max=200)])

directions = fields.String(validate=[validate.Length(max=1000)])
is_publish = fields.Boolean(dump_only=True)

created_at = fields.DateTime(dump_only=True)
updated_at = fields.DateTime(dump_only=True)
```

We can perform additional validation for a field by passing in the **validate** argument. We use **validate.Length(max=100)** to limit the maximum length of this attribute to **100**. When it exceeds **100**, it will trigger a validation error. This can prevent users from passing in an extremely long string, which will create a burden on our database. Using the **validation** function from marshmallow, that can be easily prevented.

2. Then, we define the **validate_num_of_servings(n)** method in **RecipeSchema**, which is a customized validation function. This will validate that this attribute has a minimum of **1** and cannot be greater than **50**. If its value doesn't fall within this range, it will raise an error message:

```
def validate_num_of_servings(n):
    if n < 1:
        raise ValidationError('Number of servings must be greater than
0.')
    if n > 50:
        raise ValidationError('Number of servings must not be greater than
50.')
```

3. Next, add the **num_of_servings** attribute in **RecipeSchema**. Use **validate=validate_num_of_servings** to link to our custom function, which will verify the number of servings of this recipe:

```
num_of_servings = fields.Integer(validate=validate_num_of_servings)
```

4. There is another way for us to add a customized validation method. We can add the **cooktime** attribute in **RecipeSchema**:

```
cook_time = fields.Integer()
```

5. Then, in **RecipeSchema**, use the **@validates('cook_time')** decorator to define the validation method. When validating the **cook_time** property, it will call the **validate_cook_time** method to specify that the cooking time should be between 1 minute and 300 minutes:

    ```
    @validates('cook_time')
    def validate_cook_time(self, value):
        if value < 1:
            raise ValidationError('Cook time must be greater than 0.')
        if value > 300:
            raise ValidationError('Cook time must not be greater than
    300.')
    ```

6. On top of the **schemas/recipe.py** file, import **UserSchema** from marshmallow, because we will display the author information for the recipe together when displaying the recipe information:

    ```
    from schemas.user import UserSchema
    ```

7. Then, in **RecipeSchema**, define the attribute **author**. We use **fields.Nested** to link this attribute to an external object, which is **UserSchema** in this case:

    ```
    author = fields.Nested(UserSchema, attribute='user', dump_only=True,
    only=['id', 'username'])
    ```

    To avoid any confusion, this attribute is named **author** in the JSON response, but the original attribute name is the **user**. In addition, **dump_only=True** means that this attribute is only available for serialization. Finally, add **only=['id', ' username']** to specify that we will only show the user's ID and username.

8. In addition, we add the **@post_dump(pass_many=True)** decorator so that further processing can be done when the recipe is serialized. The code is as follows:

    ```
    @post_dump(pass_many=True)
    def wrap(self, data, many, **kwargs):
        if many:
            return {'data': data}
        return data
    ```

    In the case of returning only one recipe, it will be simply returned in a JSON string. But when we are returning multiple recipes, we will store the recipes in a list and return them using the **{'data': data}** format in JSON. This format will be beneficial for us when we develop the pagination feature.

9. The code in **schemas/recipe.py** should now look like the following – please review it:

```python
from marshmallow import Schema, fields, post_dump, validate, validates,
ValidationError

from schemas.user import UserSchema

def validate_num_of_servings(n):
    if n < 1:
        raise ValidationError('Number of servings must be greater than
0.')
    if n > 50:
        raise ValidationError('Number of servings must not be greater than
50.')

class RecipeSchema(Schema):
    class Meta:
        ordered = True

    id = fields.Integer(dump_only=True)
    name = fields.String(required=True, validate=[validate.
Length(max=100)])
    description = fields.String(validate=[validate.Length(max=200)])
    num_of_servings = fields.Integer(validate=validate_num_of_servings)
    cook_time = fields.Integer()
    directions = fields.String(validate=[validate.Length(max=1000)])
    is_publish = fields.Boolean(dump_only=True)

    author = fields.Nested(UserSchema, attribute='user', dump_only=True,
only=['id', 'username'])

    created_at = fields.DateTime(dump_only=True)
    updated_at = fields.DateTime(dump_only=True)

    @post_dump(pass_many=True)
    def wrap(self, data, many, **kwargs):
        if many:
            return {'data': data}
        return data

    @validates('cook_time')
```

```
def validate_cook_time(self, value):
    if value < 1:
        raise ValidationError('Cook time must be greater than 0.')
    if value > 300:
        raise ValidationError('Cook time must not be greater than
300.'
```

Once we have completed the recipe schema, we can start to use it in the related resources.

10. We will then modify **resources/recipe.py** as follows:

```
from schemas.recipe import RecipeSchema


recipe_schema = RecipeSchema()
recipe_list_schema = RecipeSchema(many=True)
```

We first import **RecipeSchema** from **schemas.recipe**,then define the **recipe_schema** variable and **recipe_list_schema**; they are for storing single and multiple recipes.

11. Modify the **RecipeListResource get** method to return all the published recipes back to the client by using the **recipe_list_schema.dump(recipes).data** method:

```
class RecipeListResource(Resource):

    def get(self):

        recipes = Recipe.get_all_published()

        return recipe_list_schema.dump(recipes).data, HTTPStatus.OK
```

12. Modify the **RecipeListResource post** method to use the recipe schema:

```
@jwt_required
def post(self):

    json_data = request.get_json()

    current_user = get_jwt_identity()

    data, errors = recipe_schema.load(data=json_data)

    if errors:
```

```
                return {'message': "Validation errors", 'errors': errors},
        HTTPStatus.BAD_REQUEST

            recipe = Recipe(**data)
            recipe.user_id = current_user
            recipe.save()

            return recipe_schema.dump(recipe).data, HTTPStatus.CREATED
```

After receiving the JSON data, the data is verified by **recipe_schema. load(data=json_data)**. If there is an error, it will return **HTTP status code 400 Bad Request** with an error message.

If the validation is passed, **Recipe(**data)** will be used to create a **recipe** object, then specify it as the currently logged-in user's ID via **recipe.user_id = current_ user**. The recipe will then be saved to the repository via **recipe.save()**, and finally, converted to JSON using **recipe_schema.dump(recipe).data** to the client, with a HTTP status code **201 CREATED** message.

13. Because the rendering of our data has been done through marshmallow, we don't need the **data** method in the recipe, so we can delete the **data** method in **model/ recipe.py**. That is, delete the following code from the file:

```
def data(self):
    return {
        'id': self.id,
        'name': self.name,
        'description': self.description,
        'num_of_servings': self.num_of_servings,
        'cook_time': self.cook_time,
        'directions': self.directions,
        'user_id': self.user_id
    }
```

14. Now we have finished the implementation. Right-click on it to run the application. Flask will then be started up and run on the localhost (127.0.0.1) at port 5000:

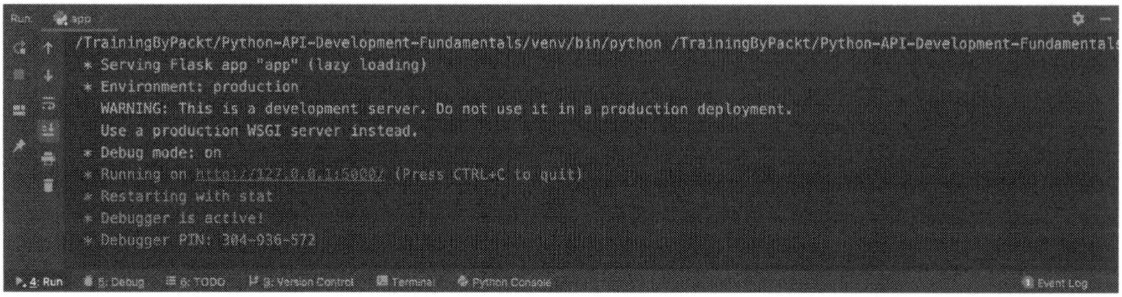

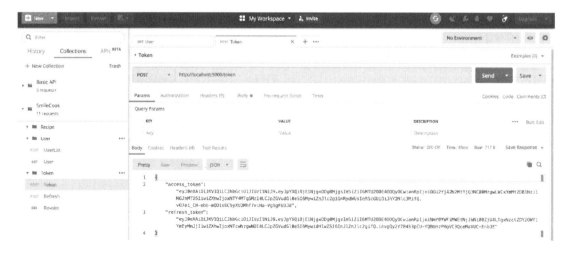

Figure 5.6: Run the application and then Flask on the localhost

So, we have just completed the work on **RecipeSchema**, as well as modifying the API endpoints to transmit the object using the serialization/deserialization approach. In the next exercise, we will test whether our implementation works.

Exercise 36: Testing the Recipe API

To test whether the serialization/deserialization of the object works, we will again need to test it in Postman. This exercise is to test creating and getting all our recipe details using Postman.

1. First, log in to the account. Our previous token was only valid for 15 minutes. If it expires, we need to log in again via **/token** or reacquire the token using the **Refresh** Token. Click on the **Collections** tab.

2. Select the **POST Token** request.

3. Click **Send** to log in. The result is shown in the following screenshot:

Figure 5.7: Log in to the account and select the POST Token request

You will then see the return response, **HTTP Status is 200 OK**, meaning the login was successful, and we will see the access token in the response body. This access token will be used in later steps.

4. Next, we will create a new recipe. Click on the **Collections** tab. Choose **POST RecipeList**.

5. Select the **Headers** tab. Enter `Authorization` in the **KEY** field and `Bearer {token}` in the **VALUE** field, where the token is the `JWT` token we got in our previous step.

6. Select the **Body** tab. Fill in the recipe details as follows:

```
{
    "name": "Blueberry Smoothie",
    "description": "This is a lovely Blueberry Smoothie",
    "num_of_servings": 2,
    "cook_time": 10,
    "directions": "This is how you make it"
}
```

7. Click **Send** to create a new recipe. The result is shown in the following screenshot:

Figure 5.8: Creating a new recipe

You will then see the return response, **HTTP Status is 201 CREATED**, meaning the new recipe has been created successfully. In the response body, we can see the recipe details. We can also see the author's details shown in a nested format.

8. Then, we will publish the recipe with `id = 4`. Click on the **Collections** tab. Choose the **PUT RecipePublish** request. Enter `http://localhost:5000/recipes/4/publish` in **Enter request URL**.

9. Select the **Headers** tab. Enter `Authorization` in the **KEY** field and `Bearer {token}` in the **VALUE** field, where the token is the JWT token we got in the previous step. Click **Send** to publish the recipe with `id = 4`. The result is shown in the following screenshot:

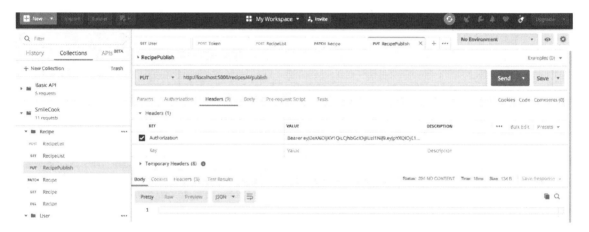

Figure 5.9: Publish the recipe with ID 4

You will then see the return response, HTTP Status is **204 NO CONTENT**, meaning it is published successfully. You will see no content in the body.

10. Then, we will get all the recipes back. Select the **GET RecipeList** request. Click
    Send to get all the recipes back. The result is shown in the following screenshot:

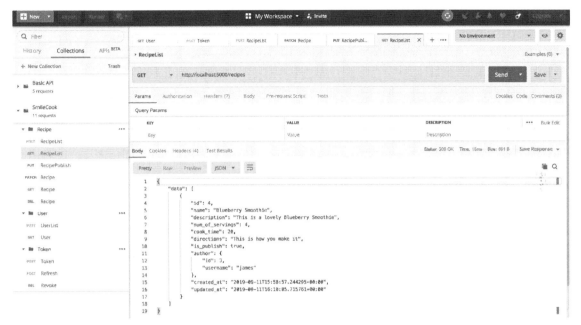

Figure 5.10: Getting all the recipes back by selecting the GET RecipeList request

You will then see the return response, HTTP Status is 200 **OK**, meaning we have
successfully retrieved all the recipe details. In the response body, we can see that there
is a list of data, which contains all the published recipes.

So, we have successfully implemented and tested the serialization (creating the recipe)
and deserialization (retrieving the recipe) on the recipe-related API endpoints. We are
making good progress here!

The PATCH Method

We have been using the **PUT** HTTP method all along for data updates. However, the actual usage of the **PUT** method is to **Replace** (**Create** or **Update**). For example, **PUT / items/1** means to replace everything in **/items/1**. If this item already exists, it will be replaced. Otherwise, it will create a new item. **PUT** must contain all attribute data for **items/1**.

This doesn't seem to work very well in all cases. If you just want to update only one of the attributes of **items/1**, you need to retransmit all the attributes of **items/1** to the server, which is not efficient at all. So, there is a new HTTP method: **PATCH**. The **PATCH** method was invented to do a partial update. With this method, we need to pass in only the attributes that need to be modified to the server.

Exercise 37: Using the PATCH Method to Update the Recipe

In this exercise, we will change the recipe update method from **PUT** to **PATCH**. We will also use the serialization/deserialization approach to transmit the recipes. Finally, we will test our changes in Postman, to make sure things work as expected. The aim of this exercise is to reduce the bandwidth and server processing resources when we update the recipe data:

1. Create the **patch** method in **RecipeListResource**. We will first use **request. get_json()** to get the JSON recipe details sent by the client, and then use **recipe_ schema.load(data=json_data, partial=('name',))** to validate the data format. We are using **partial=('name',)** because the original name is a required field in the schema. When the client only wants to update a single attribute, using **partial** allows us to specify that the **Name** attribute is optional, so no error will occur even though we are not passing in this attribute:

```
@jwt_required
 def patch(self, recipe_id):

     json_data = request.get_json()

     data, errors = recipe_schema.load(data=json_data,
partial=('name',))
```

2. Then, in the same **patch** method, we will check whether there is an error message. If any, it will return the **HTTP Status Code 400 Bad Request** error message. If the validation passes, then check whether the user has permission to update this recipe. If not, **HTTP status code Forbidden 403** will be returned:

```
if errors:
        return {'message': 'Validation errors', 'errors': errors},
HTTPStatus.BAD_REQUEST


recipe = Recipe.get_by_id(recipe_id=recipe_id)

if recipe is None:
        return {'message': 'Recipe not found'}, HTTPStatus.NOT_FOUND


current_user = get_jwt_identity()

if current_user != recipe.user_id:
        return {'message': 'Access is not allowed'}, HTTPStatus.
FORBIDDEN
```

3. We continue to work on the same **patch** method. **recipe.name = data.get('name') or recipe.name** means it will try to get the name of the key value of the data. If this value exists, it will be used. Otherwise, **recipe.name** will stay the same. This is basically how we do the update:

```
recipe.name = data.get('name') or recipe.name
recipe.description = data.get('description') or recipe.description
recipe.num_of_servings = data.get('num_of_servings') or recipe.
num_of_servings
recipe.cook_time = data.get('cook_time') or recipe.cook_time
recipe.directions = data.get('directions') or recipe.directions
```

4. In the same **patch** method, we use the **save** method to save everything to the database and return the recipe data in JSON format:

```
recipe.save()

return recipe_schema.dump(recipe).data, HTTPStatus.OK
```

5. Now we have the new **patch** method ready. Right-click on it to run the application. Flask will then be started up and run on the localhost (**127.0.0.1**) at port **5000**:

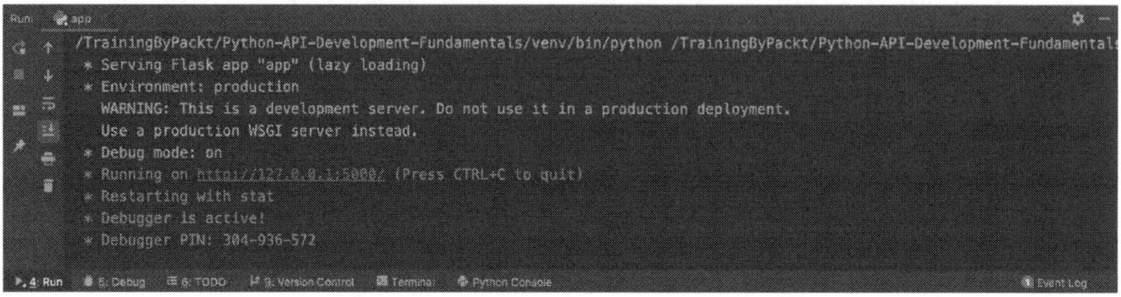

Figure 5.11: Run the application and then run Flask on the localhost

Next, we are going to update the recipe with **id** = **4**. We will update only two fields: **num_of_servings,** and **cook_time**:

6. Click on the **Collections** tab. Choose the **PUT Recipe** request. Change the **HTTP** method from **PUT** to **PATCH**.

7. Select the **Headers** tab. Enter **Authorization** in the **KEY** field and **Bearer {token}** in the **VALUE** field, where the token is the **JWT** token we got in our previous exercise.

8. Select the **Body** tab. Type the following in the **Body** field:

```
{
    "num_of_servings": 4,
    "cook_time": 20
}
```

Click **Send** to update the recipe. The result is shown in the following screenshot:

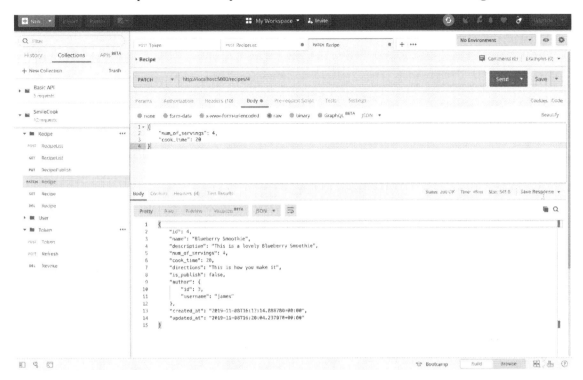

Figure 5.12: Updating the recipe

You will then see the return response **HTTP Status is 200 OK**, meaning the update was successful. In the body is the recipe details, and we can see that only `num_of_servings` and `cook_time` is updated. We can also see the `updated_at` timestamp has been automatically updated as well.

Searching for Authors and Unpublished Recipes

On the `Smilecook` platform, there will be many different foodies from around the world (here, we call them authors) to share their recipes. Among these outstanding authors, we will definitely have a favorite author, and we will definitely want to learn all of their recipes. Therefore, we have added a new endpoint (or function), which is to list the recipes of a specific author. This endpoint not only lists all the recipes published by a particular gourmet but can also allow the author to search all of their own published/unpublished recipes.

Using the webargs Package to Parse the Request Arguments

The request arguments, also known as the query string, are the arguments that we can pass in through the URL. For example, in the URL **http://localhost/testing?abc=123**, **abc=123** is the request argument.

webargs is a package for parsing request arguments. We will create a new endpoint, **GET http://localhost:5000/user/{username}/recipes**, to get all the published recipes from a particular author. For this endpoint, we will pass in the visibility request argument. The **visibility** request argument can have a value of **public**, **private**, or **all**. The default value is **public**. If it is **private** or **all**, the user needs to be authenticated first.

If you want to get only the unpublished recipes, you can add the request argument **visibility=private**. So, the URL will look like this: **http://localhost:5000/user/{username}/recipes?visibility=private**. The **webargs** package provides functions to parse this **visibility=private** argument in the URL, and then our **Smilecook** application will know this request is asking for private information in the recipe. Our **Smilecook** application will then determine whether the authenticated user is the author. If they are, it will return all the unpublished recipes. Otherwise, there is no permission for the user to see the unpublished recipes.

Exercise 38: Implementing Access Control on Recipes

In this exercise, we are going to implement access control on recipes. So, only authenticated users will be able to see all of their own recipes, including unpublished ones. The user will pass in the **visibility** mode by using the **request** argument. We use **webargs** to parse the visibility mode and return published, unpublished, or all recipes accordingly:

1. Create the **get_all_by_user** method in the **Recipe** class in **models/recipe.py**:

```
@classmethod
def get_all_by_user(cls, user_id, visibility='public'):
    if visibility == 'public':
        return cls.query.filter_by(user_id=user_id, is_publish=True).
all()

    elif visibility == 'private':
        return cls.query.filter_by(user_id=user_id, is_publish=False).
all()

    else:
        return cls.query.filter_by(user_id=user_id).all()
```

This method needs to take in **user_id** and **visibility**. If the **visibility** is not defined, the default will be **public**. If the **visibility** is **public**, it will get all the recipes by **user_id** and **is_publish=True**. If the visibility is **private**, it will search for the recipe with **is_publish=False**. If the visibility is not **public** or **private**, it will get all the recipes of this user.

2. We will install the **webargs** package, which is a package for interpreting and verifying HTTP arguments (for example, **visibility**). Please add the following package in **requirements.txt**:

   ```
   webargs==5.4.0
   ```

3. Install the package using the following command:

   ```
   pip install -r requirements.txt
   ```

   You should see a result like the following:

   ```
   Installing collected packages: webargs
   Successfully installed webargs-5.4.0
   ```

4. Import the necessary modules, functions, and classes in **resources/user.py**:

   ```
   from flask import request
   from flask_restful import Resource
   from flask_jwt_extended import get_jwt_identity, jwt_required, jwt_optional
   from http import HTTPStatus

   from webargs import fields
   from webargs.flaskparser import use_kwargs


   from models.recipe import Recipe
   from models.user import User

   from schemas.recipe import RecipeSchema
   from schemas.user import UserSchema
   ```

   First, import **webargs.fields** and **webargs.flaskparser.use_kwargs**, then we will need to use the recipe data, so we also need to import the recipe model and schema.

5. Then, we will declare the **recipe_list_schema** variable. Use **RecipeSchema** with the **many=True** parameter. This is to show that we will have multiple recipes:

   ```
   recipe_list_schema = RecipeSchema(many=True)
   ```

6. We will then create the **UserRecipeListResource** class. This resource is mainly for getting the recipes under a specific user. Please refer to the following code:

```
class UserRecipeListResource(Resource):

    @jwt_optional
    @use_kwargs('visibility': fields.Str(missing='public')})
    def get(self, username, visibility):
```

First, define **@jwt_optional** to mean that this endpoint can be accessed without a user being logged in. Then, use **@use_kwargs({'visibility': fields. Str(missing='public')})** to specify that we expect to receive the parameters of **visibility** here. If the parameter is absent, the default will be public. The **visibility** parameter will then be passed into **def get(self, username, visibility)**.

7. We will implement access control in **UserRecipeListResource.get**. If the username (the author of the recipe) is the currently authenticated user, then they can see all the recipes, including the private ones. Otherwise, they can only see the published recipes:

```
def get(self, username, visibility):

        user = User.get_by_username(username=username)

        if user is None:
            return {'message': 'User not found'}, HTTPStatus.NOT_FOUND

        current_user = get_jwt_identity()

        if current_user == user.id and visibility in ['all', 'private']:
            pass
        else:
            visibility = 'public'

        recipes = Recipe.get_all_by_user(user_id=user.id,
    visibility=visibility)

        return recipe_list_schema.dump(recipes).data, HTTPStatus.OK
```

The user is then obtained by **User.get_by_username(username=username)**. If the user cannot be found, will return a HTTP status code **404 NOT FOUND**. Otherwise, get the current user's ID using **get_jwt_identity()** and save it to the **current_user** variable.

Based on the user and their permission, we will display a different set of recipes. After the recipe is obtained, **recipe_list_schema.dump(recipes).data** is used to convert the recipes into JSON format and return to the client with HTTP Status Code is **200 OK**.

8. Then, import **UserRecipeListResource** in **app.py**:

    ```
    from resources.user import UserListResource, UserResource, MeResource,
    UserRecipeListResource
    ```

9. Finally, we add the following endpoint:

    ```
    api.add_resource(UserListResource, '/users')
    api.add_resource(UserResource, '/users/<string:username>')
    api.add_resource(UserRecipeListResource, '/users/<string:username>/
    recipes')
    ```

10. Now, we have finished the implementation. Right-click on it to run the application. Flask will then be started up and run on the localhost (**127.0.0.1**) at port **5000**:

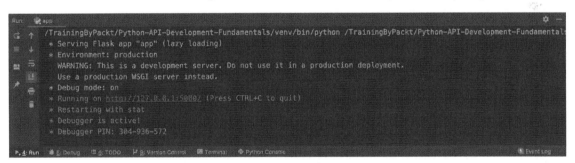

Figure 5.13: Run Flask on the localhost

Now we have learned how to use **webargs** to parse **request** arguments and have applied that to our **Smilecook** application. Next, as usual, we want to test and make sure that it works.

Exercise 39: Retrieving Recipes from a Specific Author

This exercise is to test what we implemented in our last exercise. We will make sure the API is parsing the visibility mode that the user passes in and returns different sets of recipes accordingly. We will use a specific user (James) for testing. We will see that before and after authentication, the user will be able to see different sets of recipes:

1. We will get all the published recipes for a particular user before they have logged in. First, click on the **Collections** tab.

2. Add a new request under the **User** folder. Set the **Request Name** to `UserRecipeList` and save.

3. Select the newly created **GET UserRecipeList** request. Enter `http://localhost:5000/users/james/recipes` in the **URL** field (change the username if necessary).

4. Click **Send** to check all the published recipes under this particular user (James here). The result is shown in the following screenshot:

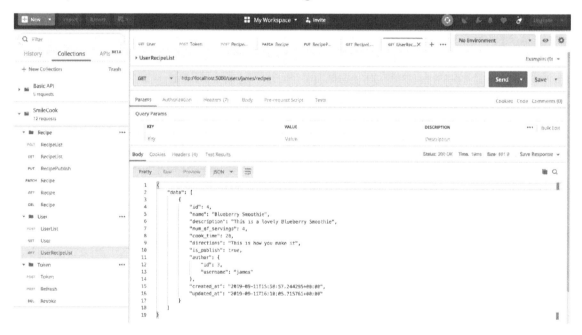

Figure 5.14: Get all the published recipes for a user before they have logged in

You will then see the return response. The HTTP status code **200 OK** here indicates that the request has succeeded and, in the body, we can see one published recipe under this author.

5. Similar to the previous step, we will see whether we can get all the recipes under a particular user before the user has logged in – it shouldn't be allowed. Select the **Params** tab. Set **KEY** to `visibility`. Set **VALUE** to `all`. Click **Send** to check all the recipes under this particular user. The result is shown in the following screenshot:

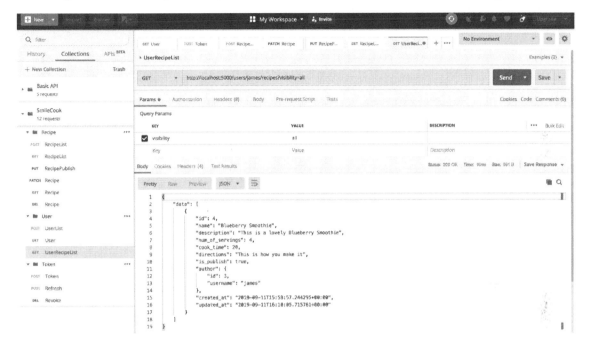

Figure 5.15: Check all the recipes under a particular user

You will then see the return response. The HTTP status code **200 OK** here indicates that the request has succeeded, and in the body again, though we are asking for all recipes, we can only see one published recipe under this author because the user hasn't logged in.

6. Log in and click on the **Collections** tab. Select the **POST Token** request. Click **Send** to check all the recipes under this particular user. The result is shown in the following screenshot:

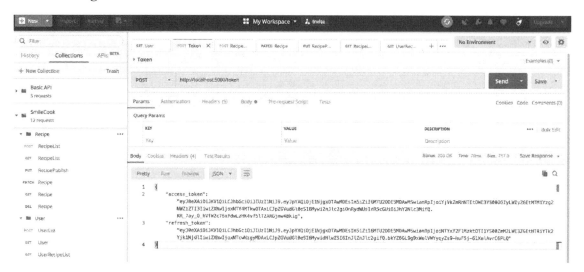

Figure 5.16: Select the POST Token request and send the request

You will then see the return response. The **HTTP status code 200 OK** here indicates that the request has succeeded, and in the body, we can get the access token and refresh token that we will use in the next step.

7. Select the **GET UserRecipeList** request. Select the **Headers** tab. Enter `Authorization` in the **Key** field and `Bearer {token}` in the **Value** field, where the token is the **JWT** token we got in our previous step. Click **Send** to query. The result is shown in the following screenshot:

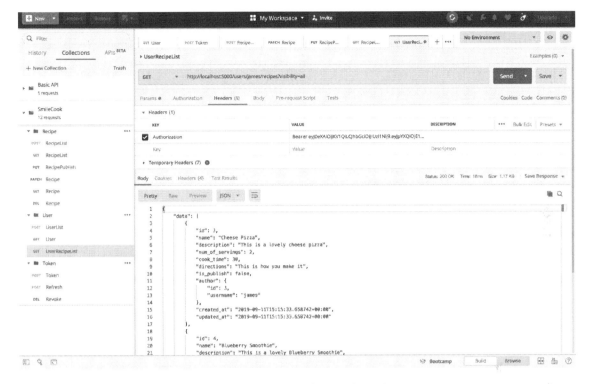

Figure 5.17: Use the JWT token and send to query

You will then see the return response. The **HTTP status code 200 OK** here indicates that the request has succeeded. In the response body, we can get all the recipes under this user, including the unpublished ones.

This testing exercise concluded what we have learned about the `webargs` package, as well as testing the new access control functions we added for viewing recipes.

Activity 8: Serializing the recipe Object Using marshmallow

In this activity, we want you to work on the serialization of the `RecipeResource.get` method. We did serialization for `User` and `RecipeList` in previous exercises. Now, it is your turn to work on this last one.

Currently, `RecipeResource.get` is returning the `recipe` object using `recipe.data()`. We want you to replace that by serializing the `recipe` object using marshmallow. The `recipe` object should be converted into JSON format and return to the frontend client-side. To do that, you will modify `recipe_schema` in `resources/recipe.py`. You are also required to test your implementation using Postman at the end.

The following are the steps to perform:

1. Modify the recipe schema, to include all attributes except for `email`.

2. Modify the `get` method in `RecipeResource` to serialize the `recipe` object into JSON format using the recipe schema.

3. Run the application so that Flask will start and run on the localhost.

4. Test the implementation by getting one specific published recipe in Postman.

> **Note**
>
> The solution for the activity can be found on page 312.

After this activity, you should have a good understanding of how to use schema to serialize objects. We have the flexibility to specify the attributes that need to be serialized, and how they are going to be serialized. Attributes that linked to another object can be serialized as well. As you can see from this activity, the author's information is included in this recipe response.

Summary

In this chapter, we have learned a lot of things. The data verification of an API through marshmallow is very important. This function should also be constantly updated in the production environment to ensure that the information we receive is correct.

In this chapter, we started with the verification of registered members and then talked about basic verification methods, such as setting mandatory fields, performing data type validation, and so on. Apart from data validation, marshmallow can be used for data filtering as well. We can use the **exclude** parameter to display the user email field. Based on what we learned, we then developed customized verifications for our application, such as verifying the length of the recipe creation time.

At the end of this chapter, we added the functionality to get all the recipes written by our favorite author. Then, we searched for different publish statuses through the **visibility** parameter and applied access control accordingly.

6

Email Confirmation

Learning Objectives

By the end of this chapter, you will be able to:

- Send out plaintext and HTML format emails using the Mailgun API
- Create a token for account activation using the itsdangerous package
- Utilize the entire workflow for user registration
- Develop applications using the benefits of environment variables

This chapter covers how to use an email package to develop an email activation feature on the food recipe sharing platform for user registration as well as email verification.

Introduction

In the previous chapter, we worked on validating APIs using marshmallow. In this chapter, we will add functionality to our application that allows us to send emails to users.

Everyone has their own email address. Some people may even have multiple mailboxes for different needs. In order to ensure the correctness of the email addresses entered by users when creating an account in our application, we need to verify their email address during registration. It is important to get their email address correct, as we may need to send emails to users in the future.

In this chapter, we will implement a function to verify a mailbox, learn how to send a message through the third-party Mailgun API, and create a unique token to ensure that it is verified by the user. This can be achieved with the `itsdangerous` package. At the end of the chapter, we will make our confidential information (for example, Mailgun API Secret Key) more secure by sorting it into environmental variables. So, when we upload our project to GitHub or other platforms down the road, this confidential information will not be shared in the project. The following is how the new user registration flow works:

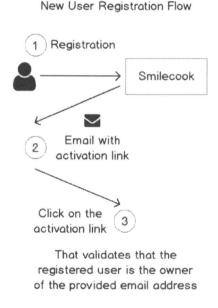

Figure 6.1: New user registration flow

In our first section, we will introduce you to the `Mailgun` platform. Without further ado, let's get started.

Mailgun

Mailgun is a third-party **SMTP** (**Simple Mail Transfer Protocol**) and API sending email provider. Through Mailgun, not only can a large number of emails be sent, but the log for every email can also be traced. You have 10,000 free quotas per month. That means, in the free plan, we can only send, at most, 10,000 emails. This will be enough for our learning purposes.

Mailgun also provides an open RESTful API, which is easy to understand and use. In the following exercise, we will register a Mailgun account, and send an email through the API.

Exercise 40: Get Started with Using Mailgun

To start with, we need to register an account in Mailgun. As we explained before, Mailgun is a third-party platform. We will register a Mailgun account in this exercise. Then, we will obtain the necessary setup information to use their email sending service API:

1. Visit the Mailgun website at https://www.mailgun.com/. Click **Sign Up** to register an account. The home page will look like the following screenshot:

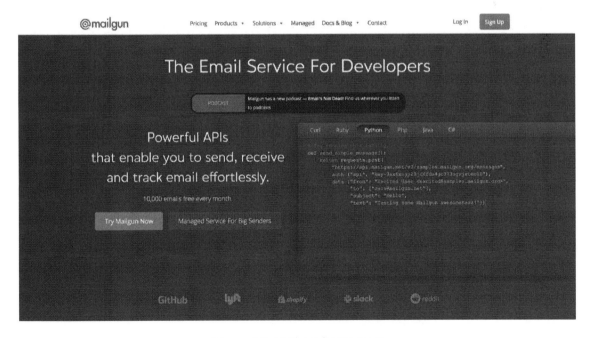

Figure 6.2: Mailgun home page

Once registration is done, Mailgun will send out a verification email with an account activation link.

2. Click on the link in the verification email to activate the account, which is shown in the following screenshot:

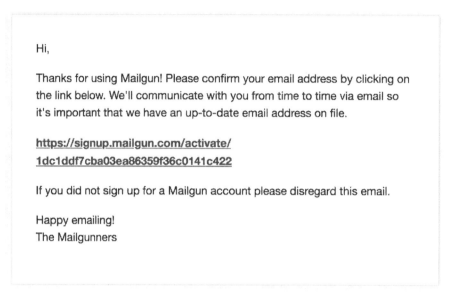

Figure 6.3: Mailgun account activation email

3. Then, we will follow the Mailgun verification process. Enter your phone number to get a verification code. Use the code to activate your account. The screen will look like this:

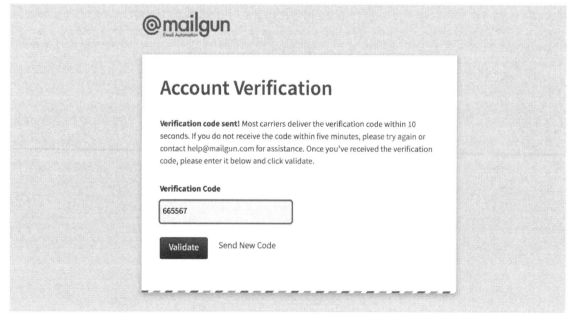

Figure 6.4: Verifying the account

4. After your account is activated, log in to your account, then go to the **Overview** screen under **Sending**. There, you can find the domain name, API key, and base URL. This information is required for our subsequent programming work. Mailgun also provides sample code for a quick start:

Figure 6.5: Mailgun dashboard

Now we have opened an account in Mailgun that will allow us to use their service to send emails to our users. The API URL and key are for our Smilecook application to connect to the Mailgun API. We will show you how to do that very soon.

> **Note**
>
> Currently, we are using the sandbox domain for testing. You can only send an email to your own email address (that is, the email address registered with Mailgun). If you want to send emails to other email addresses, you can add Authorized Recipients on the right-hand side, and it will send an email to that recipient. The recipient needs to accept you sending them email.

We will go through the process of how to send the first email in the next exercise.

Exercise 41: Using the Mailgun API to Send Out Emails

So, we have already registered an account with Mailgun. With that Mailgun account, we will be able to use the Mailgun API to send out emails to our users. In this exercise, we'll use Mailgun to send out our first test email, programmatically, in our Smilecook project:

1. Import requests and create the **MailgunApi** class in **mailgun.py**, under the **Smilecook** project:

    ```
    import requests
    class MailgunApi:
    ```

2. In the same **MailgunApi** class, set the **API_URL** to **https://api.mailgun.net/v3/{}/ messages**; this is the **API_URL** provided by Mailgun:

    ```
    API_URL = 'https://api.mailgun.net/v3/{}/messages'
    ```

3. In the same **MailgunApi** class, define the **__init__** constructor method for instantiating the object:

    ```
    def __init__(self, domain, api_key):
        self.domain = domain
        self.key = api_key
        self.base_url = self.API_URL.format(self.domain)
    ```

4. In the same **MailgunApi** class, define the **send_email** method for sending out emails using the Mailgun API. This method takes in **to**, **subject**, **text**, and **html** as the input parameters and composes the email:

    ```
    def send_email(self, to, subject, text, html=None):

        if not isinstance(to, (list, tuple)):
            to = [to, ]

        data = {
            'from': 'SmileCook <no-reply@{}>'.format(self.domain),
            'to': to,
            'subject': subject,
            'text': text,
            'html': html
        }

        response = requests.post(url=self.base_url,
                                          auth=('api', self.key),
                                          data=data)
        return response
    ```

5. Use **MailgunApi** to send the first email. Open the **PyCharm** Python console and first import **MailgunApi** from **mailgun**, then create a **mailgun** object by passing the domain name and API key provided by Mailgun in the previous exercise:

```
>>>from mailgun import MailgunApi
>>>mailgun = MailgunApi(domain='sandbox76165a034aa940feb3ef785819641871.
mailgun.org',
api_key='441acf048aae8d85be1c41774563e001-19f318b0-739d5c30')
```

6. Then, use the **send_mail()** method in **MailgunApi** to send our first email. We can pass in the **email**, **subject**, and **body** as parameters. We will get an HTTP status code **200** if the mail is sent successfully:

```
>>>mailgun.send_email(to='smilecook.api@gmail.com',
                                subject='Hello',
                                text='Testing some Mailgun awesomeness!')
<Response [200]>
```

> **Note**
>
> Please note that we need to use the same email address registered in Mailgun when we opened the account. This is because we haven't added any other email addresses to the authorized recipient list yet. So, this email address, registered in Mailgun, is the only email address that we can send out an email to now. In this case, it is **smilecook.api@gmail.com**.

7. Check the mailbox of the registered email address. You should receive an email. If you can't find it, it could be in your spam folder:

Figure 6.6: Sending an email via Mailgun

So, we have just sent out our first email using the third-party **Mailgun** API. Now we know how to add email capability to our application without setting up our own mail server. Later on, we will incorporate this email capability into our Smilecook application. We are going to use it in our user account activation workflow.

User Account Activation Workflow

We would like to add an account activation step to our recipe sharing platform so that when a user registers an account in our system, the account will not be activated by default. At this time, a user cannot log in to their account dashboard. It's only after they activate their account by clicking on the link in our activation email that they can then log in to their account dashboard:

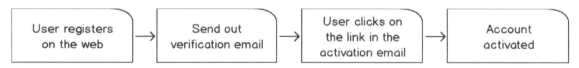

Figure 6.7: User account activation workflow

To build this workflow, we will use the **is_active** attribute in the user model to indicate whether the account is activated (whether the link of the activation email has been clicked), then create a method for sending the verification email when the user registers and the endpoint can be used to open the account. In order to create a unique link, we'll use the **itsdangerous** package, which will help us to create a unique token that will be used in the link for account activation. This package ensures that the email we generated is not modified by anyone so that we can verify the user's identity before we activate their account.

> **Note**
>
> If you are interested in understanding more about the **itsdangerous** package, please visit https://pythonhosted.org/itsdangerous/.

In the next exercise, we will generate the account activation token.

Exercise 42: Generating the Account Activation Token

As explained previously, we would like to implement a user account activation flow in our Smilecook application. This is to make sure the email address provided during registration is valid and is owned by the user. In this exercise, we will create a function to generate the activation token, as well as another function to verify the token. They will then be used later in the account activation flow:

1. Add the following line of code to **requirements.txt**:

    ```
    itsdangerous==1.1.0
    ```

2. Install the **itsdangerous** package using the following command:

    ```
    pip install -r requirements.txt
    ```

    You should see the following result returned after the packages are successfully installed:

    ```
    Installing collected packages: itsdangerous
    Successfully installed itsdangerous-1.1.0
    ```

3. Make sure the secret key is added in **config.py**; it will be useful when we use the **itsdangerous** package later:

    ```
    class Config:
        SECRET_KEY = 'super-secret-key'
    ```

4. In **utils.py**, import the **URLSafeTimedSerializer** module from **itsdangerous**:

    ```
    from itsdangerous import URLSafeTimedSerializer
    from flask import current_app
    ```

5. In **utils.py** again, define the **generate_token** function:

    ```
    def generate_token(email, salt=None):
        serializer = URLSafeTimedSerializer(current_app.config.get('SECRET_
    KEY'))
        return serializer.dumps(email, salt=salt)
    ```

    In the **generate_token** method, we used the **URLSafeTimedSerializer** class to create a token via email and the **current_app.config.get('SECRET_KEY')** secret key, which is the secret key we set in the **config.py** settings. This same secret key will be used to verify this token in the future. Also, note that the timestamp will be in this token, after which we can verify the time this message was created.

6. In **utils.py** again, define the **verify_token** function:

```
def verify_token(token, max_age=(30 * 60), salt=None):
    serializer = URLSafeTimedSerializer(current_app.config.get('SECRET_
KEY'))
    try:
        email = serializer.loads(token, max_age=max_age, salt=salt)
    except:
        return False

    return email
```

The **verify_token** function will try to extract the email address from the token, which will confirm whether the valid period in the token is within 30 minutes (30 * 60 seconds) through the **max_age** attribute.

> **Note**
>
> You can see in *steps 5* and *step 6*, that **salt** is used here to distinguish between different tokens. When tokens are created by email, for example, in the scenarios of opening an account, resetting the password, and upgrading the account, a verification email will be sent. You can use **salt='activate-salt'**, **salt='reset-salt'**, and **salt='upgrade-salt'** to distinguish between these scenarios.

Now we have these two handy functions to generate and verify the activation token, in the next exercise, we will use them in the user account activation flow.

Exercise 43: Sending Out the User Account Activation Email

Now, we have the activation token ready from our previous exercise, and we have also learned how to use the Mailgun API to send out an email. We are going to combine the two in this exercise, placing the activation token in the activation email to complete the whole account activation workflow:

1. Import **url_for**, the **MailgunAPI** class, and the **generate_token** and **verify_token** functions into **resources/user.py**:

```
from flask import request, url_for

from mailgun import MailgunApi

from utils import generate_token, verify_token
```

2. Create a **MailgunApi** object by passing in the **Mailgun** domain name and the API key that we got in the previous exercise:

```
mailgun = MailgunApi(domain='sandbox76165a034aa940feb3ef785819641871.
mailgun.org',
            api_key='441acf048aae8d85be1c41774563e001-19f318b0-739d5c30')
```

3. Add the following code in the **UserListResource** class, right after **user.save()**:

```
token = generate_token(user.email, salt='activate')
subject = 'Please confirm your registration.'
```

We first generate a token using **generate_token(user.email, salt='activate')**. Here, **salt='activate'** means that the token is mainly used to activate the account. The subject of the email is set to **Please confirm your registration**.

4. Create an activation link and define the email text in the same **UserListResource** class:

```
link = url_for('useractivateresource',
                    token=token,
                    _external=True)

text = 'Hi, Thanks for using SmileCook! Please confirm your
   registration by clicking on the link: {}'.format(link)
```

We create the activation link using the **url_for** function. It will require **UserActivateResource** (we will create that in our next step). This endpoint will need a token as well. The **_external=True** parameter is used to convert the default relative URL, **/users/activate/<string:token>**, to an absolute URL, **http://localhost:5000/users/activate/<string:token>**:

5. Finally, we use the **mailgun.send_email** method to send the email in the same **UserListResource** class:

```
mailgun.send_email(to=user.email,
                                    subject=subject,
                                    text=text)
```

6. Create a new **UserActivateResource** class under **resources/user.py** and define the **get** method in it:

```
class UserActivateResource(Resource):
    def get(self, token):

        email = verify_token(token, salt='activate')

        if email is False:
            return {'message': 'Invalid token or token expired'},
    HTTPStatus.BAD_REQUEST
```

First, this method verifies the token using **verify_token(token, salt='activate')**. The token has a default expiration time of 30 minutes. If the token is valid and not expired, we will get the user email and can proceed with the account activation. Otherwise, the email will be set to **False** and we can return an error message, **Invalid token or token expired**, with an **HTTP status code 400 Bad Request**.

7. Continue to work on the **UserActivateResource.get** method:

```
        user = User.get_by_email(email=email)

        if not user:
            return {'message': 'User not found'}, HTTPStatus.NOT_FOUND

        if user.is_active is True:
            return {'message': 'The user account is already activated'},
    HTTPStatus.BAD_REQUEST

        user.is_active = True

        user.save()
```

If we have the user's email, we can look up the **user** object and modify its **is_active** attribute. If the user account is already activated, we will simply return **The user is already activated**. Otherwise, we activate the account and save that.

8. Finally, we will return HTTP status code **204 No Content** to indicate that the request was handled successfully:

```
return {}, HTTPStatus.NO_CONTENT
```

> **Note**
>
> Usually, in a real-world scenario, the activation link in the email will point to the frontend layer of the system. The frontend layer will, in turn, communicate with the backend through the API. Therefore, when the frontend receives the HTTP status code **204 No Content**, it means the account is activated. It can then forward the user to the account dashboard.

9. Then, add the new **UserActivateResource** class to **app.py** by using the following code. First, import the **UserActivateResource** class from **resources.user**, then add the route:

```
from resources.user import UserListResource, UserResource, MeResource,
UserRecipeListResource, UserActivateResource


    api.add_resource(UserActivateResource, '/users/
activate/<string:token>')
```

10. Finally, we would like to make sure the user cannot log in to the application before their account is activated. We will change the **POST** method in **resources/token. py**. Add the following lines of code right after checking the password to return the HTTP status code **403 Forbidden** if the user account is not activated:

```
        if user.is_active is False:
            return {'message': 'The user account is not activated yet'},
    HTTPStatus.FORBIDDEN
```

11. Right-click on it to run the application. And we are ready to test the entire user registration workflow.

Congratulations! You have completed the development of the entire user registration workflow. Our Smilecook application will be able to send out an email with an activation link. Users can then click on the activation link to activate their user account.

In the next activity, we would like you to go through the whole flow and test whether it works.

Activity 9: Testing the Complete User Registration and Activation Workflow

In this activity, we will test the complete user registration and activation workflow:

1. Register a new user through Postman.

2. Log in through the API.

3. Use the link sent to the mailbox to activate the account.

4. Log in again after the account is activated.

> **Note**
>
> The solution for this activity can be found on page 314.

Setting Up Environment Variables

We are going to use environment variables to ensure that our sensitive information, such as the secret key, is safe. This ensures that we are not leaking this sensitive and confidential information when we share code with others. Environment variables are only saved in the local environment and they won't appear in code. That is a usual best practice to segregate code from confidential information.

Exercise 44: Setting Up Environment Variables in PyCharm

The environment variable is a key-value pair stored in the local system, which can be accessed by our application. In this exercise, we will set the environment variables through **PyCharm**:

1. At the top of the **PyCharm** interface, select **Run** and then click **Edit Configurations**:

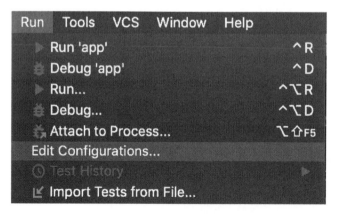

Figure 6.8: Select Run and click Edit Configurations

2. Click **Browse** next to **Environment Variables**. Then click **+** to add the MAILGUN_ DOMAIN and MAILGUN_API_KEY environment variables.

Your screen will look as follows:

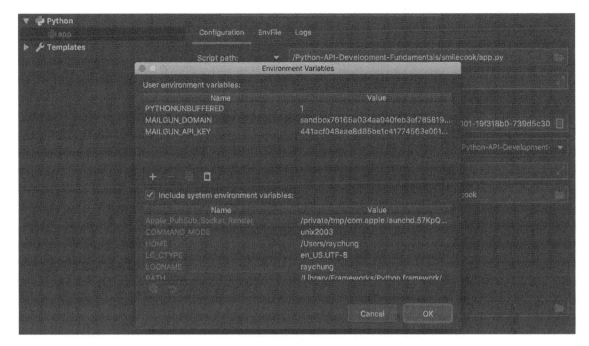

Figure 6.9: Adding the MAILGUN_DOMAIN and MAILGUN_API_KEY environment variables

> **Note**
>
> For the Python console, to read the environment variables, we can set it under *Pycharm >> Preferences >> Build, Execution, Deployment >> Console >> Python Console.*

3. We will then import the **os** package in **resources/user.py** and get the value in the environment variables using **os.environ['MAILGUN_DOMAIN']** and **os.environ['MAILGUN_API_KEY']**:

```
import os

mailgun = MailgunApi(domain=os.environ.get('MAILGUN_DOMAIN'),
                     api_key=os.environ.get('MAILGUN_API_KEY'))
```

So, this is how you can move the secret **API_KEY** and other related information out from the code. This secret data is now stored in the environment variable and is isolated from the code.

> **Note**
>
> If we get the environment variable using **os.environ['KEY']**. It will raise a **'KeyError'** if the environment variable is not defined. We can get the value using **os.environ.get('KEY')** or **os.getenv('Key')**. This will give us None if the variable is not defined. If we want to set a default value if the environment variable is not defined, we can use this syntax: **os.getenv('KEY', default_value)**.

HTML Format Email

We can add a bit of color to our email by using an HTML format email instead of plaintext email. HTML format email is everywhere. I am sure you have seen images in emails, or emails with a fancy layout. Those are HTML format emails. Theoretically, to send out HTML format email using the **Mailgun** API, it could be as simple as passing in the HTML code as a parameter to the **mailgun.send_email** method.

Please refer to the following sample code to send out an HTML format email using Mailgun. We can see that we are just adding the new **html** parameter here:

```
mailgun.send_email(to=user.email,
                   subject=subject,
                   text=text,
                   html='<html><body><h1>Test email</h1></body></
html>')
```

However, this way of coupling the HTML code with the Python code is cumbersome. If we have a fancy layout, the HTML can be pretty long and that's too much to be included in the actual Python code. To address this, we can leverage the **render_template()** function in Flask. This is a function that makes use of the Jinja2 template engine. With it, we can just place the HTML code in a separate HTML file under a **/templates** folder in the application project. We can then pass in the HTML file, also called a template file, to this **render_template** function to generate the HTML text.

From the following sample code, we can see that, with the **render_template** function, we can simplify the code a lot:

template/sample.html

```
<html><body><h1>Test email</h1></body></html>
```

We can then render the HTML with the subject set to **Test email** using the following code:

```
mailgun.send_email(to=user.email,
                          subject=subject,
                          text=text,
                          html=render_template('sample.html'))
```

The sample code here will look for the **templates/sample.html** file under the application project folder and render the HTML code for us.

The function is named **render_template** instead of **render_html** for a reason. The **render_template** function does more than just directly outputting the HTML code from the file. In fact, we can insert variable in the HTML template file and have the **render_template** function render it.

For example, we can modify **sample.html** like this (the **{{content}}** here is a placeholder):

template/sample.html

```
<html><body><h1>{{content}}</h1></body></html>
```

We can then render the HTML with the subject set to **test email** using the following code:

```
mailgun.send_email(to=user.email,
                          subject=subject,
                          text=text,
                          html=render_template('sample.html', content='Test
  email'))
```

In the next activity, we would like you to send out the activation email in HTML format.

Activity 10: Creating the HTML Format User Account Activation Email

We have previously sent out plaintext format emails. In this activity, we will create an HTML format email so that it looks more appealing to our users:

1. Put the user's email address into the **Mailgun** authorized recipient list.

2. Copy an HTML template from the **Mailgun** website.

3. Add in the activation token in the HTML template.

4. Use the **render_template** function to render the HTML code and send out the activation email using the **Mailgun** API.

5. Register a new account in Postman and get the account activation email in HTML format.

> **Note**
>
> The solution for this activity can be found on page 317.

You have now learned how to send out an email in HTML format. You can design your own HTML templates from now on.

Summary

In this chapter, we learned how to use the third-party **Mailgun** API to send a user account activation email. Later, we can send different emails, such as a notification email, using the **MailgunAPI** class. Mailgun not only provides the API for sending mail but also provides a backend dashboard for us to track the status of the emails we've sent out. It is a very handy service. User account activation is an important step to ensure we are onboarding a validated user. Though not every platform performs this kind of validation, it reduces the impact of spam and bots onboarding our platform. In this chapter, we used the **itsdangerous** package to create a unique token to confirm the ownership of the user's email address. This package contains timestamps so that we can verify whether the token has expired or not.

In the next chapter, we will continue to add more features to our Smilecook application. We will work with images in our next chapter. I am sure you will learn a lot of practical skills there. Let's continue our journey.

Working with Images

Learning Objectives

By the end of this chapter, you will be able to:

- Build a user avatar function

- Develop an image uploading API using Flask-Uploads

- Resize images using an API

- Compress images using Pillow to enhance API performance

In this chapter, we will learn how to perform image uploads so that we can let users post a profile picture and recipe cover image to our Smilecook application.

Introduction

In the previous chapter, we completed the account opening workflow by activating the user accounts via email. In this chapter, we will develop a function so that we can upload pictures. These pictures are the user's profile picture and the recipe cover images. Aside from uploading images, we will also discuss image compression. Pillow is an image processing package that we are going to use to compress images up to 90%. This can greatly enhance the performance of our API without compromising on the image's quality.

Technically speaking, we will introduce two Python packages, Flask-Uploads and Pillow, in this chapter. Flask-Uploads allows us to quickly develop image uploading functions. For image compression, we will be using Pillow. It can generate images in our specified format and compress them accordingly.

Building the User Avatar Function

In our Smilecook application, there are user profile pages that list user information. While this is useful enough, it would be much better if we could allow users to upload a profile picture (avatar) to their profile page. This would make the application more sociable.

To store the user avatar, we will create a new attribute (`avatar_image`) in the user model. We are not going to store the image directly in this attribute. Instead, we are going to store the image on the server, and the new attribute will have the filename of the image. Later, when our API gets a client request asking for the image, we will find the filename in this attribute and generate the URL to point to the image location and then return it to the frontend client-side. The frontend client will then base on the image URL and fetch it from the server:

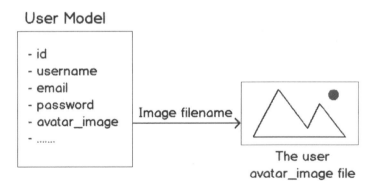

Figure 7.1: Building a user model avatar diagram

We are going to create a new endpoint, **http://localhost:5000/users/avatar**, that will take **PUT** requests. The reason we have designed it to accept **PUT** requests is that there should be only one avatar picture for each user. So, every time there is a client request, it should be either replacing an empty image with the new image for the first time, or it will be replacing the old image with a new one. This is a replacement action. In this case, we should use the HTTP verb, PUT.

Now, let's add the **avatar_image** attribute in our model. We will have to use Flask-Migrate to update the underlying database table.

Exercise 45: Adding the avatar_image Attribute to the User Model

In this exercise, we will work on changing the user model. First, we will create an additional attribute (**avatar_image**) in the user model. Then, we will reflect it in the database schema and use the Flask-Migrate Python package to create the corresponding field in the database table. Finally, we will confirm the change is successful by using pgAdmin. Let's get started:

1. Add the **avatar_image** attribute to the user model. The code file is **models/user** **.py**:

    ```
    avatar_image = db.Column(db.String(100), default=None)
    ```

    The **avatar_image** attribute is designed to store the filename of the uploaded image. Due to this, it is a string with a length of **100**. The default is **None**.

2. Run the following command to generate the database migration script:

    ```
    flask db migrate
    ```

    You will see that a new column called **user.avatar_image** has been detected:

    ```
    INFO  [alembic.runtime.migration] Context impl PostgresqlImpl.
    INFO  [alembic.runtime.migration] Will assume transactional DDL.
    INFO  [alembic.autogenerate.compare] Detected added column 'user.avatar_
    image'
      Generating /TrainingByPackt/Python-API-Development-Fundamentals/
    Lesson07/smilecook/migrations/versions/7aafe51af016_.py ... done
    ```

3. Check the content in **/migrations/versions/7aafe51af016_.py**, which is the database migration script that we generated in the previous step:

```
"""empty message

Revision ID: 7aafe51af016
Revises: 983adee75c9a
Create Date: 2019-09-18 20:54:51.823725

"""
from alembic import op
import sqlalchemy as sa

# revision identifiers, used by Alembic.
revision = '7aafe51af016'
down_revision = '983adee75c9a'
branch_labels = None
depends_on = None

def upgrade():
    # ### commands auto generated by Alembic - please adjust! ###
    op.add_column('user', sa.Column('avatar_image', sa.String(length=100),
nullable=True))
    # ### end Alembic commands ###

def downgrade():
    # ### commands auto generated by Alembic - please adjust! ###
    op.drop_column('user', 'avatar_image')
    # ### end Alembic commands ###
```

From its content, we can see that two functions have been generated in the script: **upgrade** and **downgrade**. The **upgrade** function is used to add the new **avatar_image** column to the database table, while the **downgrade** function is used to remove the **avatar_image** column so that it can go back to its original state.

4. Run the following **flask db upgrade** command to update the database schema:

```
flask db upgrade
```

You will see the following output:

```
INFO  [alembic.runtime.migration] Context impl PostgresqlImpl.
INFO  [alembic.runtime.migration] Will assume transactional DDL.
INFO  [alembic.runtime.migration] Running upgrade 983adee75c9a ->
7aafe51af016, empty message
```

5. Check the schema **change** in pgAdmin. *Right-click* on the **user** table and choose **Properties**. A new window will appear. Then, click the **Columns** tab to check the columns:

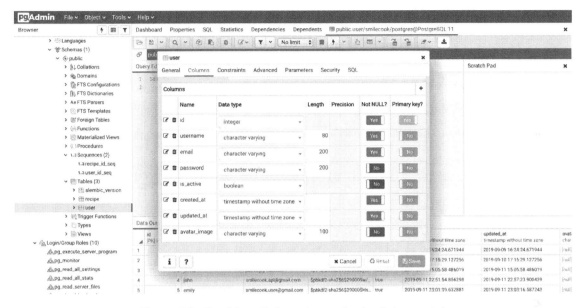

Figure 7.2: Checking all the columns in the Columns tab

Here, we can see the new **avatar_image** column being added to the **user** table. Now, our Smilecook application is ready to take in the image path of the user avatar.

Flask-Uploads

We will be using the Flask-Uploads package to complete our image upload function. This is a very powerful package that simplifies most of the tedious coding for us. By simply calling a few methods provided by the package, it allows us to efficiently and flexibly develop the file upload function. Flask-Uploads can handle various common file types out of the box. What we need to define is the Set that classifies the types of uploaded files, such as **IMAGES**, **DOCUMENT**, **AUDIO**, and so on. Then, we simply need to set the destination of the uploaded files.

Let's look at a few basic concepts and functions in Flask-Uploads before we implement them.

Upload Sets

Before we upload any files, we need to define the **UploadSet**. An upload set is a single collection of files. Take **images** as an example; we can define the image upload set as follows, where **'images'** is the name of the upload set:

```
image_set = UploadSet('images', IMAGES)
```

Once you have the **image_set**, you can use the **save** method to save the uploaded image from the incoming HTTP request, like so:

```
image_set.save(image, folder=folder, name=filename)
```

An upload set's configuration also needs to be stored on an app. We can use the **configure_uploads** function from Flask-Uploads to do that:

```
configure_uploads(app, image_set)
```

In addition, you can also use **patch_request_class** to restrict the maximum upload size of the uploaded file. In the next exercise, we will work on the image upload function together. The image user is going to upload their avatar picture. We will define the destination as **static/images/avatars**.

Exercise 46: Implementing the User Avatar Upload Function

In this exercise, we will start by installing the Flask-Uploads package to our virtual environment. Then, we will do some simple configurations and get to work on the image upload function development. By completing this exercise, we will see an image URL being returned to the client. Let's get started:

1. Add the following line in **requirements.txt**:

    ```
    Flask-Uploads==0.2.1
    ```

2. Run the following command to install the Flask-Uploads package in the PyCharm console:

    ```
    pip install -r requirements.txt
    ```

    You will see the following installation result:

    ```
    Installing collected packages: Flask-Uploads
    Running setup.py install for Flask-Uploads ... done
    Successfully installed Flask-Uploads-0.2.1
    ```

3. Import **UploadSet** and **IMAGES** into **extensions.py**:

```
from flask_uploads import UploadSet, IMAGES
```

4. In the same **extensions.py** file, define a set called **'images'** and an extension called **IMAGES**. This will cover the common image file extensions (**.jpg**, **.jpeg**, **.png**, and so on):

```
image_set = UploadSet('images', IMAGES)
```

5. Set the image destination in **Config.py**:

```
UPLOADED_IMAGES_DEST = 'static/images'
```

> **Note**
>
> The **UPLOADED_IMAGES_DEST** attribute name is decided by the name of the upload set. Since we set the upload set name to be **'images'**, the attribute name here must be **UPLOADED_IMAGES_DEST**.

6. Import **configure_uploads**, **patch_request_class**, and **image_set** into **app.py**:

```
from flask_uploads import configure_uploads, patch_request_class
from extensions import db, jwt, image_set
```

7. Using the **configure_uploads** function that we have just imported, pass in the **image_set** that we want to upload:

```
configure_uploads(app, image_set)
```

8. Set the maximum file size allowed for uploads as 10 MB using **patch_request_class**. This step is important because, by default, there is no upload size limit:

```
patch_request_class(app, 10 * 1024 * 1024)
```

9. Import the **url_for** function in **schemas/user.py** and add the **avatar_url** attribute and **dump_avatar_url** method under the **UserSchema** class:

```
from flask import url_for

class UserSchema(Schema):

    avatar_url = fields.Method(serialize='dump_avatar_url')

    def dump_avatar_url(self, user):
```

```
        if user.avatar_image:
            return url_for('static', filename='images/avatars/{}'.
format(user.avatar_image), _external=True)
        else:
            return url_for('static', filename='images/assets/default-
avatar.jpg', _external=True)
```

The **url_for** function is used to help generate the URL of the image file. The **dump_avatar_url** method is used to return the URL of the user avatar after serialization. If no image is being uploaded, we will simply return the URL of the default avatar.

10. Create a folder called **assets** under **static/images** and place the **default-avatar.jpg** image inside it. This image is going to be our default user avatar:

Figure 7.3: Folder structure after adding the image

> **Note**
>
> You can put any image you like in here. We have also provided a default avatar image in our sample code folder.

11. Import the **uuid** extension, and **image_set** into **utils.py**. You will see how these modules/methods are used next:

```
import uuid

from flask_uploads import extension

from extensions import image_set
```

12. Add the **save_image** function to **utils.py**:

```
def save_image(image, folder):

    filename = '{}.{}'.format(uuid.uuid4(), extension(image.filename))
    image_set.save(image, folder=folder, name=filename)

    return filename
```

In the **save_image** method, we used the **uuid** function to generate the filename for the uploaded image. We got the file extension from the uploaded image using the extension function from Flask-Uploads. Then, we saved the image using the **image_set.save** function; the saving destination is **static/images**. If we pass in **folder='avatar'** as the parameter, the destination will be **static/images/avatar**.

13. Import the **image_set** and **save_image** functions from **utils** into **resources/user.py**:

```
from extensions import image_set

from utils import generate_token, verify_token, save_image
```

14. Add **user_avatar_schema** to **resources/user.py**. This schema is just to show the **avatar_url**:

```
user_avatar_schema = UserSchema(only=('avatar_url', ))
```

15. Create the **UserAvatarUploadResource** class, in **resources/user.py**, and define the **put** method inside it:

```
class UserAvatarUploadResource(Resource):

    @jwt_required
    def put(self):

        file = request.files.get('avatar')

        if not file:
            return {'message': 'Not a valid image'}, HTTPStatus.BAD_
REQUEST

        if not image_set.file_allowed(file, file.filename):
            return {'message': 'File type not allowed'}, HTTPStatus.BAD_
REQUEST

        user = User.get_by_id(id=get_jwt_identity())

        if user.avatar_image:
            avatar_path = image_set.path(folder='avatars', filename=user.
avatar_image)
            if os.path.exists(avatar_path):
                os.remove(avatar_path)
```

The **@jwt_required** decorator before the **put** method means that login is required before this method is triggered. In the **put** method, we got the avatar image file from **request.files**. Then, we validated whether the image file exists and whether the file extension is permitted. If everything is okay, we will get back the user object and check whether an avatar already exists. If so, that will be removed before we replace it with our uploaded image.

16. Then, we used **save_image** to save the uploaded image. Once the image is saved, we will get the filename of the image and save it to **user.avatar_image**. Then, we used **user.save()** to save the update to the database:

```
filename = save_image(image=file, folder='avatars')

user.avatar_image = filename
user.save()
```

17. Use **user_avatar_schema.dump(user).data** to return the image URL and the HTTP status code, **200 OK**:

```
return user_avatar_schema.dump(user).data, HTTPStatus.OK
```

18. Import the **UserAvatarUploadResource** class into **app.py**:

```
from resources.user import UserListResource, UserResource, MeResource,
UserRecipeListResource, UserActivateResource, UserAvatarUploadResource
```

19. Link the resource to the route, that is **/users/avatar in app.py**:

```
api.add_resource(UserAvatarUploadResource, '/users/avatar')
```

We have successfully created the user avatar image upload function in our Smilecook application. Now, we can upload an image to the user profile page. In the next exercise, we will test that using Postman.

Exercise 47: Testing the User Avatar Upload Function Using Postman

In the previous exercise, we finished developing the avatar uploading function. To make sure things are working as expected, we need to test the function from the client-side. We will be using Postman to send the client request, which will have the user avatar image in it. Let's get started:

1. First, log in to a user account. Now, click on the **Collections** tab and select the **POST Token** request. Then, click the **Send** button. The result can be seen in the following screenshot:

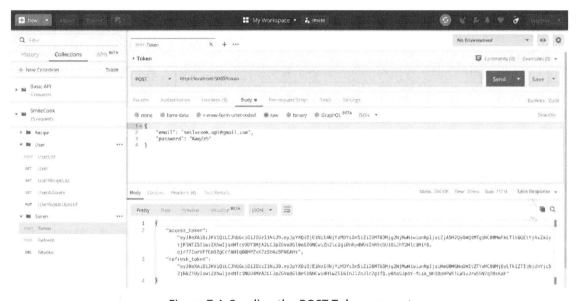

Figure 7.4: Sending the POST Token request

2. Next, we are going to use the **PUT** method to upload an avatar. Send an HTTP **PUT** request to the following URL: `http://localhost:5000/users/avatar`. Click on the **Collections** tab. *Right-click* on ... next to the **User** folder, and then create a new request.

3. Set the **Request Name** to `UserAvatarUpload` and save it in the **User** folder.

4. Select **PUT** as the HTTP method and type in `http://locaohost:5000/users/avatar` as the request URL.

5. Now, select the **Headers** tab and put `Authorization` into the **KEY** field and `Bearer {token}` into the **VALUE** field, where the token is the access token we got in the previous step.

6. Select the **Body** tab. Then, select the **form-data** radio button and put "avatar" as the **KEY**.

7. Select **File** in the drop-down menu next to **Key** and select the image file to upload.

8. Now, click the **Save** button and then the **Send** button. The result can be seen in the following screenshot:

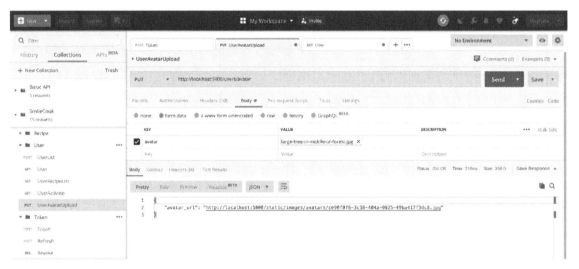

Figure 7.5: Sending a request to upload an avatar

We can see `avatar_url` in the response, meaning that our image upload request was successful.

9. Clicking on **avatar_url** should bring you to the uploaded image. Check the path, **static/images/avatars**, in PyCharm. You should see the uploaded image there:

Figure 7.6: Checking the uploaded image

10. Send a request to get a user back by their **username**. Click on the **Collections** tab and select the **GET User** request.

11. Type **http://localhost:5000/users/john** into the URL field. You can replace the username, that is, **John**, with any username that is appropriate and then click the **Send** button. The result can be seen in the following screenshot:

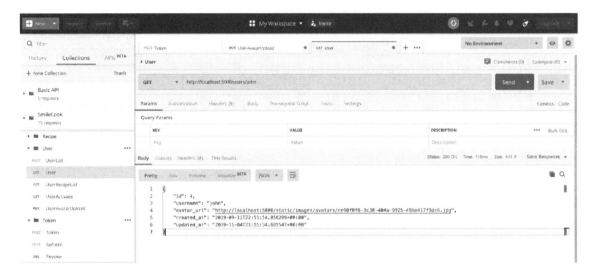

Figure 7.7: Checking the user avatar URL

Here, we can see the new avatar URL attribute in the user.

This testing exercise proves that the image upload function is working as expected. We can also look up the user by placing the username in the endpoint URL.

> **Note**
>
> You can test two more aspects of the **avatar image upload** functions. The first one is to upload an image that's greater than 10 MB in size. The second is to test whether the default avatar image (that is, **default-avatar.jpg**) will be used for a user account that has no uploaded avatar.

Image Resizing and Compression

The size of the image will affect the speed of the website. Imagine looking at a picture that's 10 MB in size. If there are 10 pictures on one page, this website will be 100 MB in size, and so it will take a lot of time to get a page. Due to this, a good practice to reduce the size of the image and compress it so that it's around 500 KB in size instead.

In addition, we will also convert the image into JPEG (it has the `.JPG` file extension). JPEG is an image compression technology that can remove unnoticeable, insignificant details in an image, thus achieving a smaller file size. Besides, it is often regarded as acceptable to have a lower image quality for web use.

In our Smilecook application, we will convert all our uploaded images into JPG format and compress them. We will do this through the Pillow package.

> **Note**
>
> We cannot have a transparent image in JPEG format. If we save an image with the background removed as a JPEG, the background will become white, instead of transparent. The other two commonly used image formats, PNG and GIF. These two image formats will support transparency in images.
>
> In our Smilecook application, however, we won't be displaying a transparent image, so using JPG images will be good enough here.

Introduction to Pillow

Pillow, previously known as the **Python Imaging Library** (**PIL**), is an image processing package in Python. The most important class in this package is `Image`. We can use `Image.open` to create an object from an `image` file. We can then get the image dimension in pixels by using the attribute `size`. We can also find out the color mode of the image by using the attribute mode.

Some common color modes you should expect to see include L for black and white, RGB for red-green-blue, and CMYK for cyan-magenta-yellow-black:

```
>>>image = Image.open('default-avatar.jpg')
>>>image.size
(1600, 1066)
>>>image.mode
'RGB'
```

If we want to change the color mode of the picture to RGB, use the **convert** function. We usually change the color mode to ensure the color accuracy of our images. RGB is the most commonly used color mode for computer monitors:

```
>>>image = image.convert("RGB")
```

If we want to resize an image so that it has smaller dimensions, we should use the **thumbnail** method. This method can maintain the aspect ratio of the image, and at the same time make sure that each side of the image is less than our defined limit.

As an example, the resultant image's sides will be less than **1600** px, while keeping the aspect ratio intact:

```
>>>maxsize = (1600, 1600)
>>>image.thumbnail(maxsize)
```

When we save our changes using the Pillow package, we can pass in a **quality** parameter. This is done to specify how much JPEG compression we want. The quality can range from 1 to 100, with 1 being the worst and 95 being the best. We should avoid putting in a value higher than 95 because that means almost no compression. The default quality value is 75:

```
>>>image.save('compressed_image.jpg', optimize=True, quality=85)
```

Let's complete an exercise in order to implement image compression.

Exercise 48: Implementing Image Compression in Our Smilecook Application

Now that we've learned about the theory and the tools we can use to perform image compression, let's apply that to our Smilecook application. We would like to compress the user's avatar. We will be using the Pillow package to do this. Let's get started:

1. Add the **Pillow** package to **requirements.txt**:

    ```
    Pillow==6.2.1
    ```

2. Install the **Pillow** package by running the **pip install** command, as follows:

```
pip install -r requirements.txt
```

You should see the following installation result after running the preceding command:

```
Installing collected packages: Pillow
Successfully installed Pillow-6.2.1
```

3. Import the necessary package and module into **utils.py**:

```
import os

from PIL import Image
```

4. In **utils.py**, define the **compress_image** function, which takes the filename and **folder** as parameters.

First, we will use **image_set.path(filename=filename, folder=folder)** to get the actual image file's location. Then, by using **Image.open(file_path)**, we will create the **image** object from the image file:

```
def compress_image(filename, folder):

    file_path = image_set.path(filename=filename, folder=folder)

    image = Image.open(file_path)
```

5. Change the color mode to **RGB** and resize it so that each side is no bigger than **1600** px:

```
if image.mode != "RGB":
    image = image.convert("RGB")

if max(image.width, image.height) > 1600:
    maxsize = (1600, 1600)
    image.thumbnail(maxsize, Image.ANTIALIAS)
```

6. Generate the new filename and path for our compressed image:

```
compressed_filename = '{}.jpg'.format(uuid.uuid4())
compressed_file_path = image_set.path(filename=compressed_filename,
folder=folder)
```

7. Save the compressed image with **quality = 85**:

```
image.save(compressed_file_path, optimize=True, quality=85)
```

8. Use **os.stat(file_path)** to get the size in bytes. By doing this, we will have the original size for a before and after comparison in our testing:

```
original_size = os.stat(file_path).st_size
compressed_size = os.stat(compressed_file_path).st_size
percentage = round((original_size - compressed_size) / original_size *
100)

print("The file size is reduced by {}%, from {} to
{}.".format(percentage, original_size, compressed_size))
```

> **Note**
>
> The **os.stat** method is a Python method that returns basic folder/file information (for example, owner ID, group owner ID, and file size).

9. Remove the original image and then return the compressed image filename by using the following code:

```
os.remove(file_path)

return compressed_filename
```

10. Finally, in the **save_image** function, under **utils.py**, call the **compress_image** function right after the image is saved:

```
def save_image(image, folder):

    filename = '{}.{}'.format(uuid.uuid4(), extension(image.filename))
    image_set.save(image, folder=folder, name=filename)

    filename = compress_image(filename=filename, folder=folder)

    return filename
```

Here, we have created our compress_image function. The function just needs to know where the image file is, and it will compress the image for us.

In the next exercise, we will test the image compression function.

Exercise 49: Testing the Image Compression Function

So far, we have developed an image compression function that can compress the avatar that was uploaded by the user. In this exercise, we will test and see how the image compression function does. Let's get started:

1. First, we are going to use the **PUT** method to upload an avatar. We will send an HTTP **PUT** request to the following URL: `http://localhost:5000/users/avatar`. Click on **PUT UserAvatarUpload** and select the **Body** tab.

2. Select a large image file to upload and click the **Send** button. The result can be seen in the following screenshot:

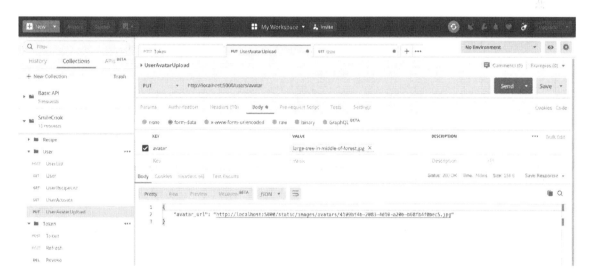

Figure 7.8: Uploading an avatar using the PUT method

3. From the application log in PyCharm, we can see that the original size of the uploaded image was 7.6 MB; it is reduced to 618 KB after compression:

Figure 7.9: Image size after compression

By doing this, we can see that the image compression function that we implemented previously works. Now, the image size has been significantly reduced. In the next activity, we will implement the recipe cover image upload function.

Activity 11: Implementing the Recipe Cover Image Upload Function

So far, we have learned how to develop the image upload and compression function. In this activity, we are going to work on the recipe cover image upload function for the Smilecook application. We want to make our recipe more attractive by providing a cover image for it. Similar to the user avatar, only one cover image is allowed per recipe. Follow these steps to complete this activity:

1. Add the `cover_image` attribute to the user model in `models/recipe.py`.

2. Update the corresponding DB schema using the `flask db migrate` command.

3. Create the `recipe_cover_schema` to show the `cover_url` in the HTTP response.

4. Create the `RecipeCoverUploadResource` for the recipe cover image upload function.

> **Note**
>
> The solution to this activity can be found on page 323.

Activity 12: Testing the Image Upload Function

In this activity, we are going to test the recipe cover image uploading function. First, we will create a new recipe, upload a recipe cover image, and verify whether it has been uploaded by fetching the recipe back. Follow these steps to complete this activity:

1. Log in to the Smilecook user account using Postman.

2. Send a client request to our API to create a recipe.

3. Upload the recipe images.

4. Check whether the image is compressed in PyCharm.

5. Check the uploaded image in `static/images/recipes`.

6. Get the recipe back and confirm that the `cover_url` attribute is populated.

> **Note**
>
> The solution to this activity can be found on page 328.

Summary

In this chapter, we have learned how to use Flask-Uploads to upload images for our user avatar and recipe cover. Since our maximum uploaded image size is 10 MB, this allows users to upload huge images, thereby slowing down the performance of the website. To address this performance issue, we introduced the concept of image resizing and compression. From here, we worked on developing the function using the Pillow package.

Apart from learning about new techniques regarding image manipulation, we also revisited things we learned in the previous chapters, such as updating the database schema using Flask-Migrate and displaying the URL of the uploaded image during deserialization using marshmallow's schema.

We have completed most of the key functionality of our Smilecook recipe sharing platform. In the next chapter, we will develop the recipe searching and pagination functions.

8

Pagination, Searching, and Ordering

Learning Objectives

By the end of this chapter, you will be able to:

- Implement the pagination function using Flask-SQLAlchemy

- Serialize the paginated result using marshmallow for the frontend display

- Build the API with search function

- Sort and order the returned records in your own way

- Test all these features using Postman

This chapter covers pagination and how to change the order in which recipes are listed, as well as how to add search functionality for recipes and ingredients.

Introduction

In the previous chapter, we implemented the **user avatar** and **recipe cover image upload** functions. We worked on the image compression function to improve the performance of image loading speed. Once an image has been uploaded, users can retrieve the URL of the image through an API.

In this chapter, we will work on paginating recipe data. We will explain why we need to perform pagination. This is an important step in optimizing our API. We will also discuss some more important functions, including searching and ordering, which I am sure you have come across in other online applications.

Pagination

In the testing environment, we may only have a few developers putting recipes on the Smilecook platform. There are only a handful of recipes there and performance is never a concern. However, in the production environment, that is, after the platform has been launched for public use, there could be thousands of users sharing recipes on the platform. If you consider social media platforms such as Facebook, then the volume will be even bigger.

That's why we need to introduce pagination. Pagination means instead of querying the whole population of records from the database, we just query a handful of them. When the user wants to see more, they can always go to the next page. For example, when you're browsing a shopping site, usually, you will view the items for sale a page at a time. Each page may display 40 items, and you have to navigate to subsequent pages to view all the items that are available. This is the nature of pagination.

The number of records that are shown per page is limited by the page's size. This way, there will be a huge saving in server loading time and data transfer time, and, most importantly, it will enhance the user's navigation experience.

The good thing here is that we are using a web framework to build our API. This kind of common function has already been thought of. We just need to use Flask-SQLAlchemy to help us build a paginated API.

Paginated APIs

A paginated API means that when you query the API, only the data records on the current page will be returned. It also includes other information, such as the total number of records, the total number of pages, links to other pages, and so on. The following is a sample response from a paginated API. It is a serialized pagination object, so it is in JSON format:

```
{
    "links": {
        "first": "http://localhost:5000/recipes?per_page=2&page=1",
        "last": "http://localhost:5000/recipes?per_page=2&page=5",
        "prev": "http://localhost:5000/recipes?per_page=2&page=1",
        "next": "http://localhost:5000/recipes?per_page=2&page=3"
    },
    "page": 2,
    "pages": 5,
    "per_page": 2,
    "total": 9,
    "data": [
        {
            "data": "data"

        },
        {
            "data": "data"
        }
    ]
}
```

Here, you can see the following attributes in the HTTP response:

- **first**: The link to the first page
- **last**: The link to the last page
- **prev**: The link to the previous page
- **next**: The link to the next page
- **page**: The current page
- **pages**: The total number of pages
- **per_page**: The number of records per page
- **total**: The total number of records
- **data**: The actual data records on this page

These attributes are automatically generated by the pagination object in Flask-SQLAlchemy. We just need to serialize the pagination object using marshmallow so that we can return the result in JSON format to the frontend client.

Exercise 50: Implementing Pagination on the Published Recipes Retrieval Function

Now that we've discussed the importance of pagination, we want to add this functionality to our Smilecook platform. We'll begin to work on that in this exercise. Let's get started:

1. Create **pagination.py** in the **schema** folder and import the necessary modules and functions:

```
from flask import request
from marshmallow import Schema, fields
from urllib.parse import urlencode
```

2. Create the **PaginationSchema** class:

```
class PaginationSchema(Schema):

    class Meta:
        ordered = True
```

```
links = fields.Method(serialize='get_pagination_links')

page = fields.Integer(dump_only=True)
pages = fields.Integer(dump_only=True)

per_page = fields.Integer(dump_only=True)
total = fields.Integer(dump_only=True)
```

In this step, we can see that **PaginationSchema** inherits from **marshmallow. Schema**. **PaginationSchema** is used to serialize the pagination object from Flask-SQLAlchemy. The **links** attribute is a custom field, which means that we can specify how we are going to serialize it. The **get_pagination_links** function will be created in *step 4*.

> **Note**
>
> We've explained the other attributes here already. These attributes are required in the HTTP response, and so we need to add them to the schema.
>
> We can have a different key name in the final JSON response. For example, if we want to show **total_count** as the key name instead of **total**, we can use the **attribute** parameter like this: **total_count = fields.Integer(dump_only=True, attribute='total')**.

3. Add the following **get_url** method to **PaginationSchema**:

```
@staticmethod
def get_url(page):

    query_args = request.args.to_dict()
    query_args['page'] = page

    return '{}?{}'.format(request.base_url, urlencode(query_args))
```

The **PaginationSchema.get_url** method is used to generate the URL of the page based on the page number. It is taking in the page number parameter and adding that to the **request** argument's dictionary. Finally, it encodes and returns the new URL, including the page number, as an argument.

> **Note**
>
> An example of this is if **request.base_url** is **http://localhost:5000/recipes**, and **urlencode (query_args)** is giving us **per_page=2&page=1**. The format function will stitch them together and return the new URL, that is, **http://localhost:5000/recipes?per_page=2&page=1**.

4. Add the **get_pagination_links** method to **PaginationSchema**:

```
def get_pagination_links(self, paginated_objects):

    pagination_links = {
        'first': self.get_url(page=1),
        'last': self.get_url(page=paginated_objects.pages)
    }

    if paginated_objects.has_prev:
        pagination_links['prev'] = self.get_url(page=paginated_
objects.prev_num)

    if paginated_objects.has_next:
        pagination_links['next'] = self.get_url(page=paginated_
objects.next_num)

    return pagination_links
```

The **PaginationSchema.get_pagination_links** method is used to generate URL links to different pages. It gets the page's information from **paginated_objects** and relies on the **get_url** method we built in *step 3* to generate the links.

5. Next, import **PaginationSchema** in **schemas/recipe.py**:

```
from schemas.pagination import PaginationSchema
```

6. Delete the following code in **schemas/recipe.py**:

```
@post_dump(pass_many=True)
def wrap(self, data, many, **kwargs):
    if many:
        return {'data': data}
    return data
```

This part of the code has been removed because we are building a pagination function. We no longer need to wrap multiple data records with the **data** key.

7. Define **RecipePaginationSchema**, which inherits from **PaginationSchema** in **schema/pagination.py**:

```
class RecipePaginationSchema(PaginationSchema):
    data = fields.Nested(RecipeSchema, attribute='items', many=True)
```

As you may recall, the attribute name in the final JSON response will be **data** here, because that is how it has been defined in **RecipePaginationSchema**. **attribute = 'items'** means that it is getting the source data from the **items** to attribute in **the pagination** objects.

8. Now, import **acs** and **desc** from **sqlalchemy** into **model/recipe.py** and modify the **get_all_published** method:

```
from sqlalchemy import asc, desc


    @classmethod
    def get_all_published(cls, page, per_page):

        return cls.query.filter_by(is_publish=True).order_by(desc(cls.
created_at)).paginate(page=page, per_page=per_page)
```

The **get_all_published** method we built here is used to leverage the **paginate** method from Flask-SQLAlchemy. We will filter and order the records, then the paginate method takes the **page** and **per_page** parameters and generates a pagination object.

9. Import **fields, use_kwargs** and **RecipePaginationSchema** into **resources/recipe.py**:

```
from webargs import fields
from webargs.flaskparser import use_kwargs
from schemas.recipe import RecipeSchema, RecipePaginationSchema
```

10. Declare the **recipe_pagination_schema** attribute in **resources/recipe.py** in order to serialize the paginated recipes:

```
recipe_pagination_schema = RecipePaginationSchema()
```

11. Modify the **RecipeListResource.get** method in **resources/recipe.py** in order to return the paginated recipes:

```
class RecipeListResource(Resource):

        @use_kwargs({'page': fields.Int(missing=1),
                            'per_page': fields.Int(missing=20)})
    def get(self, page, per_page):

        paginated_recipes = Recipe.get_all_published(page, per_page)

        return recipe_pagination_schema.dump(paginated_recipes).data,
    HTTPStatus.OK
```

Here, we have added the **@user_kwargs** decorator to the **RecipeListResource. get** method. The default value for the **page** parameter is 1, while the default value for the **per_page** parameter is 20. This means that if nothing is passed in, we will be getting the first page with the first 20 recipe records.

Then, we pass these two parameters into the **get_all_published** method to get the pagination object back. Finally, the paginated recipes will be serialized and returned to the frontend client.

Here, we have successfully implemented the pagination function and displayed the result. In the next exercise, we will test the pagination functions.

Exercise 51: Testing the Pagination Functions

In this exercise, we will test the pagination functions that we have just built. We will be creating eight recipes in our Smilecook application, and we will publish all of them. Then, we will simulate a user scenario in which we will get back all the recipes, page by page. Let's get started:

1. Click on the **Collections** tab.

2. Then, select the **POST Token** request and **Send** a request. This is to login to a user account. The result is shown in the following screenshot:

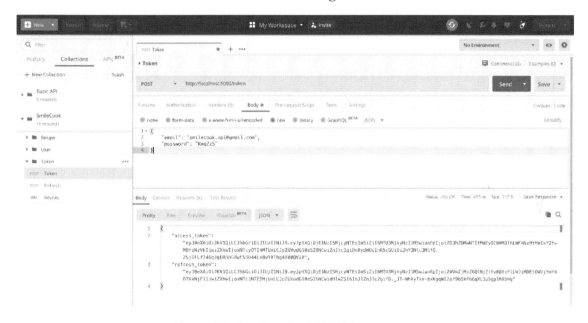

Figure 8.1: Sending the POST Token request

3. Create eight recipes by running the following **httpie** command in the PyCham console. The **{token}** placeholder should be replaced with the access token we obtained in *step 2*:

```
http POST localhost:5000/recipes "Authorization: Bearer {token}"
name="Vegetable Paella" description="This is a lovely vegetable paella"
num_of_servings=5 cook_time=60 directions="This is how you make it"

http POST localhost:5000/recipes "Authorization: Bearer {token}"
name="Minestrone Soup" description="This is a lovely minestrone soup" num_
of_servings=4 cook_time=60 directions="This is how you make it"

http POST localhost:5000/recipes "Authorization: Bearer {token}"
name="Thai Red Curry" description="This is a lovely thai red curry"
```

```
num_of_servings=4 cook_time=40 directions="This is how you make it"

http POST localhost:5000/recipes "Authorization: Bearer {token}"
name="Coconut Fried Rice" description="This is a lovely coconut fried
rice" num_of_servings=2 cook_time=30 directions="This is how you make it"

http POST localhost:5000/recipes "Authorization: Bearer {token}"
name="Vegetable Fried Rice" description="This is a lovely vegetable fried
rice" num_of_servings=2 cook_time=30 directions="This is how you make it"

http POST localhost:5000/recipes "Authorization: Bearer {token}"
name="Burrito Bowls" description="This is a lovely coconut fried rice"
num_of_servings=5 cook_time=60 directions="This is how you make it"

http POST localhost:5000/recipes "Authorization: Bearer {token}"
name="Fresh Huevos Rancheros" description="This is a lovely fresh huevos
rancheros" num_of_servings=4 cook_time=40 directions="This is how you make
it"

http POST localhost:5000/recipes "Authorization: Bearer {token}"
name="Bean Enchiladas" description="This is a lovely coconut fried rice"
num_of_servings=4 cook_time=60 directions="This is how you make it"
```

Note

You can also create the recipes one by one using Postman. We are using the
httpie command here because it's faster.

4. Publish all eight recipes using the following **httpie** command. Replace the **{token}** placeholder with the access token. Make sure that the recipe IDs in the URLs are referring to the recipes we created in the previous step:

```
http PUT localhost:5000/recipes/6/publish "Authorization: Bearer {token}"
http PUT localhost:5000/recipes/7/publish "Authorization: Bearer {token}"
http PUT localhost:5000/recipes/8/publish "Authorization: Bearer {token}"
http PUT localhost:5000/recipes/9/publish "Authorization: Bearer {token}"
http PUT localhost:5000/recipes/10/publish "Authorization: Bearer {token}"
http PUT localhost:5000/recipes/11/publish "Authorization: Bearer {token}"
http PUT localhost:5000/recipes/12/publish "Authorization: Bearer {token}"
http PUT localhost:5000/recipes/13/publish "Authorization: Bearer {token}"
```

Now we have created and published eight recipes. Next, we will get the recipes back page by page with a page size of two recipes.

5. Click on **GET RecipeList** and select the **Params** tab. Then, put a key-value pair (**per_page**, 2) into **Query Params** and **Send** the request. The result is shown in the following screenshot:

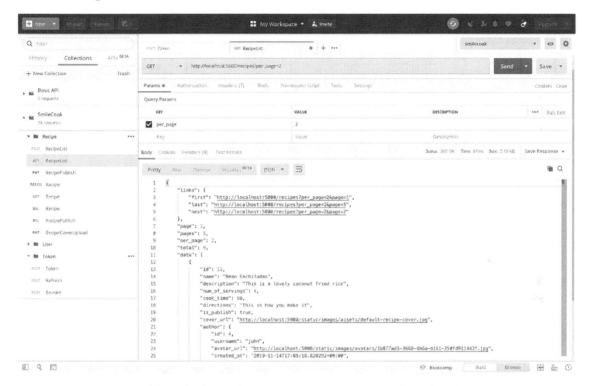

Figure 8.2: Adding the key-value pair to Query Params and sending the request

In the details of the recipe, we can see that there are links with the URLs of the **first**, **last**, and **next** pages. We can't see **prev** here because we are on the first page. There is a total of five pages, and we have two records per page. You can also see the **sorted** recipe details in the HTTP response.

6. Next, let's test whether the links in the recipes are working properly. We just need to click on the **next** URL link, which will open a new tab in Postman with the request URL populated (`http://localhost:5000/recipes?per_page=2&page=2`). Then, we just need to click on **Send** to send the request. The result is shown in the following screenshot:

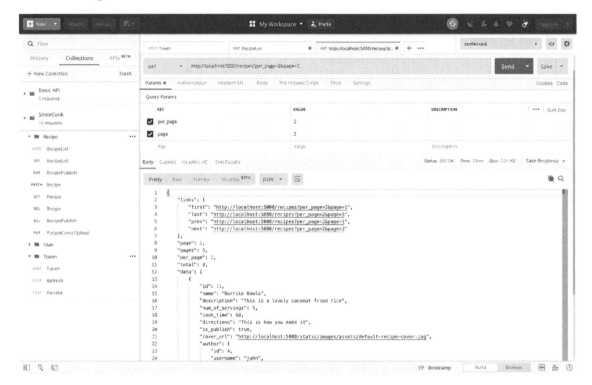

Figure 8.3: Testing the links in the recipes

Here, we can see that there are links to the **first**, **last**, **next**, and **prev** pages. We can also see that we are currently on page 2. All the recipe data is there as well.

We have successfully created our pagination function. Now, I will leave it to your capable hands to test it.

The benefit of pagination is that you are able to segregate thousands of records into pages. Data is retrieved in a page by page manner, and that will reduce the server's workload. But what if the user is setting a page size of, say, 100,000? How can we prevent a user from exploiting the system loophole? What we can do is pass the `max_per_page` parameter for pagination. That will limit the maximum page size the user can set. If the user is setting a page size bigger than the maximum page size, then the maximum page size will be used.

Activity 13: Implementing Pagination on the User-Specific Recipe Retrieval API

We implemented and tested the pagination function on our all published recipe retrieval APIs in the previous exercise. In this activity, we will work on the pagination function in the user-specific recipe retrieval API. The corresponding API can be found in `UserRecipeListResource`, which is used to get the recipes from a specific author. Follow these steps to complete this activity:

1. Modify the `get_all_by_user` method in `model/recipe.py`.

2. Import `RecipePaginationSchema` into `resources/user.py`.

3. Declare the `recipe_pagination_schema` attribute in `resources/user.py`.

4. Modify the `UserRecipeListResource.get` method in `resources/user.py`.

5. Add the `@user_kwargs` decorator for `UserRecipeListResource.get`. It takes a few parameters, including `page`, `per_page`, and `visibility`.

> **Note**
>
> The solution to this activity can be found on page 332.

Now, you should have completed the pagination function for the user recipe. Let's follow the same routine and test the function in the next activity.

Activity 14: Testing Pagination on the User-Specific Recipe Retrieval API

In this activity, we will test the user recipe pagination function that we just built. We published eight recipes in the previous exercise. We will use them here as our test subjects. We are going to create a request in Postman and test whether we can get them back, page by page. Follow these steps to complete this activity:

1. Get all the recipes by the author from the previous exercise using Postman, page by page, with a page size of two.

2. Click the next URL in the `links` to query for the next two records.

> **Note**
>
> The solution to this activity can be found on page 334.

Recipe Searching

In the previous exercises, we implemented the **pagination** function and also saw the benefits of using it. This can greatly reduce the number of recipes that are going back to users in one go. From the user's perspective, they can browse through different pages to look for the recipe they want.

A better way for the user to look for a recipe is by searching. The search function is an essential function on the internet. Look at the search giant Google; their search engine brings in huge amounts of revenue. Of course, we are not going to implement anything of the scale of Google in our Smilecook application. We will be just doing a simple text matching search here.

In the next exercise, we will implement the search function in our Smilecook platform. We will build a recipe searching API that allows the client to provide a **q** parameter to search for specific recipes by name or recipe description. This can be done by using the **LIKE** comparison operator. The **LIKE** operator works by matching the search string with the target string. We can use **%** in the search string as a wildcard. If it's not a exact match here it is more like a **SIMILAR TO** matching. So, the **%Chicken%** search string will match with the **Hainanese Chicken Rice** string.

Perhaps a better choice of comparison operator would be **ILIKE**. **LIKE** is case-sensitive, while **ILIKE** is case-insensitive. For example, we can't match **Thai Red Curry** with **%curry%** using the **LIKE** operator. You can see that **C** is uppercase here. However, if we use **ILIKE**, it will match perfectly fine.

Take a look at the following table to see how the comparison operator works:

Search String	Target String	Operator	Result
%curry%	The Red Curry	LIKE	not match
%curry%	The Red Curry	ILIKE	match
red%	The Red Curry	ILIKE	not match
%yellow%	The Red Curry	ILIKE	not match

Figure 8.4: Comparison operators

In our Smilecook platform, we don't want our search to be that strict. The search should be case-insensitive. Now, let's see how we can add this function to our Smilecook platform.

Exercise 52: Implementing the Search Function

Having learned about the recipe searching concept, we want to implement this as a function in our Smilecook platform. To do this, we will be adding a **q** parameter that will pass the search string into the API. Then, we will use the search string to look for the recipes we require. Let's get started:

1. Import **or_** from **sqlalchemy** into **models/recipe.py**:

   ```python
   from sqlalchemy import asc, desc, or_
   ```

2. Modify the **Recipe.get_all_published** method in **models/recipe.py** so that it gets all the published recipes that satisfy the search criteria:

   ```python
   @classmethod
   def get_all_published(cls, q, page, per_page):

       keyword = '%{keyword}%'.format(keyword=q)

       return cls.query.filter(or_(cls.name.ilike(keyword),
                   cls.description.ilike(keyword)),
                   cls.is_publish.is_(True)).\
                   order_by(desc(cls.created_at)).paginate(page=page, per_
   page=per_page)
   ```

   The preceding code is used to assign the search pattern to the variable **keyword**. Then, it searches the **name** and **description** fields by this keyword.

3. Modify **RecipeListResource** in **resources/recipe.py**:

   ```python
   class RecipeListResource(Resource):
       @use_kwargs({'q': fields.Str(missing='),
                                    'page': fields.Int(missing=1),
                                    'per_page': fields.Int(missing=20)})
       def get(self, q, page, per_page):

           paginated_recipes = Recipe.get_all_published(q, page, per_page)

           return recipe_pagination_schema.dump(paginated_recipes).data,
   HTTPStatus.OK
   ```

We added the **q** parameter to the **user_kwargs** decorator and the **get** function. The default for this **q** value is an empty string. The **q** parameter will also be passed into the **get_all_published** function.

Now we are done with the search function. Next, we are going to test this function.

Exercise 53: Testing the Search Function

In this exercise, we will be testing the search function that we have just built. We will test by searching for recipes that contain the **fried rice** string in the name or description. Let's get started:

1. Click on the **RecipeList** request and select the **Params** tab.

2. Insert the first key-value pair (**q**, **fried rice**).

3. Insert the second key-value pair (**per_page**, **2**).

4. Send the request. The result is shown in the following screenshot:

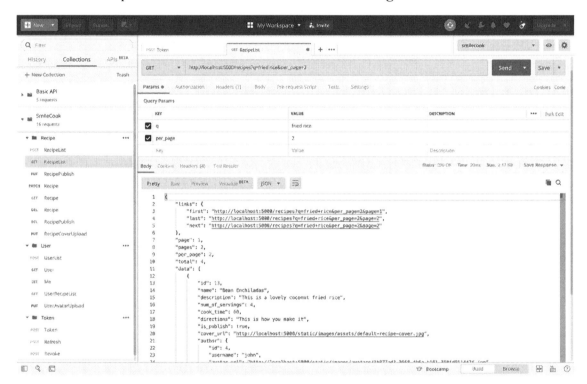

Figure 8.5: Searching for recipes that contain the "fried rice" string in the name or description

Here, we can see four fried rice recipe records, divided into two pages.

5. Next, test whether the links in the recipes are still working properly. We just need to click on the next URL link, which will open a new tab in Postman with the request URL populated (**http://localhost:5000/recipes?q=fried+rice&per_page=2&page=2**). Then, we just need to click on **Send** to send the request. The result is shown in the following screenshot:

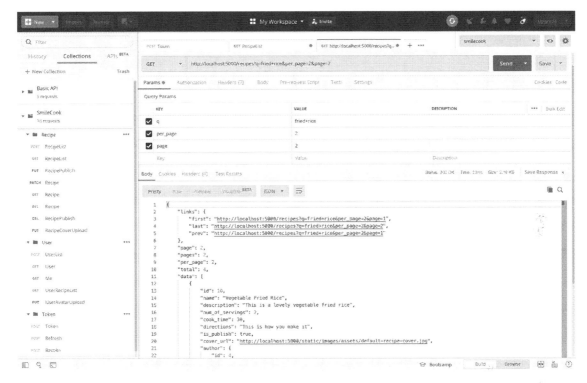

Figure 8.6: Testing whether the links in the recipes are working

From the result, we can that we are now on **page** 2. The recipe records are also sorted by creation time. The latest recipe is placed on the top.

So far, we have created the pagination and searching functions. This is a great achievement, but we are not done yet. We need to continue enhancing our Smilecook application. Without further ado, let's move on.

Sorting and Ordering

Sorting is another important feature that helps user navigation. Again, when we build any application, we need to keep the user experience in mind. Our application could eventually store millions of recipes, so we need to provide an easy way for our users to navigate the recipes and find the recipe they want.

Previously, the recipes that we sent back were sorted by time by default. Let's implement some other sorting criteria in our Smilecook application. We can still keep the default sorting criteria such as time, but we want to allow the user to define the searching criteria they want; for example, they can specify that they want the recipes to be sorted by cooking time. This is a possibility as the user may want to cook a quick meal, which means they will only be interested in recipes with short cooking times.

For our Smilecook application, sorting and ordering can be done by adding the **sort** and **order** parameters. We can put the sorting criteria (for example, **created_at**, **cook_time**, or **num_of_servings**) into the **sort** parameter, and we can use **created_at** as the default. The **order** parameter is used to specify whether it is **asc** (ascending order) or **desc** (descending order). We can put **desc** as the default.

In terms of the syntax, if we want our SQLAlchemy query result to be sorted in ascending order, we can do the following:

```
Import asc


sort_logic_asc = asc(getattr(cls, sort))


cls.query.filter(cls.is_publish=True).order_by(sort_logic_asc)
```

If we want it to be sorted in descending order, we can just use **desc**:

```
Import desc


sort_logic_desc = desc(getattr(cls, sort))


cls.query.filter(cls.is_publish=True).order_by(sort_logic_desc)
```

> **Note**
>
> Instead of **cls.is_published=True**, you can also use the SQLAlchemy column operator, that is, **cls.is_published.is_(True)**. You will get the same result.

In the next exercise, we will implement the sorting and ordering functions in our Smilecook platform. This will make our application more user-friendly.

Exercise 54: Implementing Sorting and Ordering

In this exercise, we will implement the sorting and ordering functions in our Smilecook platform. We will be adding the **sort** and **order** parameters to the get all published recipes API so that users can perform sorting and ordering on the published recipes. Let's get started:

1. In **resources/recipe.py**, use the **use_kwargs method** in the decorator to add two parameters (**sort**, **order**) to the **RecipeListResource.get** method. Set the default values for these two parameters to **created_at** and **desc**, respectively:

```
@use_kwargs({'q': fields.Str(missing='),
                        'page': fields.Int(missing=1),
                        'per_page': fields.Int(missing=20),
                        'sort': fields.Str(missing='created_at'),
                        'order': fields.Str(missing='desc')})
def get(self, q, page, per_page, sort, order):
```

2. Restrict the **sort** parameter to accept only the **created_at**, **cook_time**, and **num_of_servings** values. If other values are passed in, then we'll default to **created_at**:

```
if sort not in ['created_at', 'cook_time', 'num_of_servings']:
    sort = 'created_at'
```

3. Restrict the **order** parameter to accept only the **asc** and **desc** values. If other values are passed in, then we'll default to **desc**:

```
if order not in ['asc', 'desc']:
    order = 'desc'
```

4. Pass the **sort** and **order** parameters into the **get_all_published** function:

```
paginated_recipes = Recipe.get_all_published(q, page, per_page,
sort, order)
```

5. Modify the **get_all_published** method in **models/recipe.py** so that it looks as follows. It takes in two additional parameters, that is, **sort** and **order**, to define the logic:

```python
@classmethod
def get_all_published(cls, q, page, per_page, sort, order):

    keyword = '%{keyword}%'.format(keyword=q)

    if order == 'asc':
        sort_logic = asc(getattr(cls, sort))
    else:
        sort_logic = desc(getattr(cls, sort))

    return cls.query.filter(or_(cls.name.ilike(keyword),
                                cls.description.ilike(keyword)),
                            cls.is_publish.is_(True)).\
        order_by(sort_logic).paginate(page=page, per_page=per_page)
```

Here, we have created the sorting and ordering functions. Not many changes were made to the code. Next, we are going to test our implementation using Postman.

Exercise 55: Testing the Sorting and Ordering Feature

In the previous exercise, we created customized ordering functions. Users should be able to order the recipe records in our Smilecook platform by their specified column, and in either ascending or descending order. In this exercise, we will test whether that is really the case. We will pass the **sort** and **order** parameters into Postman and verify them. Let's get started:

1. We will send a request to get all the recipe records back. Then, sort the data by **cook_time** in ascending order. First, click on the **RecipeList** request and select the **Params** tab.

2. Insert the first key-value pair (**sort**, **cook_time**).

3. Insert the second key-value pair (**order**, **desc**).

4. Send the request. The result is shown in the following screenshot:

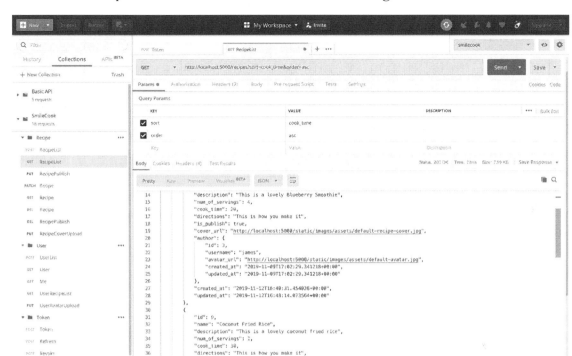

Figure 8.7: Sending a request to get all the recipe records back

From the preceding search result, we can see that the recipe's **cook_time** is sorted in ascending order. The first recipe's **cook_time** is 20 minutes, whereas the second one is 30 minutes.

5. Send a request to get all the recipe records back. Then, sort the data by **num_of_servings** in descending order. Click on **RecipeList** and select the **Params** tab.

6. Insert the first key-value pair (**sort**, **num_of_servings**).

7. Insert the second key-value pair (**order**, **desc**).

8. Send the request. The result is shown in the following screenshot:

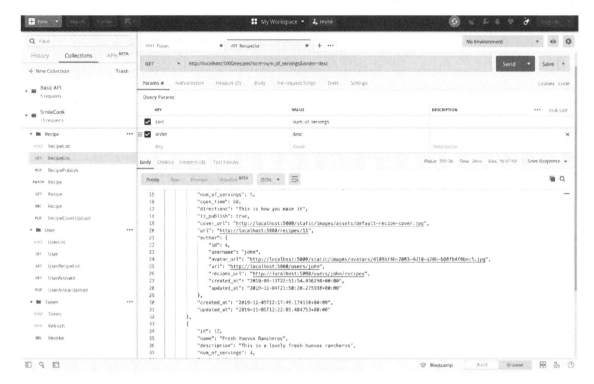

Figure 8.8: Sending a request and sorting the data by num_of_servings in descending order

9. From the preceding search result, we can see that the recipe's **num_of_servings** has been sorted in descending order. The first recipe's **num_of_servings** is for five people, whereas the second one is for four people.

Now, you have finished developing and testing all the functions you have learned about in this chapter. Next, we will complete an activity to ensure you have the flexibility to use what we have learned so far.

Activity 15: Searching for Recipes with Specific Ingredients

In this activity, we will search the recipes using a specific attribute. We will add a new **ingredients** attribute and then pass in parameters to search through the recipe. Follow these steps to complete this activity:

1. Add the ingredients attribute to the **Recipe** model.

2. Run Flask-Migrate to update the database.

3. Add the `ingredients` attribute to `RecipeSchema`.

4. Modify the `RecipeResource.patch` method to support the `ingredients` attribute update.

5. Modify the `Recipe.get_all_published` method so that you can search through the ingredients.

6. Create two recipes with the `ingredients` attribute and publish them.

7. Search for the recipes using the `ingredients` attribute.

> **Note**
>
> The solution to this activity can be found on page 336.

Congratulations! You have completed this activity. Now, please work on the assessments to test your understanding of this chapter.

Summary

We have implemented a lot of great features in this chapter that allows users to find the recipe information they want in a simple and efficient manner. The pagination function we implemented allows the user to quickly find out how many recipes there are in total and navigate them page by page. It also saves the server's resources as it doesn't need to render thousands of recipes in one go.

The search function is another time-saving feature. Users can now look for the recipes they want by performing a simple search. We have also completed the sorting and ordering functions in the Smilecook application, which provide a better browsing experience for users.

So far, we have created almost all of the user functions we need. Our Smilecook platform development is nearing its end. In the next chapter, we will work on internal system optimization, such as HTTP caching and rate-limiting.

Building More Features

Learning Objectives

By the end of this chapter, you will be able to:

- Use caching to improve API performance and efficiently get the latest information
- Add the cache function to the Smilecook application using the Flask-Caching package
- Implement rate-limiting functionality to an API
- Use IP address to perform rate limiting

In this chapter, we will cover caching to improve performance and get accustomed to using the rate-limiting function.

Introduction

We added pagination, searching, and ordering functions to our Smilecook application in our last chapter so that users can navigate to their recipes much easier. This also helps to reduce the server burden and improve performance. We have explained how making our APIs snappy is important in today's world.

In this chapter, we will be further improving our API performance from another aspect. We will be adding in the **cache** function, which will temporarily save data to the application memory. This will allow us to save the time required to query the database every time. This can greatly improve API performance and reduce server burden. There is a Flask extension package, Flask-Caching, that can help us in implementing the caching function. We will first talk about the theory behind caching, and through practical exercises, we show you how to implement this function in our Smilecook application.

Besides caching, we will implement a rate-limiting function. That will prevent certain high-usage users from jeopardizing the whole system by limiting their usage. Ensuring fair usage of our APIs is crucial to guarantee service quality. We will be using a Flask extension package, **Flask-Limiter**, for that.

These two caching and rate-limiting functions are very common and powerful in real-world scenarios. Let's learn about how they work.

Caching

Caching means storing data in a temporary space (a cache) so that it can be retrieved faster in subsequent requests. The temporary space can be application memory, server hard disk space, or something else. The whole purpose of caching is to lighten the workload by avoiding any heavy processes for querying the data again. For example, in our Smilecook application, if we reckon that the recipes from a popular author will always get queried by the users, we can cache these recipes. So, the next time that users ask for these recipes, we can just send back the recipes in the cache instead of querying against our database. You can see caching everywhere. Almost all applications have caching implemented nowadays. Even in our local browsers, we save website results on the local hard disk to achieve faster access next time.

For server-level caching, most of the time, the cache is stored in the same web server as the application. But technically speaking, it can be stored in another server as well, such as **Redis** (**Remote Dictionary Server**) or **Memcached** (a high-performance distributed cached memory). They are all in-memory data storage systems that allow key-value storage as well as storing data. For simple applications and easy implementation, we can also use a single global dictionary as a cache (simple cache).

Benefit of Caching

Through caching, not only can we reduce the volume of data to be transferred, but we can also improve the overall performance. This is done by reducing the bandwidth required, reducing the server loading time, and more. Take our Smilecook application as an example: if we have a low traffic, caching may not be a lot of help, because the cache will pretty much expire before the next query comes in. But imagine that we have high traffic, say, 10,000 requests per minute, coming in asking for recipes. If these recipes are all cached and the cache has not expired, we will be able to simply return the recipes in the cache to the client frontend. In this scenario, we would be saving 10,000 database queries, which could be a substantial cost-saving measure.

Flask-Caching

Flask-Caching is a Flask extension package that allows us easily implement caching functionality. You can imagine a **cache** as a dictionary object that contains key-value pairs. The key here is used to specify the resource to **cache**, whereas the value is used to store the actual data to be cached. Take the resource for retrieving all the recipes as an example. The flow contains the following stages:

1. Request the get **/recipes** resource.

2. Use the key to search for the existing cache (Flask-Caching will be using **request.path** and **hashed_args** to be the key value, for example, **recipesbcd8b0c2eb1fce714eab6cef0d771acc**).

3. If the recipes were previously cached, return the cached data.

4. If no cache for these recipes exists, follow the standard flow to get the recipes from the database.

5. Save the result (the recipe data) in the cache.

6. Return the recipe data.

The process is better illustrated through the following figure:

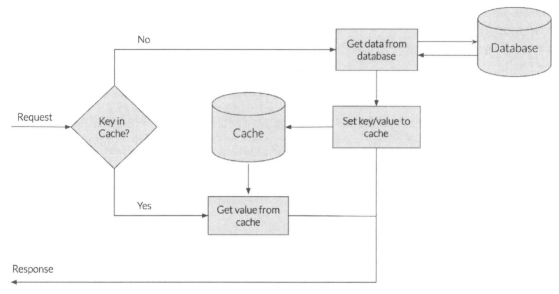

Figure 9.1: Flask-Caching process flow chart

By following this flow, you can see that data that is cached can be served before we query against the database.

I hope you have a better understanding of the theory behind caching. Let's roll up our sleeves and work on bringing this feature and our Smilecook application together, through the coming exercises.

Exercise 56: Implementing Caching Functionality Using Flask-Caching

In this exercise, we will be installing the Flask-Caching package. Then, we will implement the **cache** function in **RecipeListResource**. We will also add two decorators, @ **app.before_request** and @**app.after_request**, to print application logs for easier testing:

1. Add the Flask-Caching package and version in **requirements.txt**:

   ```
   Flask-Caching==1.7.2
   ```

2. Run the **pip** command to install the package:

   ```
   pip install -r requirements.txt
   ```

   Once we have run the **install** command, we should see the following result:

   ```
   Installing collected packages: Flask-Caching
   Successfully installed Flask-Caching-1.7.2
   ```

3. Import **Cache** in **extensions.py** and instantiate it:

```
from flask_caching import Cache


cache = Cache()
```

4. Import **cache** from **extensions** in **app.py**:

```
from extensions import db, jwt, image_set, cache
```

5. In **app.py**, put in **cache.init_app(app)** under the **register_extensions** function. Pass in the **app** object to initialize the caching function:

```
def register_extensions(app):
    db.app = app
    db.init_app(app)
    migrate = Migrate(app, db)
    jwt.init_app(app)
    configure_uploads(app, image_set)
    patch_request_class(app, 10 * 1024 * 1024)
    cache.init_app(app)
```

6. Add the caching-related configuration in **config.py**:

```
CACHE_TYPE = 'simple'
CACHE_DEFAULT_TIMEOUT = 10 * 60
```

The default **CACHE_TYPE** is **Null**, meaning there is no cache. Here, we set **CACHE_TYPE** as **simple**, which means we are going to use the **SimpleCache** strategy. The default expiration time is **10 * 60** seconds, which is 10 minutes.

7. Import **cache** from **extensions** in **resources/recipe.py**:

```
from extensions import image_set, cache
```

8. In **resources/recipe.py**, put the **cache** decorator in the **get** method of **RecipeListResource**:

```
class RecipeListResource(Resource):

    @use_kwargs({'q': fields.Str(missing=''),
                            'page': fields.Int(missing=1),
                            'per_page': fields.Int(missing=20),
                            'sort': fields.Str(missing='created_at'),
                            'order': fields.Str(missing='desc')})
    @cache.cached(timeout=60, query_string=True)
    def get(self, q, page, per_page, sort, order):
```

We are setting the cache expiration time (**timeout**) to be **60** seconds here. **query_string = True** means it allows the passing in of arguments.

9. For testing, print a line of **Querying database** in the **RecipeListResource.get** method:

```
def get(self, q, page, per_page, sort, order):
    print('Querying database...')
```

10. For testing, in **app.py**, add in the following decorator definition at the bottom of the **register_extensions(app)** function:

```
@app.before_request
    def before_request():
        print('\n===================== BEFORE REQUEST
=====================\n')
        print(cache.cache._cache.keys())
        print('\n=====================================================
=\n')

    @app.after_request
    def after_request(response):
        print('\n===================== AFTER REQUEST
=====================\n')
        print(cache.cache._cache.keys())
        print('\n=====================================================
=\n')
        return response
```

We have already completed our first caching function on **RecipeListResource**. That should reduce the frequency of having to get recipes from the database. Let's test it out in our next exercise to make sure it works.

Exercise 57: Testing the Caching Function with Postman

In this exercise, we will be using Postman to test the caching function. And we will verify whether it works or not in the PyCharm console:

1. First, get all the recipe details back. Click on **GET RecipeList**.

2. Then, send the request. The result is shown in the following screenshot:

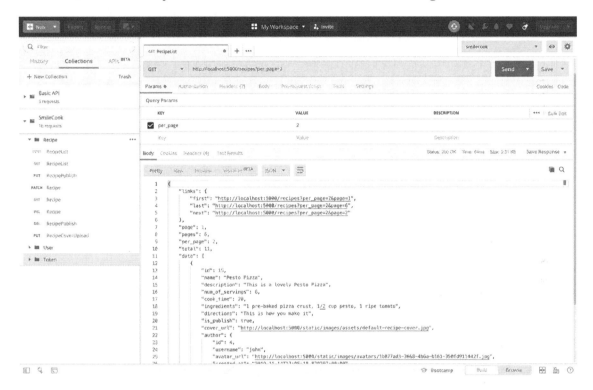

Figure 9.2: Getting all recipe details

3. Check the application log in the PyCharm console.

Figure 9.3: Checking the application log

In the console, we can see that before the request, the cache is empty. After the database query, the data is cached and returned to the frontend client.

4. Get all the recipe details back again one more time and check the result in the PyCharm console:

Figure 9.4: Getting all the recipe details again

Because this is the second time that we are requesting the data, we get it from the cache rather than the database; the previous result was cached. We can see from the PyCharm console that the result was cached and no query to the database was fired.

So, we have completed the implementation and testing of the caching function here. Since we are just caching one record here, the performance gain may not be obvious. But imagine we were getting thousands of requests of the same kind in a short period of time; this caching functionality can greatly reduce the workload of our database.

> **Note**
>
> If we want to see the data in the cache, we can use this line of code: `print(cache.cache._cache.items())`, to check the key-value stored there. There we can see that the value in the cache is the JSON data that we return to the client frontend.

Clearing the Cache when Data Updates

When data is updated, the data that was cached before becomes stale immediately. For example, if the cover image of a recipe is updated, the old cover image is removed. But in the cache, there would still be the URL of the old cover image, which would no longer work. Therefore, we need a mechanism for clearing the old cache and storing the URL of the new cover image to our cache instead.

Activity 16: Getting Cache Data after Updating Recipe Details

When we get all the recipe details, they will be stored in the cache and can be used directly in the next request. In this activity, we will check to see what will happen when we try to get recipe details after updating the recipe data:

1. First, get all the recipe details back.

2. Update one of the recipe details.

3. Get all the recipe details back again and check the recipe details.

> **Note**
>
> The solution for this activity can be found on page 340.

In our next exercise, we shall find all the resources that are involved in updating data. We shall add a step to clear the cache after data is updated.

Exercise 58: Implementing Cache-Clearing Functionality

In this exercise, we will try to clear the cache when recipe data is updated. There are quite a few resources involved here. We shall tackle them one by one:

1. Import cache from extensions in utils.py:

    ```
    from extensions import image_set, cache
    ```

2. Create a new function under **utils.py** that is for clearing the cache. The function should clear the cache with a specific prefix:

    ```
    def clear_cache(key_prefix):

        keys = [key for key in cache.cache._cache.keys() if key.
    startswith(key_prefix)]
        cache.delete_many(*keys)
    ```

    Here, the code is to use the **for** loop for **key** in **cache.cache._cache.keys()** to iterate all the keys in the cache. If the key is prefixed with the passed-in prefix, it will be placed on the **keys** list. Then, we will be using the **cache.delete_many** method to clear the cache. The single star, *, in the preceding code, is for unpacking the list into positional arguments.

3. Import the **clear_cache** function in **resources/recipe.py**:

    ```
    from utils import clear_cache
    ```

4. Invoke **clear_cache('/recipes')** in the resources that update recipe data. In the **RecipeResource.patch**, **RecipeResource.delete**, **RecipePublishResource.put**, **RecipePublishResource.delete**, and **RecipeCoverUploadResource.put** methods, add in **clear_cache('/recipes')** before **return**:

    ```
    clear_cache('/recipes')
    ```

    So, here, if done properly, the old cache data will be cleared when the data is updated. Next time, when this updated data is requested, it will be stored in the cache again.

5. Import the **generate_token**, **verify_token**, **save_image**, **clear_cache** function in **resources/user.py**:

    ```
    from utils import generate_token, verify_token, save_image, clear_cache
    ```

6. Invoke `clear_cache('/recipes')` in `UserAvatarUploadResource.put` to clear the cache when data is updated:

```
clear_cache('/recipes')
```

When the user updates their avatar image, that will change the `avatar_url` attribute. Therefore, we will need to clear the stale cache there as well.

After this exercise, I believe that you will have a much better understanding of how the whole flow of caching works. We build the caching function here to improve performance, but at the same time, we want to make sure that the cache is refreshed to ensure data quality.

Exercise 59: Verifying the Cache-Clearing Function

In our previous exercise, we added the step to clear the cache to the resources that are involved in data updates. In this activity, we will verify the cache-clearing function that we have implemented. We can test it by updating the data and seeing whether the API returns the updated data:

1. Get all the recipe data back. Click on **RecipeList** and send the request. The result is shown in the following screenshot:

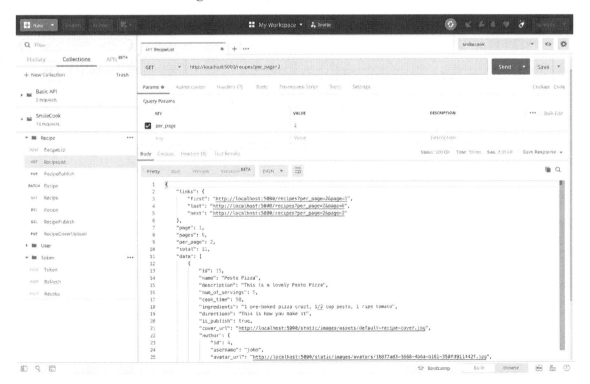

Figure 9.5: Get all the recipe data back and send the request

2. Check the PyCharm console for the application log:

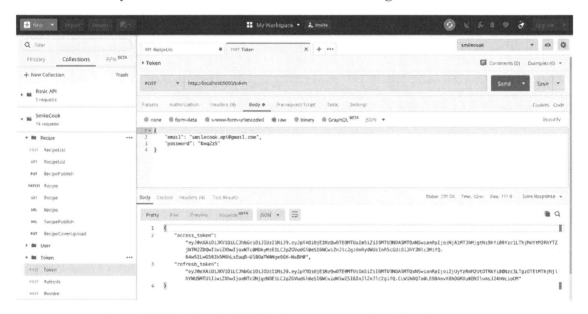

Figure 9.6: Checking the PyCharm console for the application log

We can see that the cache is empty before the request. Then, after querying the database, the new data is cached.

3. Log in to your account. Click on the **Collections** tab and select the **POST Token** request.

4. Send the request. The result is shown in the following screenshot:

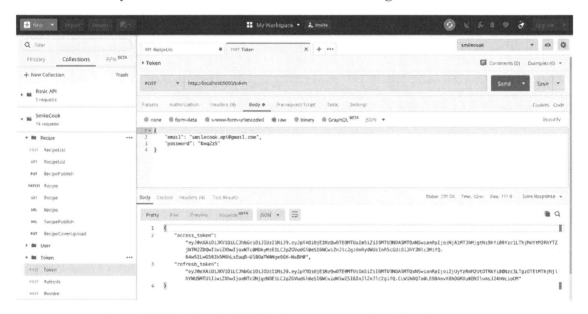

Figure 9.7: Selecting the POST Token request and sending the request

5. Modify a recipe record using the **PATCH** method. First, select the **PATCH Recipe** request. Now, select the **Headers** tab and modify **Bearer {token}**; the token should be the access token.

6. Select the **Body** tab and modify **num_of_servings** to **10** and **cook_time** to **100**. Please check the following:

```
{
    "num_of_servings": 10,
    "cook_time": 100
}
```

7. Send the request. The result is shown in the following screenshot:

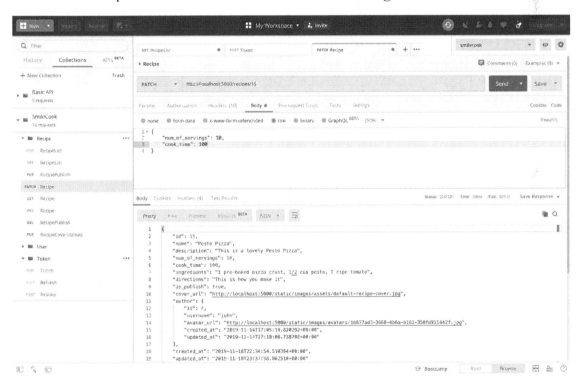

Figure 9.8: Modifying the recipe record using the PATCH method

8. Check the PyCharm console for the application log:

Figure 9.9: Checking the application log

We can see that the cache is there before the request. But after the recipe record is updated, the cache becomes stale and is removed.

So, in this exercise, we have completed the testing of the cache-clearing function. This will ensure that we are getting the latest data.

> **Note**
>
> The printing of the application log is for testing only. Before we go on, we need to comment on the **print** command in **before_request** and **after_request**. We can do that by using *command + /* on a Mac, or *Ctrl + /* on a Windows machine.

API Rate Limiting

When we provide an API service, we need to ensure fair usage for every user so that the system resources are effectively and fairly serving all. We want to make sure that the majority of users are getting good server performance; therefore, we need to apply restrictions. By limiting a small number of high-traffic users, we can make sure that the majority of users are satisfied.

The way to do that is to set a limit per user. For example, we can limit the number of requests per user to be no more than 100 per second. This number will be enough for the normal usage of our API. If there is any particular case where a user is firing 100+ requests per second, the excess requests will not be handled. This is to reserve system resources (such as CPU processing and bandwidth resources) for other users.

To achieve this, we introduce the concept of rate-limiting. By limiting the "rate" of our API service per user, we guarantee that the majority of our users are able to enjoy the service performance they deserve.

HTTP Headers and Response Codes

We can use HTTP headers to display rate limit information. The following attributes in the HTTP headers can tell us the number of requests (the rate) allowed, the remaining quota, and when the limit will be reset:

- **X-RateLimit-Limit**: Shows the rate limit of this API endpoint

- **X-RateLimit-Remaining**: Shows the number of remaining requests allowed before the next reset

- **X-RateLimit-Reset**: When the rate limit will be reset (in UTC epoch time)

- **Retry-After**: The number of seconds before the next reset

When a user starts to violate the rate limit, the API will return the HTTP status code **429 Too Many Requests**, with the error message in the response body:

```
{
    "errors": "Too Many Requests"
}
```

To implement this rate limit function, we can use the Flask extension package Flask-Limiter. The Flask-Limiter package can help us easily add the rate limit function to our APIs.

Flask-Limiter

Flask-Limiter is a Flask extension package that can let us easily add rate-limiting functionality to an endpoint. Apart from limiting the rate, it can also put the rate limit information in the HTTP header by using the **RATELIMIT_HEADERS_ENABLED** configuration. We, therefore, don't need to code the HTTP header information ourselves. Besides that, it also supports a configurable backend for storage with current implementations for Redis, in-memory, Memcached, and others.

We can even set multiple limits; we just need to delimit them using a delimiter. For example, we can set the limit to be **100** requests per minute and **1000** requests per hour, at the same time.

Use the following syntax to set up the rate limit for our API endpoint:

```
[count] [per|/] [n (optional)] [second|minute|hour|day|month|year]
```

Here are some examples:

```
100 per minute
```

```
100/minute
```

```
100/minute;1000/hour;5000/day
```

Now we understand how rate limits work. We will work on a practical exercise together to add this useful functionality to our Smilecook application.

Exercise 60: Implementing API Rate-Limiting Functionality

In this exercise, we will implement API rate-limiting functionality using **Flask-Limiter**. We will install and set **Flask-Limiter**, and then add the limit in rate-limit to **RecipeListResource**:

1. Add **Flask-Limiter** version **1.0.1** to **requirements.txt**:

   ```
   Flask-Limiter==1.0.1
   ```

2. Install the package using the **pip install** command:

   ```
   pip install -r requirements.txt
   ```

   You should be seeing the following installation result:

   ```
   Installing collected packages: limits, Flask-Limiter
     Running setup.py install for limits ... done
     Running setup.py install for Flask-Limiter ... done
   Successfully installed Flask-Limiter-1.0.1 limits-1.3
   ```

3. Import **Limiter** and **get_remote_address** in **extensions.py** and instantiate a **limiter** object:

   ```
   from flask_limiter import Limiter
   from flask_limiter.util import get_remote_address

   limiter = Limiter(key_func=get_remote_address)
   ```

   The **get_remote_address** function will return the IP address for the current request. If the IP address is not found, it will return **127.0.0.1**, which means the localhost. Here, our strategy is to limit the rate per IP address.

4. In **app.py**, import **limiter** from **extensions**:

```
from extensions import db, jwt, image_set, cache, limiter
```

5. In **app.py**, initialize the **limiter** object under **register_extensions**. Pass in the **app** object to the **limiter.init_app** method:

```
limiter.init_app(app)
```

6. In **config.py**, set **RATELIMIT_HEADERS_ENABLED** to **True**:

```
RATELIMIT_HEADERS_ENABLED = True
```

This will allow Flask-Limiter to put in rate limit-related information in the HTTP header, including **X-RateLimit-Limit**, **X-RateLimit-Remaining**, **X-RateLimit-Reset**, and **Retry-After**.

7. In **resources/recipe.py**, import **limiter** from **extensions**:

```
from extensions import image_set, cache,  limiter
```

8. In **RecipeListResource**, put the **limiter.limit** function in the **decorators** attribute:

```
class RecipeListResource(Resource):
    decorators = [limiter.limit('2 per minute', methods=['GET'], error_
message='Too Many Requests')]
```

We are setting the number of requests to be only two per minute. The HTTP method is **GET** and the error message is **Too Many Requests**.

9. Click **Run** to start the Flask application; then, we are ready to test it:

Figure 9.10: Start the Flask application and then test it

Now that this exercise is complete, our API has rate-limiting functionality. In the next exercise, we have to test our rate limit function.

Exercise 61: Verifying the Rate-Limit Function

In the last exercise, we set the API for getting all recipe details, which can only be obtained twice per minute. So, in this exercise, we will see whether the result is what we expected:

1. Get all the recipe data back. Click on GET **RecipeList** and send the request.

2. Select the **Header** tab in **Response**. The result is shown in the following screenshot:

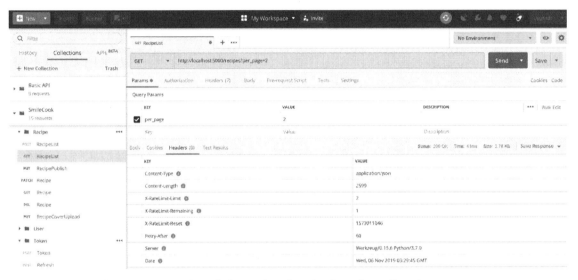

Figure 9.11: Getting all the recipe data back and sending the request

In the HTTP response, we can see that the rate limit for this endpoint is **2**, while we only have one remaining request quota. And the limit is going to be reset **60** seconds later.

3. Get all the recipe data back again and send the request twice more.

4. Select the **Body** in the HTTP response. The result is shown in the following screenshot:

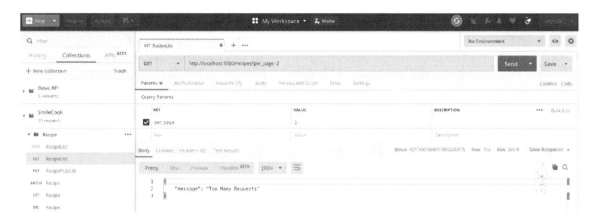

Figure 9.12: Getting all the recipe data back again and sending the request twice

We can see that at the third request, we will receive the error HTTP status code **429 TOO MANY REQUESTS**. That means the rate limit is working.

In this exercise, we have completed the rate limit function. By restricting a small number of abusive users, we ensure that the majority of users can enjoy high servicing performance.

Exercise 62: Adding a Whitelist

We want to ease the rate limit for our developers, the testers of the API, because they may indeed need to fire frequent requests to the APIs for testing. What should we do in this case? In this exercise, we shall see how we can use Flask-Limiter to satisfy this requirement.

We would like to set up an IP whitelist that can allow certain IP addresses to use the API without any rate limit:

1. In **app.py**, import **request**:

   ```
   from flask import Flask, request
   ```

2. In **app.py**, use the **@limiter.request_filter** decorator and set up the whitelist function. Put **127.0.0.1** (localhost) in the whitelist:

   ```
   @limiter.request_filter
   def ip_whitelist():
       return request.remote_addr == '127.0.0.1'
   ```

3. Run **app.py**:

Figure 9.13: Running the app.py file

4. Test the application by firing a **GET** all recipe request, and check the HTTP header for the rate limit. Click on **GET RecipeList** and send the request. Select the **Header** tab in **Response**. The result is shown in the following screenshot:

Figure 9.14: Checking the HTTP header for rate limit

We can see that the rate-limit restriction is gone. In this exercise, you have seen that the rate-limiting function can be flexible. It can be enacted or withdrawn depending on different situations.

Activity 17: Adding Multiple Rate-Limit Restrictions

In this activity, we are going to add multiple rate-limit restrictions to the same resource. But remember, we added a whitelist to the previous exercise. We need to comment out that code, so we can test it:

1. In `UserRecipeListResource`, add the rate limit. The limit is **3** times per minute, **30** times per hour, and **300** times a day.

2. Comment out the whitelist code.

3. Test the rate limit function using Postman.

> **Note**
>
> The solution for this activity can be found on page 343.

Congratulations! Now that you have completed this activity, you know how to flexibly use the rate-limiting function.

Summary

In this chapter, we have learned about and implemented caching and rate-limiting functions in our Smilecook API. Such functions make our APIs even more efficient. Our Smilecook application is saving the cache in application memory, though, which means the cache will be gone after a server reboot. To address this, we can work with Redis or Memcached in the future, which can persist the cache even after a server reboot. They also support sharing the cache with multiple servers. This is something we encourage you to explore outside of this book. The most important thing at the moment is for you to learn all the fundamental concepts covered in this book. So, later, if you want to extend to more advanced implementation, it shouldn't be too hard for you.

In the next and final chapter, we will build the Smilecook frontend client for you to work with the backend API. Through this frontend client, we will understand the whole picture better. You will see how the frontend and backend interact. Finally, we will deploy the whole application to the Heroku cloud platform, which means our Smilecook application will be used by everybody.

10

Deployment

Learning Objectives

By the end of this chapter, you will be able to:

- Explain the application deployment process to the cloud

- Explain the difference between SaaS, PaaS, and IaaS

- Set up different configurations between development and production environments

- Set up the Heroku cloud platform

- Install and configure Heroku Postgres

- Use the Heroku command-line interface (Heroku CLI) to deploy an application

- Set up the Postman environment variable

In this chapter, we are going to deploy our application to Heroku and test it using Postman.

Introduction

In the previous chapter, we added the cache and rate limit functions to our Smilecook applications. These last two functions are very useful, especially when we are dealing with huge volumes of traffic. Caching and rate-limiting can improve response speeds and can also raise the security level.

In this chapter, we will discuss how we can deploy our application to a cloud server. Deploying an application is like publishing a book or releasing a movie. It is like releasing our application on the market. Nowadays, a lot of cloud services provide free usage quotas. They allow developers to deploy their application to their cloud platform for free provided the resource usage is below a certain threshold. For our Smilecook application, what we need to do is simply make a few minor changes to the code and some configuration files. Everything else will be handled by the cloud platform. You will see how simple this is very soon.

We will first make minor modifications to the application code to segregate the production and development environment configurations. Then, we will talk about the Heroku cloud service platform, on which we are going to deploy the Smilecook application. We will walk you through the account registration, configuration, and deployment processes in the Heroku cloud service platform.

Once the deployment is done, we will use Postman to test the APIs directly in the production environment. Isn't that exciting?! Without further ado, let's get started.

Deployment

What is **deployment** for? The API application we wrote earlier just runs the code on the local machine. Using one of the ports on the local machine, we can send the request from the client to the local server. This is good for development purpose. We can quickly test and adjust our application in a development environment. However, our local machine is not intended to be a server; others can't access it. And they cannot send HTTP requests to APIs hosted on our local machine.

If we want to open this API service to external users, we need to host it on a server. The server should be connected to the internet, with a domain and URL that allow others to access it.

Moving an application from a local machine to a server that runs on the internet is called deployment. This will involve work such as environment setting, dependent package installation, and building a web server.

Comparing SaaS, PaaS, and IaaS

In the past, it was expensive to set up your own web server. There are lots of considerations, including network connectivity, storage, server configuration, and OS setup. Nowadays, cloud computing services are here to provide all the infrastructure services, which lowers costs significantly, especially for individual developers and small- and medium-sized companies. There are three main categories of cloud computing services out there. These are **Software as a Service** (**SaaS**), **Platform as a Service** (**PaaS**), and **Infrastructure as a Service** (**IaaS**). There are pros and cons for each, and these will be discussed in this section.

IaaS: Users do not need to purchase their own servers, software, network devices, and so on. These infrastructures are provided as a service, and users do not need to care about setup and maintenance. They still have the ability to configure these services, such as installing software and setting up firewall. Example of IaaS include **AWS EC2** and **Google Compute Engine** (**GCE**).

Compared with the past, this IaaS model can greatly reduce the hardware and network setup costs, and all other costs relating to space and resources surrounding that. Individual developers, or small- and medium-sized companies often do not need that many system resources. This model, therefore, allows them to rent the infrastructure as a service; they just need to pay for the resources that they need.

- Pros: Developers have much more flexibility. IaaS provides the necessary computing resources for applications to run on. Developers can easily request additional resources, or trim down resources, according to the needs of the application. This is easily customizable.

- Cons: Developers need to spend time learning how to configure the cloud platform according to their needs.

PaaS: PaaS is somewhere between SaaS and IaaS. There is no need for users to manage and maintain infrastructures. Service providers already package all these infrastructure and related services together as a platform and rent them out as a service to users. Users do not need to worry about the backend setup required, nor aspects such as extending the number of servers and load balancing. Users (developers) just need to focus on their development and deploy their work accordingly to the cloud platform. Example of PaaS include Heroku, Windows Azure, and AWS Elastic Beanstalk.

- Pros: Reduced setup time. By leveraging the services provided by the platform, developers can zero in on development.

- Cons: There could be an unnecessary charge incurred. Compared to IaaS, PaaS is less flexible in the sense that you have less control over the infrastructure setup and configuration. As the whole platform is packaged as a service, some unused packaged resources could go to waste. In this case, the charge could be comparatively higher than IaaS.

SaaS: SaaS basically refers to web applications available on the internet. Users are not required to maintain the software. The software is provided as a service. A very typical example is Gmail. Example of SaaS include Dropbox, Salesforce, and Slack.

- Pros: The cost is low as we don't need to care about hardware purchases and other setup costs. If a user has a specific requirement that can be addressed by this service, SaaS could be the easiest and most effective solution.

- Cons: Since the vast amount of user data will be stored in the cloud platform, there could be some concerns regarding data security. Also, we need to consider service availability once the application is deployed.

As individual developers, we need a stable and scalable server for us to deploy our application. PaaS is the best option here. It provides the computing platform for applications to run on, and developers do not need to worry about hardware maintenance since service providers take care of all of this. Hence, it is a time and cost-saving solution for developers. Developers can focus on developing good software.

The Heroku Platform

Heroku is a popular PaaS. We can deploy our APIs there so that they can be accessed by anyone in the world. And it doesn't just support Python, but also other programming languages, including Ruby and Go.

Heroku provides a free plan for developers to deploy and test their applications there. Certainly, they do have paid plans as well, and with many more powerful functions that can make our APIs more secure and efficient. Later on, if you need these powerful features and system resources for your application, you can consider that. But right now, for teaching purposes, a free plan is good enough.

> **Note**
>
> Apart from Heroku, there are other cloud service providers. Some of the market leaders in cloud services are **Amazon Web Services** (**AWS**), **Google Cloud Platform** (**GCP**), IBM Cloud, Microsoft Azure, and Rackspace Cloud.

Configuration Handling in Smilecook

Most applications require multiple configurations; at least one is required for a production server, and one for development use. There will be differences between them, such as the debug mode, secret key, and database URL. We can use a default configuration that is always loaded, and a separate configuration for the production server and development environment to inherit the default configuration depending on the environment. For environment-specific configurations, we will create two new classes – `DevelopmentConfig` and `ProductionConfig`.

Exercise 63: Configuration Handling for the Production and Development Environments

In this exercise, we will segregate our application configurations between the development and production environments. For configurations such as `DEBUG`, we will require different values for the two environments. The same goes for the database URL as well. We are therefore going to create two sets of configurations, `DevelopmentConfig` and `ProductionConfig`. The former is for development and system enhancement in a development environment, while the latter is to be run in the production environment. Perform the following steps to complete the exercise:

1. First, in `config.py`, add a default configuration that will be used in all environments:

```
import os
class Config:
    DEBUG = False

    SQLALCHEMY_TRACK_MODIFICATIONS = False
```

```
JWT_ERROR_MESSAGE_KEY = 'message'

JWT_BLACKLIST_ENABLED = True
JWT_BLACKLIST_TOKEN_CHECKS = ['access', 'refresh']

UPLOADED_IMAGES_DEST = 'static/images'

CACHE_TYPE = 'simple'
CACHE_DEFAULT_TIMEOUT = 10 * 60

RATELIMIT_HEADERS_ENABLED = True
```

2. Add **DevelopmentConfig** after the **Config** class:

```
class DevelopmentConfig(Config):
    DEBUG = True

    SECRET_KEY = 'super-secret-key'

    SQLALCHEMY_DATABASE_URI = 'postgresql+psycopg2://your_name:your_
password@localhost:5432/smilecook'
```

The new **DevelopmentConfig** class extends the parent **Config** class. The **DEBUG** value is set to **True**. That will allow us to see the error messages while we are developing.

3. Add **ProductionConfig** after the **Development Config** class:

```
class ProductionConfig(Config):

    SECRET_KEY = os.environ.get('SECRET_KEY')

    SQLALCHEMY_DATABASE_URI = os.environ.get('DATABASE_URL')
```

The **ProductionConfig** class here also extends the parent **Config** class. Similar to the **DevelopmentConfig** class, we have **SECRET_KEY** and **SQLALCHEMY_DATABASE_URI** set here. In the production environment, these values are obtained from the environment variables. We will teach you how to set these on a cloud platform later.

4. In **app.py**, import **os**:

```
import os
```

5. In **app.py**, make the following change to get the configurations dynamically:

```python
def create_app():

    env = os.environ.get('ENV', 'Development')

    if env == 'Production':
        config_str = 'config.ProductionConfig'
    else:
        config_str = 'config.DevelopmentConfig'

    app = Flask(__name__)
    app.config.from_object(config_str)


    ...


    return app
```

The **ENV** environment variable will be obtained via **os.environ.get**. If it is **Production**, the production environment configuration will be used. In addition, the development environment configuration will be used.

6. Right-click on PyCharm and run the application. Because we haven't set up the **ENV** environment variable in the local machine, Flask will pick up **config.DevelopmentConfig** and execute it. We can see from the output that **Debug mode: on**:

```
 app                                                                              ⚙ —
/TrainingByPackt/Python-API-Development-Fundamentals/venv/bin/python /TrainingByPackt/Python-API-Development-Fundament
 * Serving Flask app "app" (lazy loading)
 * Environment: production
   WARNING: This is a development server. Do not use it in a production deployment.
   Use a production WSGI server instead.
 * Debug mode: on
 * Running on http://127.0.0.1:5000/ (Press CTRL+C to quit)
 * Restarting with stat
 * Debugger is active!
 * Debugger PIN: 304-936-572
```

Figure 10.1: Running an application in the development environment

So, we have separated the configurations between the production and development environments. In the future, if there are common configurations shared among the two environments, we will put them in the **Config** class. Otherwise, they should be placed under the corresponding **DevelopmentConfig** or **ProductionConfig** class.

Exercise 64: Adding a Staging Configuration Class

In order to facilitate internal testing, in this exercise, we need to add a `StagingConfig` class. This configuration will extend the common `Config` class. The staging environment will not be much different from production, because it is mainly designed to imitate the production environment for testing. And we will obtain the secret key and database URI from the environment variables:

1. In `config.py`, create a `StagingConfig` class that extends `Config`:

   ```
   class StagingConfig(Config):

       SECRET_KEY = os.environ.get('SECRET_KEY')

       SQLALCHEMY_DATABASE_URI = os.environ.get('DATABASE_URL')
   ```

2. In `app.py`, modify the conditional statements for `StagingConfig`:

   ```
   if env == 'Production':
       config_str = 'config.ProductionConfig'
   elif env == 'Staging':
       config_str = 'config.StagingConfig'
   else:
       config_str = 'config.DevelopmentConfig'
   ```

Hence, we have set up the configuration for the staging environment. But it is not completed yet, since the environment variables will need to be obtained from the cloud server. Next, we will start to work on the cloud platform, **Heroku**.

Heroku Application

Before we deploy to Heroku (the cloud platform), we will first create an account and set up the environment there. We will create a new Heroku application. Then, we will need to install the Postgres database on Heroku. The installation process can be done within the Heroku platform; everything is integrated. Finally, we set up the virtual environment variables, such as the database URL and the secret key. Once all these precursors are completed, we will then start the deployment process.

Exercise 65: Creating a New Application in Heroku

In this exercise, we will first register a Heroku account. Then, we will create a new app on it. Heroku provides a nice user interface with an easy-to-follow setup flow. We just need to click a few buttons and that's it. As Heroku is a PaaS, we don't need to manage any hardware nor set up the OS. These are all taken care of by Heroku:

1. Visit the Heroku website, https://www.heroku.com/, and click **Sign up**:

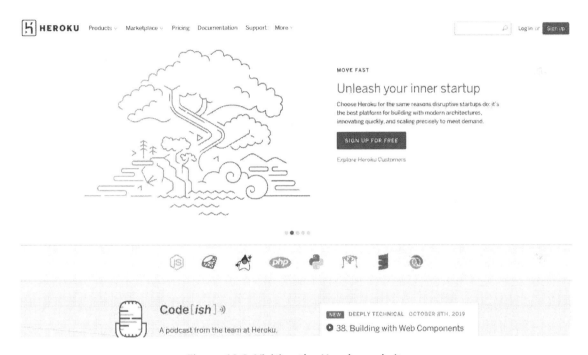

Figure 10.2: Visiting the Heroku website

2. Once the signup process is complete, click **Log in** and access the dashboard. Click **Create new app** to create a new application in Heroku:

Figure 10.3: Logging in and accessing the Heroku dashboard

3. Type in the app name, and then select the server region (right now, the only options are the United States and Europe; please select the one that is closer to your target users). Then, click **Create app** to continue:

Figure 10.4: Typing in the app name and selecting the server region

> **Note**
>
> The app name will be used in the application URL provided by Heroku, for example, `https://{app_name}.herokuapp.com/`. Users can then access our APIs using this URL.

After the application is created, we can see the app administration screen, along the lines of the following:

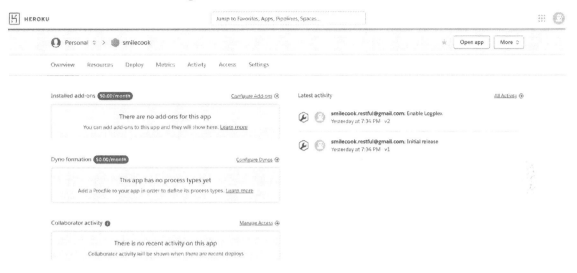

Figure 10.5: Heroku app administration screen

The app administration screen provides information for us to understand the application status:

Overview: For us to see the cost incurred or other collaborators' activities

Resources: For managing add-ons and the **Procfile** setting

Deploy: For choosing the deployment method

Metrics: For showing the metrics of the app

Activity: For tracking user activity

Access: For managing collaborator access

Settings: Includes environment variable configurations, buildpack settings, and other advanced features

> **Note**
>
> At the heart of the Heroku platform is the ability to run the applications using the lightweight container Dynos. Containerization is a standard way to package your application's code, configuration, and dependencies into a single object. Containerization can reduce the burden on the managing hardware, virtual machine, or environment setup, and so on.

Once the application has been created, we will install the Postgres repository in Heroku and we will install it directly via Heroku add-ons.

Heroku Add-Ons

Heroku has a rich add-ons library. Add-ons are like plugins, which provide tools and services for developing, extending, and operating your apps, including data stores, monitoring, logging, analytics, and security. For our Smilecook application, we will use Heroku Postgres from Heroku, which is a reliable and powerful database as a service based on PostgreSQL. The starter tier is free and offers a 10,000-row limit and provides an expected uptime of 99.5%. This is suitable for developing hobby applications.

Exercise 66: Installing Heroku Postgres

In this exercise, we will install Heroku Postgres. It is more convenient to install Postgres from Heroku, compared to installing it from the Postgres official website. We only need to go to the **Data Stores** category in **Heroku add-ons** and then select **Heroku Postgres** directly to install. Heroku provides a backend management interface so that we can see the database status at a glance:

1. Switch to the **Resources** tab in Heroku, and then right-click on the **Find more add-ons** button:

Figure 10.6: Switching to the Resources tab in Heroku

2. In the **Add-ons** page, click on **Data Stores** and select **Heroku Postgres**:

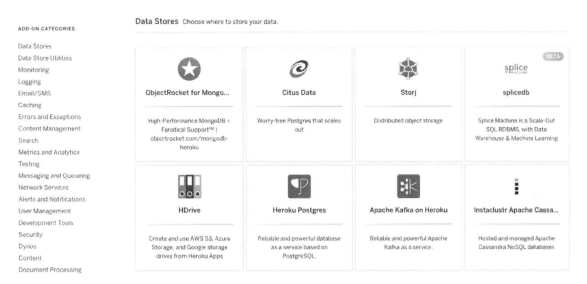

Figure 10.7: Add-ons page in Heroku

3. Then, click on **Install Heroku Postgres** to install the add-on in our cloud server:

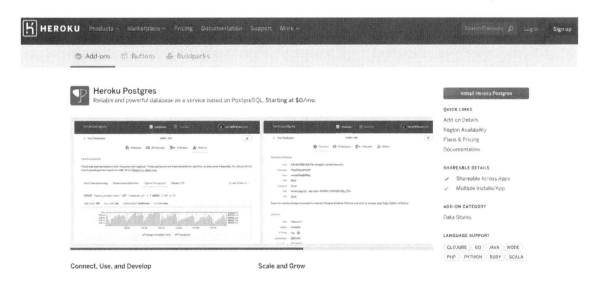

Figure 10.8: Installing the Heroku Postgres add-on

4. Select the default, **Hobby Dev - Free Plan**. This plan is free. In **App to provision to**, put in the app name we used in the previous exercise, and then click **Provision add-on**:

Figure 10.9: Selecting the Heroku Postgres add-on plan

5. Once that is done, we can check whether **Heroku Postgres** is installed on the **Add-ons** page:

Figure 10.10: Checking that Heroku Postgres is installed

6. Then, click on **Heroku Postgres add-on** to enter the management page:

Figure 10.11: Heroku Postgres management page

The **Overview** allows us to check the database status, utilization rate, and so on. **Durability** allows us to manage data security and backup. **Settings** stores the database credentials and other advanced settings. **Data clips** allow you to query the database data using the SQL command online. You can export or share the result there.

As you can see, it is pretty straightforward to install Postgres on Heroku; it just takes a few steps. Next, we will work on setting up the environment variables in the cloud platform.

Setting Up Environment Variables for the Heroku App

We previously modified `config.py` and added `ProductionConfig` there. Now we have to add the environment variables in Heroku, including the secret key and database URL. In addition to these, let's not forget the Mailgun API key and the Mailgun domain as well. We will set up all of these together in the next exercise.

Exercise 67: Setting Up the App Environment Variables

In this exercise, we will set up the environment variables in the production environment. Fortunately, because we are using Heroku Postgres, the database URL environment variable has already been set up for us. We only need to set **ENV**, **SECRET_ KEY**, **MAILGUN KEY**, and **DOMAIN**. Then, once the setting is complete, after the **Deploy** code is completed, the application will read the newly added environment variables in **App config**:

1. Generate the secret key using the following two lines of code in the Python console in PyCharm:

   ```
   >>>import os
   >>>os.urandom(24)
   ```

   Note

   A secret key should be as random as possible. There are a lot of random generators out there that we can leverage. But perhaps the easiest way to do so is to generate that in the Python console in PyCharm.

2. Go to the **Settings** tab and set up the **ENV**, **MAILGUN_API_KEY**, **MAILGUN_ DOMAIN**, and **SECRET_KEY** environment variables as the following:

Figure 10.12: Setting up environment variables in Heroku

Now that we have finished the necessary preparatory setup in Heroku, we will go straight to the deployment process.

Deployment Using Heroku Git

Heroku provides a guideline on how we can deploy our application. The guide can be found in the **Deploy** tab. It is mainly divided into three parts. They are **Install the Heroku CLI**, **Create a new Git repository**, and **Deploy your application**. The details are as follows:

Figure 10.13: Deployment using the Heroku Git guideline

There are three parts to the guideline in the **Deploy** tab:

Install the Heroku CLI

- `heroku login` – For logging into Heroku using the Heroku CLI tool provided.

Create a new Git repository

- `cd my-project/` – Change directory to the `my-project` folder.

- `git init` – Initialize `git`, which is a version control system. We will discuss this soon.

- `heroku git:remote -a smilecook` – Add the app (Smilecook) repository to the remote repository list of the local Git.

Deploy your application

- `git add .` – To add all files and folders to the current directory and subfolder to Git.

- `git commit -am "make it better"` – Commit a change and insert the commit message to `make it better`.

- `git push heroku master` – This will upload the local repository content to the remote repository, which is the repository in Heroku. Once it is pushed, Heroku will run the app start-up procedure.

Before we start deploying our application, there are still a few bits of terminology that require explanation.

What is Git?

Git is a distributed version control system. A version control system is mainly a system that can keep track of every version of your source code. Any changes in the source code will be recorded in the system. It allows developers to easily restore the previous version. No manual backup is required.

Git also supports collaboration and other advanced features. If you are interested, you can go to the official Git website to learn more about it: https://git-scm.com.

What is gitignore?

gitignore is a file that contains a list of files and folders that Git should ignore. Files and folders in this list will not be stored in Git. Usually, we will include the environment configs, logs, and so on in this list.

What is Procfile?

Procfile is a file that will be executed during the app start-up process in Heroku. Developers will put in the commands they want Heroku to run during the app start-up process. Usually, we will put the setup scripts and server start-up scripts here.

What is Gunicorn?

Gunicorn is a Python WSGI HTTP server that is compatible with various web applications. It can be used as an interface between web servers and web applications. Gunicorn can communicate with multiple web servers or start multiple web applications. It is a powerful and fast HTTP server.

Now that we have learned about the deployment flow as well as some key concepts and terminology, we will work on the deployment together in our next exercise.

Exercise 68: Setting Up the Git and the Heroku CLI

In this exercise, we will deploy our Smilecook application to the production environment. We will download and install the Heroku CLI and Git first so that we can run the deployment command in the local machine. Then, we will add the `gitignore` file to ensure that some files will not be uploaded to Heroku. Finally, we will add `main.py` and `Procfile` to the root directory of the project and then deploy it to Heroku:

1. Install the **Heroku CLI** from https://devcenter.heroku.com/articles/heroku-cli. Pick the version for your OS and download it:

Download and install

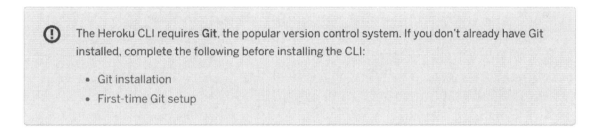

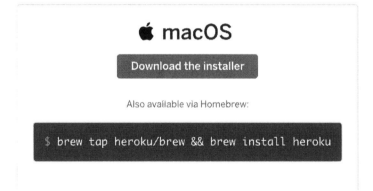

Figure 10.14: Installing the Heroku CLI

2. If you haven't installed Git, please install it from https://git-scm.com/:

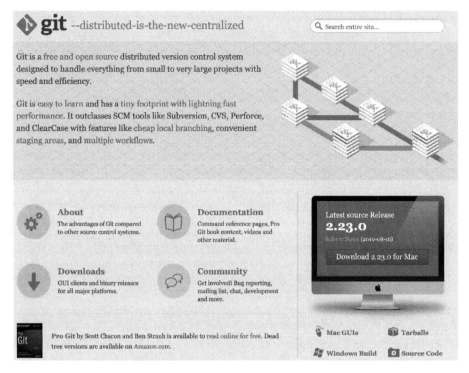

Figure 10.15: Installing Git

3. At the bottom of PyCharm, open the terminal. Run the `git --version` command to confirm that Git has installed successfully:

```
$ git --version
 git version 2.19.1 // You may see a different value inside the brackets
depending on your OS
```

4. Right-click to create a `.gitignore` file in the project. This file will contain a list of files or folders that we don't want to be added to Git:

```
static/images/avatars/*
static/images/recipes/*
.idea/
venv/
```

static/images/avatars/* – We do not want to include all the testing images that we created in the previous chapters to be uploaded to the production environment.

static/images/recipes/* – We do not want to include all the testing images that we created in the previous chapters to be uploaded to the production environment.

.idea/ – This is the IDE project-specific settings folder. We don't need it in production.

venv/ – This is the virtual environment.

5. Log in to your Heroku account:

    ```
    $ heroku login
    ```

6. Then, type in the following **git init** command to initialize Git. This is to add version control to our project:

    ```
    $ git init
    ```

7. Add the Heroku repository to the Git remote repository (please replace **your-heroku-app** with the name of your Heroku app).

    ```
    $ heroku git:remote -a your-heroku-app
    ```

    > **Note**
    >
    > Before adding in the remote repository, all our changes can only be committed to the local repository.

8. In **requirements.txt**, add in the **gunicorn** package, which is going to be our HTTP server:

    ```
    gunicorn==19.9.0
    ```

9. Create **main.py** under the project root folder. This will be executed by Gunicorn to start up our web application:

    ```
    from app import create_app

    app = create_app()
    ```

10. Right-click to create a file under the project root folder. Name it **Procfile** without an extension and then insert the following two commands:

    ```
    release: flask db upgrade
    web: gunicorn main:app
    ```

    This **Procfile** file is for Heroku to run during the app start-up process. The first line is to ask Heroku to run **flask db upgrade** after every deployment. This is designed to ensure that our database schema is always up to date.

The second line is to have Heroku recognize it as the task that starts the webserver.

11. Run **git add** . in the Python console under PyCharm. This will add our source code to Git, for version control and deployment:

```
$ git add .
```

12. Run the **git commit** command to commit our source code. The **-a** parameter tells Git to stage files that have been modified or deleted. The **-m** parameter is for incorporating the commit message:

```
$ git commit -am "first commit"
```

13. Deploy the application by using **git push** to push the source code to the Heroku repository:

```
$ git push heroku master
```

Heroku will automatically set up the environment. We can see the following output:

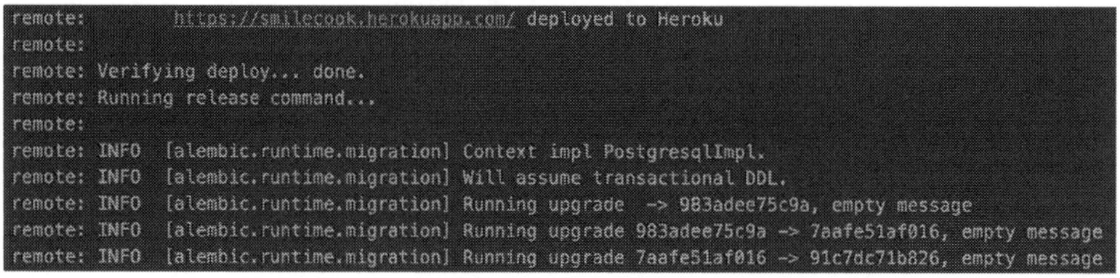

```
remote:            https://smilecook.herokuapp.com/ deployed to Heroku
remote:
remote: Verifying deploy... done.
remote: Running release command...
remote:
remote: INFO   [alembic.runtime.migration] Context impl PostgresqlImpl.
remote: INFO   [alembic.runtime.migration] Will assume transactional DDL.
remote: INFO   [alembic.runtime.migration] Running upgrade  -> 983adee75c9a, empty message
remote: INFO   [alembic.runtime.migration] Running upgrade 983adee75c9a -> 7aafe51af016, empty message
remote: INFO   [alembic.runtime.migration] Running upgrade 7aafe51af016 -> 91c7dc71b826, empty message
```

Figure 10.16: Deploying the application to Heroku

> **Note**
>
> During the deployment process, if we want to know more about what's happening behind the scenes, we can check the application logs by clicking the **More** button in the top right-hand corner, and then clicking **VIEW logs**.

Figure 10.17: Deploying the application to Heroku

From the preceding log, we can see that after the database is upgraded, it will run Gunicorn. And finally, you can see the message **State changed from starting to up**.

We have successfully deployed our Smilecook application to Heroku, which means it is ready to serve the public. Later, we will test it using Postman.

> **Note**
>
> In the future, when there is a new version, we only need to use three commands to redeploy the application. First, use `git add .` to add our source code to Git, and then use `git commit -am "make it better"`. Lastly, use `git push heroku master` to push the source code to Heroku.

Exercise 69: Checking the Heroku Postgres Tables in pgAdmin

In the last exercise, we completed deployment. We will now need to check whether the tables have been created in the database. So, in this exercise, we are going to use **pgAdmin** to connect to Heroku Postgres:

1. Get the credentials of the database in Heroku Postgres, go to **Add-ons** > **Settings**, then click **View Credentials**, and you will see the following screen:

Figure 10.18: Getting the credentials of the database in Heroku Postgres

2. Right-click on **Servers** and then create a new server in pgAdmin:

Figure 10.19: Creating a new server in pgAdmin

3. In the **General** tab, name the server **Heroku**:

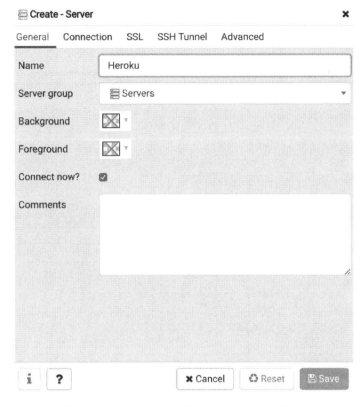

Figure 10.20: Entering the name for the server in the General tab

4. In the **Connection** tab, enter the credentials, including the **Host name/address**, **Port**, **Maintenance database**, **Username**, and **Password**, and then click **Save**:

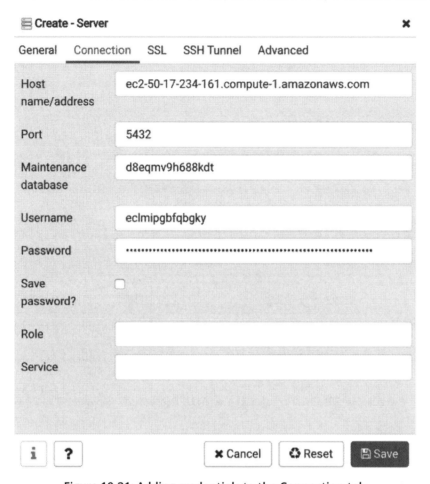

Figure 10.21: Adding credentials to the Connection tab

5. Now, check the database tables in pgAdmin. Go to **Heroku** >> **Databases** >> (your database name) >> **Schemas** >> **Public** >> **Tables** to verify this:

Figure 10.22: Checking the database tables in pgAdmin

Now we can see whether the tables have been created in the database. If you can see that the tables have been created successfully, we can continue to the next step, which is using Postman to test our APIs.

Setting Up Variables in Postman

We have successfully deployed our project to Heroku. Now you can test them in Postman using all the saved requests that we set up before. However, the requests we have saved previously in Postman are all running against localhost. Instead of changing the URL bit by bit to the production URL, we can leverage the variables in Postman. We can set up a **url** variable and assign the production URL to it in Postman, then replace the URL with **{{url}}** from the saved request. Postman will then substitute **{{url}}** with the production URL for us dynamically.

Exercise 70: Setting Up Variables in Postman

In this exercise, we will set up variables in Postman so that we can dynamically incorporate the appropriate value depending on the environment. We will set up the URL as a variable so that when we are testing in the development environment, we simply need to change the URL variable to **http://localhost:5000**. And if we are testing in a production environment, we can change that to **https://your_heroku_app. herokuapp.com**:

1. Click **Manage environments** in the top right-hand corner of Postman. Then, click **Add**, and insert **Smilecook** as the environment name. Then, create a **url** variable with the value **https://your_heroku_app.herokuapp.com**. If the current value is not set, it will automatically assume the initial value. Please replace **your_heroku_app** with the name of your Heroku app, and then click **Update**:

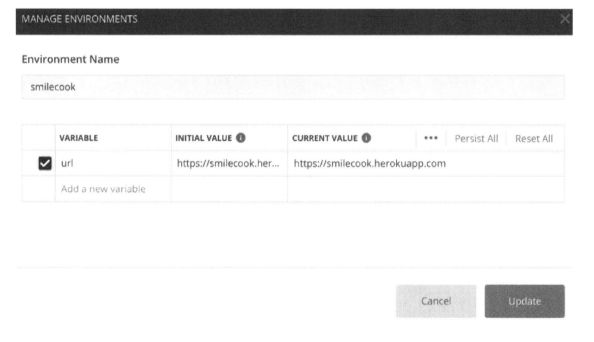

Figure 10.23: Adding an environment variable in Postman

2. Once it is added, verify the variable by clicking on the eye icon in the top right-hand corner:

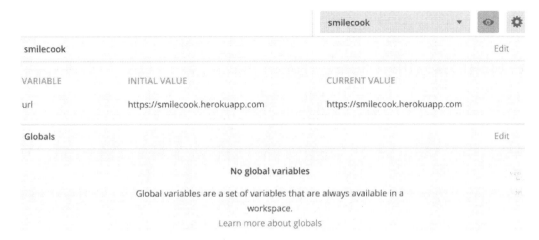

Figure 10.24: Verifying the environment variable in Postman

3. In the **UserList** request, update the URL to **{{url}}/users** and then click **Send** to register a user account. You should see the following output (Postman will then dynamically replace the placeholder to be **https://your_heroku_app.herokuapp.com/users** when the request is sent):

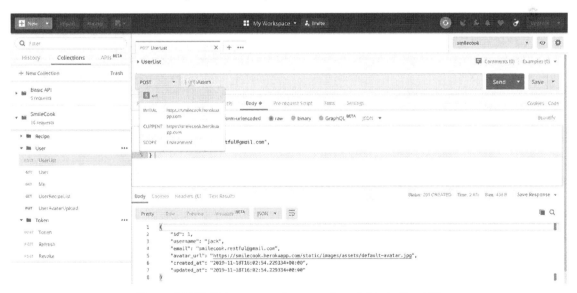

Figure 10.25: Using an environment variable in the URL

Postman is a very powerful testing tool. It can even allow us to effectively test our API endpoints on different environments. In the future, if you want to test other API endpoints in the production environment, you just need to change the URL in the previously saved requests. In the next activity, we will test your knowledge of this.

Activity 18: Changing access_token to a Variable in Postman

In the previous exercise, you learned how to change a URL to a variable. In this activity, we would like you to do the same for **access_token**:

1. Get an access token by using the previously saved **POST Token** request.

2. Add **access_token** as a variable in Postman.

3. Test a Smilecook API endpoint that requires the access token.

> **Note**
>
> The solution to this activity can be found on page 345.

That's great. When you are done with this activity, that means that you have already deployed and tested the Smilecook API in production. This is the final activity in the book and we are glad that you made it to this point!

Now, we will setup the Smilecook frontend website, which will work with the APIs that you have just developed.

Setting up the Front-end Interface to Work with the Smilecook API

Please download the **smilecook-vuejs** folder, which contains the frontend website source code, from https://github.com/TrainingByPackt/Python-API-Development-Fundamentals/tree/master/Lesson10/Frontend:

1. Create a new app in the Heroku platform, which is for deploying our frontend web interface:

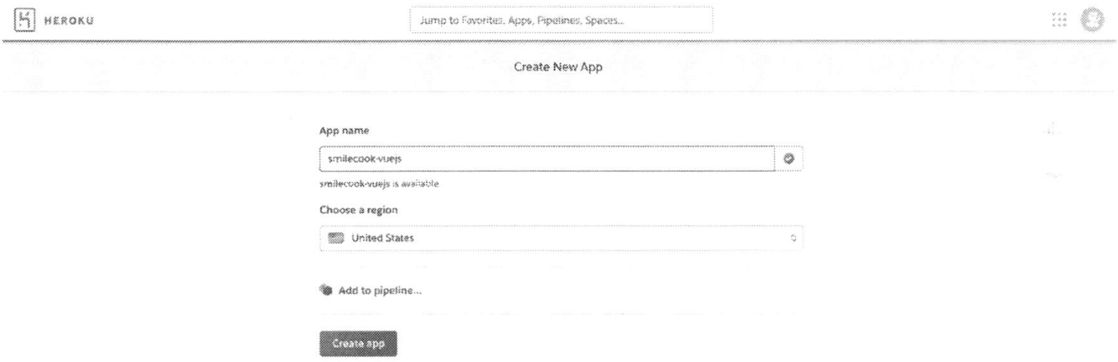

Figure 10.26: Creating a new app in the Heroku platform

2. Once the app is created, we go to the **Settings** tab and then **Config Vars**. Here, we are going to set up an environment variable, which will be used to store the backend API URL:

Figure 10.27: Setting up an environment variable

3. Set the variable name to be **VUE_APP_API_URL**, and insert the backend Smilecook API URL here.

4. Open the **smilecook-vuejs** project in PyCharm.

5. In the PyCharm console, type in the following command to log in to the Heroku CLI:

```
$ heroku login
```

6. Then, initialize **git** and add the Heroku repository to the **git:remote** repository:

```
$ git init
$ heroku git:remote -a your_heroku_app_name
```

7. Then, add the source code to **git**, commit, and push them to Heroku.

```
$ git add .
$ git commit -am "make it better"
$ git push heroku master
```

8. When deployment is complete, you should see the following message on screen:

```
remote: -----> Compressing...
remote:        Done: 30M
remote: -----> Launching...
remote:        Released v1
remote:        https://your_heroku_app_name.herokuapp.com/ deployed to
Heroku
remote:
remote: Verifying deploy... done.
To https://git.heroku.com/your_heroku_app_name.git
   59c4f7f..57c0642  master -> master
```

9. Type **https://your_heroku_app_name.herokuapp.com/** in the browser; we can see that the frontend interface has been set up successfully:

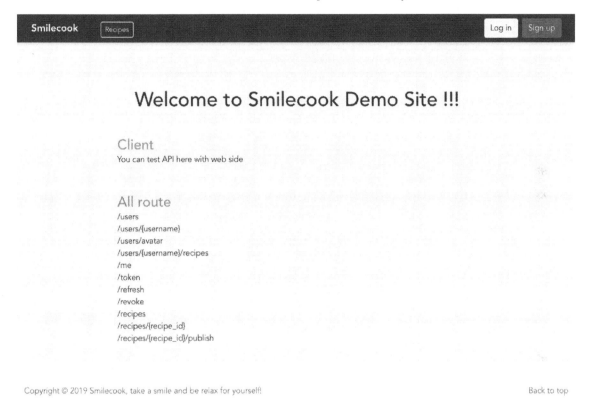

Figure 10.28: Successful frontend setup

Now, you can interact with the Smilecook API using this frontend website interface.

Summary

In this chapter, we successfully deployed the Smilecook API to the Heroku cloud server. The deployment process is simple as we are leveraging the service provided by Heroku. We do not need to worry about purchasing hardware, setting up the server OS, connecting the server to the internet, and so on. Everything is provided by Heroku. A cloud platform service can quickly help developers to deploy their applications/APIs to the internet. This easy deployment process allows developers to focus on development and not the infrastructure/platform setup. And once the API is deployed, millions of users on the internet can connect to the API through their client-side app.

Of course, Heroku is just one of the many cloud services available out there. As to which cloud service should be chosen, you should consider important factors such as cost, additional services provided, and the scale of our application. We do not limit you to a particular platform. In fact, we hope that this book is a starting point for your journey as a professional developer. With the fundamental knowledge that you have learned, you should be able to explore and further develop new skills and use new tools to build more advanced APIs.

Congratulations! We have completed the whole book. Not only have you learned what an API is, but you have also developed and deployed a real-life API service, Smilecook, yourself. Throughout the entire book, you have learned about setting up a development environment, building an API, interacting with a database, object serialization, security tokens, interacting with third-party APIs, caching, and finally deployment. We have covered many different topics horizontally, and we have also explored each topic in-depth vertically. Apart from learning the theory, you have also practiced actual coding in the exercises and activities. You also tested your work thoroughly.

Your next steps should involve continuing to learn by working on development projects. The most important thing is to have hands-on development experience, together with an inquiring mind. Look for a better solution whenever you encounter a problem. You should not be satisfied with just getting things done. Instead, you should aim at doing things right. That's what will take you to the next level.

We hope you enjoyed the learning journey with us. Thank you!

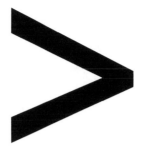

Appendix

About

This section is included to assist the students to perform the activities in the book.
It includes detailed steps that are to be performed by the students to achieve the objectives of
the activities.

Chapter 01: Your First Step

Activity 1: Sending Requests to Our APIs Using Postman

Solution

1. First, we will get all of the recipes. Select **GET** as our **HTTP** method in the drop-down list.

2. Enter the request URL `http://localhost:5000/recipes`.

3. Click the **Send** button. The result can be seen in the following screenshot:

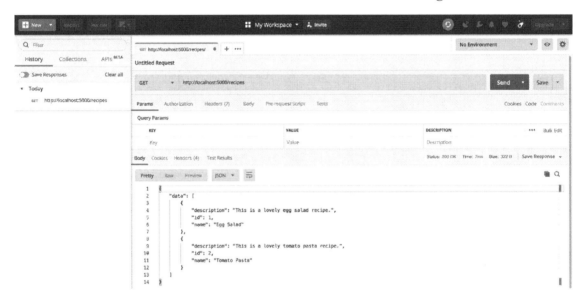

Figure 1.14: Getting all the recipes

In the HTTP response, you will see the HTTP status **200 OK** in the top-right corner of the response panel. That means the request has been successful. The time next to it shows **7ms**, which is the time spent on the request. And the size of the response, including the header and body, is **322** bytes. The details of the recipes, in JSON format, are shown in the Body panel.

4. Next, we are going to use the POST method to create a recipe. We will send an HTTP **POST** request to `http://localhost:5000/recipes`.

5. Create a new tab next to the Get Request Tab by clicking on the **+** button. Select **POST** as the HTTP method. Type in `http://localhost:5000/recipes` as the request URL.

6. Select the Body Tab. Also, select the **raw** radio button.

7. Choose **JSON (application/json)** in the right drop-down menu. Type the following data in JSON format in the **Body** content area. Click the **Send** button:

```
{
    "name": "Cheese Pizza",
    "description": "This is a lovely cheese pizza"
}
```

The result can be seen in the following screenshot:

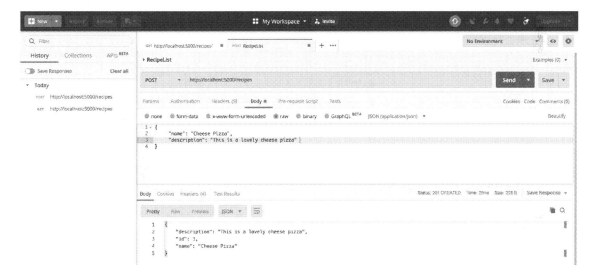

Figure 1.15: Creating a recipe

You should see the following information in the HTTP response in the Postman interface, Status **201** OK, meaning the creation has been successful and we can see our new recipe in JSON format. You will also notice that the ID assigned to the recipe is **3**.

8. Now, get all the recipes from the server application again. We want to see if we have three recipes there now. In the history panel, select our previous request that gets all recipes, clicks on it, and resends.

In response, we can see that there are three recipes. They are shown in the following screenshot:

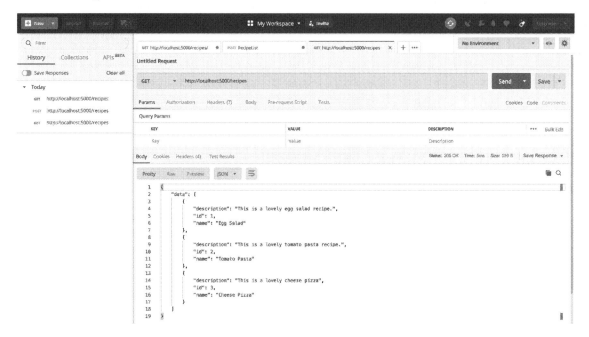

Figure 1.16: Getting all the recipes from the server application

9. Then, modify the recipe that we have just created. To do this, create a new tab next to the **Get** Request Tab by clicking on the **+** button. Select **PUT** as the HTTP method.

10. Type in **http://localhost:5000/recipes/3** as the request URL.

11. Select the **Body** Tab and then select the **raw** radio button.

12. Choose **JSON (application/json)** in the right drop-down menu. Type the following data in JSON format in the **Body** content area. Click **Send**:

```
{
"name": "Lovely Cheese Pizza",
"description": "This is a lovely cheese pizza recipe."
}
```

The result is shown in the following screenshot:

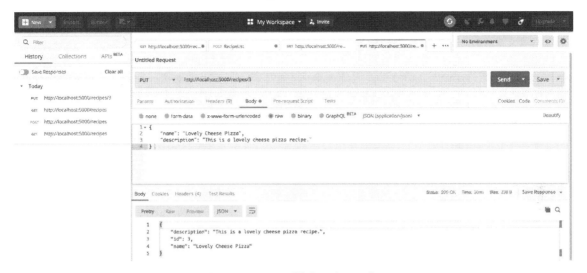

Figure 1.17: Modifying the recipe

In the HTTP response, you will see the **200 OK** HTTP status, meaning the update has been successful. You can also see the time spent on the request in milliseconds. You should also see the size of the response (header and body). The content of the response is in JSON format. We can see our updated recipe here in JSON format.

13. Next, we will see if we can look for a recipe using its ID. We only want to see the recipe with ID **3** in the response. To do this, create a new tab next to the **Get Request** Tab by clicking on the **+** button.

14. Select **GET** as the HTTP method. Type in `http://localhost:5000/recipes/3` as the request URL.

15. Click **Send**. The result is shown in the following screenshot:

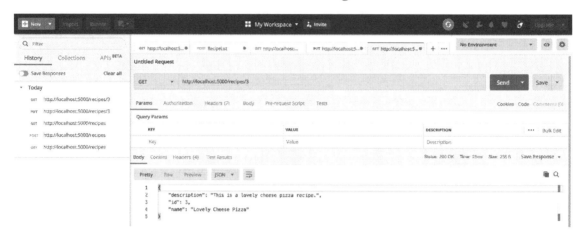

Figure 1.18: Looking for the recipe with ID

We can see in the response that only the recipe with ID **3** is returned. It has the modified details that we just set as well.

16. When we search for a recipe that doesn't exist, we will see the following response, with a message **recipe not found**. Search by using the `http://localhost:5000/recipes/101` endpoint. The result is shown in the following screenshot:

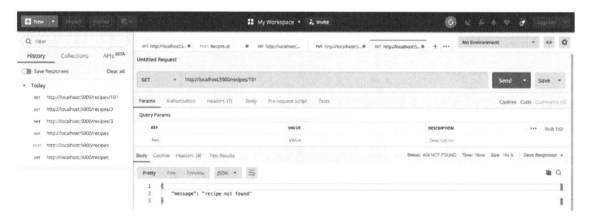

Figure 1.19: Response showing "recipe not found"

Activity 2: Implement and Test the delete_recipe Function

Solution

1. The **delete_recipe** function removes a recipe from the memory. Use **recipe = next((recipe for recipe in recipes if recipe['id'] == recipe_id), None)** to get the recipe with the specific ID:

```
@app.route('/recipes/<int:recipe_id>', methods=['DELETE'])
def delete_recipe(recipe_id):
    recipe = next((recipe for recipe in recipes if recipe['id'] == recipe_id), None)

    if not recipe:
        return jsonify({'message': 'recipe not found'}), HTTPStatus.NOT_FOUND

    recipes.remove(recipe)

    return '', HTTPStatus.NO_CONTENT
```

2. Similar to the **update_recipe** function shown in earlier, if you can't find the recipe, then return "**recipe not found**" together with HTTP status **NOT_FOUND**. Otherwise, we will go ahead and remove the recipe with the given ID from our recipe collection with HTTP status **204 No Content**

3. Once the code is done, *right-click* on the **app.py** file and click **run** to start the application. The Flask server will start up, and our application is ready to be tested.

4. Use httpie or curl to delete the recipe with **ID = 1**:

```
http DELETE localhost:5000/recipes/1
```

Following is the **curl** version of the command which does the same thing.

```
curl -i -X DELETE localhost:5000/recipes/1
```

The `@app.route('/recipes/<int:recipe_id>', methods=['DELETE'])` route will catch the client request and invoke the `delete_recipe(recipe_id)` function. The function will look for recipes with the `recipe_id` ID and, if it finds one, it will delete it. In response, we can see that the deletion has been successful. And we see that the HTTP status is `204 NO CONTENT`:

```
HTTP/1.0 204 NO CONTENT
Content-Type: text/html; charset=utf-8
Date: Fri, 06 Sep 2019 05:57:50 GMT
Server: Werkzeug/0.15.6 Python/3.7.0
```

5. Lastly, use Postman to delete the recipe with `ID = 2`. For that, create a new tab next to the **Get Request** Tab by clicking on the **+** button.

6. Select **DELETE** as the `HTTP` method. Type in `http://localhost:5000/recipes/2` as the request URL.

7. Click **Send**. The result is shown in the following screenshot:

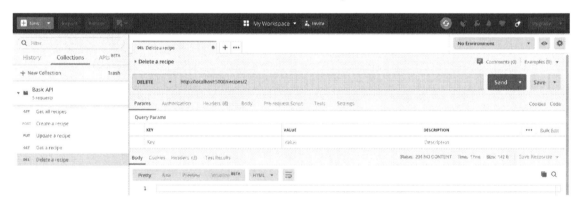

Figure 1.20: Deleting the recipe

And then we can see the response with the HTTP status **204 NO CONTENT**. That means the recipe was successfully removed.

Chapter 02: Starting to Build Our Project

Activity 3: Testing the APIs Using Postman

Solution

1. First, build a client request that asks for a new recipe. Then, make use of the collection function in Postman to make the testing more efficient.

2. Click on the **Collection** tab and then create a new collection by clicking on **+**.

3. Type in **Smilecook** as the name and click **Create**.

4. *Right-click* on **...** next to **Smilecook**, create a new folder under **Smilecook**, and type **Recipe** in the name field.

5. *Right-click* on **Recipe** to create a new request. Then, set the name to **RecipeList** and save it under the **Recipe** collection.

6. Select **POST** in the drop-down list as the HTTP method and type `http://local-host:5000/recipes` in the request URL field.

7. Now, go to the **Body** tab and select **raw**. Then, choose **JSON (application/json)** in the drop-down menu and type the following code into the **body** field:

```
{
    "name": "Cheese Pizza",
    "description": "This is a lovely cheese pizza",
    "num_of_servings": 2,
    "cook_time": 30,
    "directions": "This is how you make it"
}
```

8. **Save** and send the recipe. The result is shown in the following screenshot:

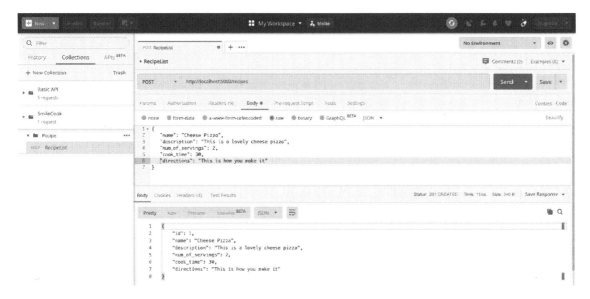

Figure 2.10: Creating our first recipe by sending the details in JSON format

In the HTTP response, you will see the HTTP status **201 Created**, meaning that the request was successful, and, in the body, you should see the same recipe that we just created. The ID of the recipe should be 1.

9. Create the second recipe by sending over a client request. Next, we will create our second recipe by sending the following details in JSON format:

```
{
    "name": "Tomato Pasta",
    "description": "This is a lovely tomato pasta recipe",
    "num_of_servings": 3,
    "cook_time": 20,
    "directions": "This is how you make it"
}
```

10. Click **Send**. The result is shown in the following screenshot:

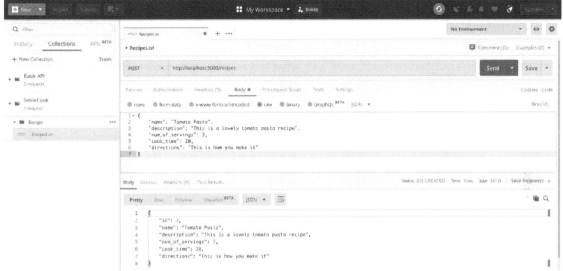

Figure 2.11: Creating our second recipe by sending the details in JSON format

In the HTTP response, you will see the HTTP status **201 Created**, meaning that the request was successful, and, in the body, you should see the same recipe that we just created. The ID of the recipe should be 2.

So far, we have created two recipes. Let's retrieve these recipes using Postman and confirm whether the two recipes are in the application memory.

11. Create a new request under the **Recipe** folder, name it **RecipeList**, and then save it.

12. Select the **RecipeList** that we just created (the one with the HTTP method set to GET).

13. Type **http://localhost:5000/recipes** in the request URL. Then, click **Save** and send the request. The result is shown in the following screenshot:

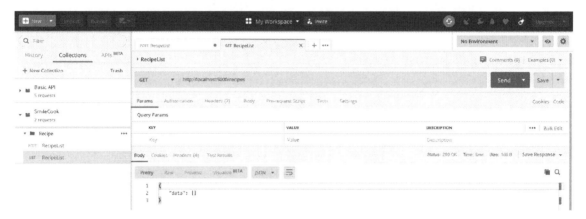

Figure 2.12: Retrieving all the recipes using Postman and confirming whether they are in the application's memory

In the HTTP response, you will see the HTTP status **200 OK**, meaning that the request was successful, and, in the body, you should see no data because the two recipes that we have created haven't been set to published yet. Now, we know that we can only retrieve published recipes. Let's set the recipe with **ID = 1** to published.

14. Create a new request under the **Recipe** folder, and name it **RecipePublish**, and then save it.

15. Click on the **RecipePublish** request that we just created (the one with the HTTP method set to GET).

16. Select **PUT** as the HTTP method in the drop-down list and type **http://localhost:5000/recipes/1/publish** in the request URL. Then, click **Save** and send the request. The result is shown in the following screenshot:

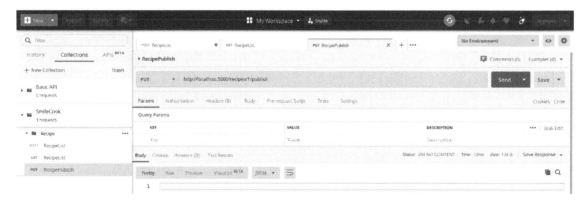

Figure 2.13: Retrieving the published recipe

In the HTTP response, you will see the HTTP status **204 NO CONTENT**, meaning that the request has been successfully published and that no data has been returned in the response body.

17. Retrieve all the recipes using Postman again. Select **RecipeList (GET)** from the left-hand panel and send the request. The result is shown in the following screenshot:

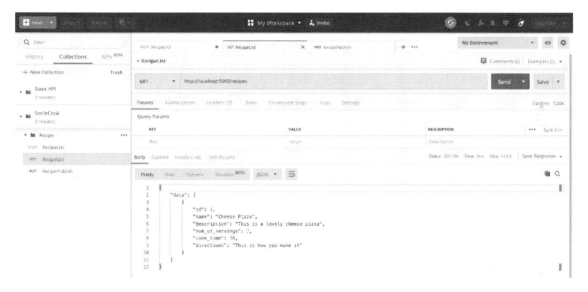

Figure 2.14: Retrieving all the recipes using Postman

In the HTTP response, you will see the HTTP status **200 OK**, meaning that the request was successful. The body should contain a published recipe. It should be the same recipe that we set to published previously.

We will modify the recipe with ID 1 by using the PUT method to send the modified recipe data to the URL route, that is, `localhost:5000/recipes/1`.

18. Create a new request under the **Recipe** folder, set the **Request Name** to **Recipe**, and save it. Then, change the HTTP method to **PUT** and type `http://local-host:5000/recipes/1` in the request URL.

19. Now, go to the **Body** tab and select raw, choose **JSON (application/json)** from the drop-down menu, and insert the following code into the body field. This is the modified recipe:

```
{
    "name": "Lovely Cheese Pizza",
    "description": "This is a lovely cheese pizza recipe",
    "num_of_servings": 3,
    "cook_time": 60,
    "directions": "This is how you make it"
}
```

20. **Save** and send it. The result is shown in the following screenshot:

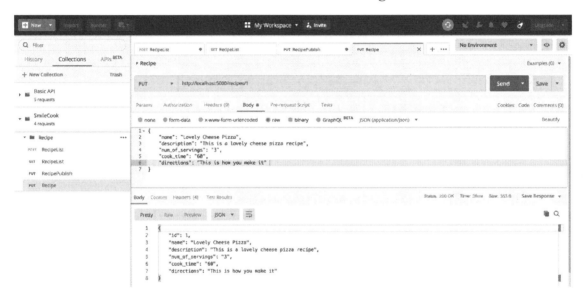

Figure 2.15: Modifying the recipe with ID 1

In the HTTP response, you will see the HTTP status **200 OK**, meaning that the modification was successful. The body should contain the updated details of recipe 1 in JSON format. We will retrieve the recipe with ID 1.

21. Create a new request under the **Recipe** folder, set the **Request Name** to **Recipe**, and save it. Then, change the HTTP method to **GET** and type `http://local-host:5000/recipes/1` in the request URL.

22. **Save** and send it. The result is shown in the following screenshot:

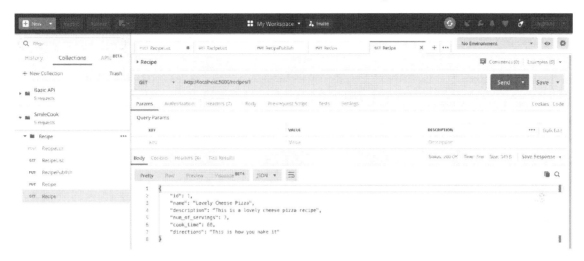

Figure 2.16: Retrieving the recipe with ID 1

In the HTTP response, you will see the HTTP status **200 OK**, meaning that the request is successful. The body should contain the details of `recipe 1` in JSON format.

Activity 4: Implementing the Delete Recipe Function

Solution

1. Add the **delete** function to **RecipeResource**. Implement the **delete** method by following the sample code:

```
def delete(self, recipe_id):
    recipe = next((recipe for recipe in recipe_list if recipe.id ==
recipe_id), None)

    if recipe is None:
        return {'message': 'recipe not found'}, HTTPStatus.NOT_FOUND

    recipe_list.remove(recipe)

    return {}, HTTPStatus.NO_CONTENT
```

The third method we built here has been deleted. We do this by locating the recipe with the respective recipe ID and then remove it from the recipe list. Finally, we return the HTTP status **204 NO CONTENT**.

2. *Right-click* on the **app.py** file and click **run** to start the application. The Flask server will start up and our application will be ready for testing. Now, create the first recipe using Postman. We will build a client request that asks for a new recipe.

3. First, select the **RecipeList POST** request. Now, send the request by clicking the **Send** button, as shown in the following screenshot:

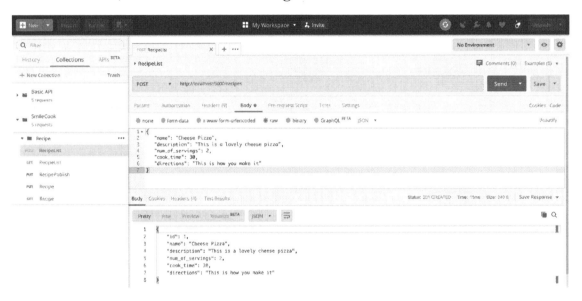

Figure 2.17: Creating the first recipe using Postman

4. Now, we will delete a recipe using Postman. To do that, delete the recipe with ID 1.

5. Create a new request under the **Recipe** folder. Then, set the **Request Name** to **Recipe** and **save** it.

6. Change the **HTTP** method to **DELETE** and type **http://localhost:5000/recipes/1** in the request URL. Then, save and send the request. The result is shown in the following screenshot:

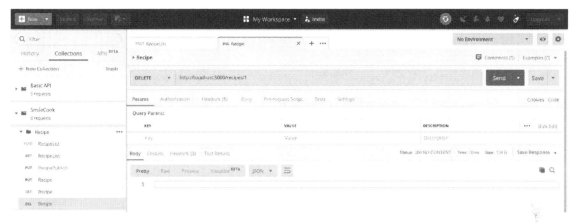

Figure 2.18: Deleting a recipe using Postman

In the HTTP response, you will see the HTTP status **204 NO CONTENT**, meaning that the delete is successful with empty body content. The following table shows the methods that we have built for the **RecipeResource** class in this activity:

| DELETE | Deletes a recipe | RecipeResource.delete | http://localhost:5000/recipes/1 |

Figure 2.19: The method that we built for the RecipeResource class

Chapter 03: Manipulating a Database with SQLAlchemy

Activity 5: Creating a User and a Recipe

Solution

1. Open the Python console at the bottom of PyCharm and type in the following code to import the necessary modules and classes:

```
from app import *
from models.user import User
from models.recipe import Recipe
app = create_app()
```

2. Create a **user** object and save that to the database by typing in the following code in the Python console:

```
user = User(username='peter', email='peter@gmail.com', password='WkQa')
db.session.add(user)
db.session.commit()
```

3. Next, we will create two recipes using the following code. One thing to note is the fact that the **user_id** attribute of the recipe is set to **user.id**. This is to indicate that the recipe was created by the user **Peter**:

```
carbonara = Recipe(name='Carbonara', description='This is a lovely
carbonara recipe', num_of_servings=4, cook_time=50, directions='This is
how you make it', user_id=user.id)
db.session.add(carbonara)
db.session.commit()

risotto = Recipe(name='Risotto', description='This is a lovely risotto
recipe', num_of_servings=5, cook_time=40, directions='This is how you make
it', user_id=user.id)
db.session.add(risotto)
db.session.commit()
```

4. We can see a new record there in the **user** table:

Data Output	Explain	Messages	Notifications					
id [PK] integer	username character varying (80)	email character varying (200)	password character varying (200)	is_active boolean	created_at timestamp without time zone	updated_at timestamp without time zone		
1	1 jack	jack@gmail.com	WkQa	false	2019-09-09 16:24:24.671944	2019-09-09 16:24:24.671944		
2	2 peter	peter@gmail.com	WkQa	false	2019-09-10 17:15:29.127256	2019-09-10 17:15:29.127256		

Figure 3.18: New record in the user table

5. We will then check whether the two recipes have been created in the database

| 3 | | 3 | Carbonara | This is a lovely carbo... | 4 | 50 | This is how you ma... | false | 2019-09-11 15:15... | 2019-10-09 10:16... | 2 |
| 4 | | 4 | Risotto | This is a lovely risott... | 5 | 40 | This is how you ma... | false | 2019-09-11 15:58... | 2019-09-11 16:10... | 2 |

Figure 3.19: Checking whether the two recipes have been created

Activity 6: Upgrading and Downgrading a Database

Solution

1. Add a new attribute to the **user** class:

   ```
   bio= db.Column(db.String())
   ```

2. Now, run the **flask db migrate** command to create the database and tables:

   ```
   flask db migrate
   ```

   Flask-Migrate detected the new column and created a script for that:

   ```
   INFO  [alembic.runtime.migration] Context impl PostgresqlImpl.
   INFO  [alembic.runtime.migration] Will assume transactional DDL.
   INFO  [alembic.ddl.postgresql] Detected sequence named 'user_id_seq' as
   owned by integer column 'user(id)', assuming SERIAL and omitting
   INFO  [alembic.ddl.postgresql] Detected sequence named 'recipe_id_seq' as
   owned by integer column 'recipe(id)', assuming SERIAL and omitting
   INFO  [alembic.autogenerate.compare] Detected added column 'user.bio'
     Generating /Python-API-Development-Fundamentals/smilecook/migrations/
   versions/6971bd62ec60_.py ... done
   ```

3. Now, check **/migrations/versions/6971bd62ec60_.py** under the **versions** folder. This file is created by Flask-Migrate. Note that you may get a different revision ID here. Please review the file before you run the **flask db upgrade** command. That's because, sometimes, it may not detect every change you make to your models:

   ```
   """empty message

   Revision ID: 6971bd62ec60
   Revises: 1b69a78087e5
   Create Date: 2019-10-08 12:11:47.370082

   """
   from alembic import op
   import sqlalchemy as sa
   ```

```
# revision identifiers, used by Alembic.
revision = '6971bd62ec60'
down_revision = '1b69a78087e5'
branch_labels = None
depends_on = None


def upgrade():
    # ### commands auto generated by Alembic - please adjust! ###
    op.add_column('user', sa.Column('bio', sa.String(), nullable=True))
    # ### end Alembic commands ###


def downgrade():
    # ### commands auto generated by Alembic - please adjust! ###
    op.drop_column('user', 'bio')
    # ### end Alembic commands ###
```

There are two functions in this autogenerated file; one is upgraded, and this is to add the new recipe and user to the table, while the other is downgraded, which is to go back to the previous version.

4. We will then execute the **flask db upgrade** command, which will upgrade our database to conform with the latest specification in our models:

```
flask db upgrade
```

This command will invoke **upgrade()** to upgrade the database:

```
INFO  [alembic.runtime.migration] Context impl PostgresqlImpl.
INFO  [alembic.runtime.migration] Will assume transactional DDL.
INFO  [alembic.runtime.migration] Running upgrade a6d248ab7b23 ->
6971bd62ec60, empty message
```

5. Check whether the new field is created in the database. Go to **smilecook** >> **Schemas** >> **Tables** >> **user** >> **Properties to verify**:

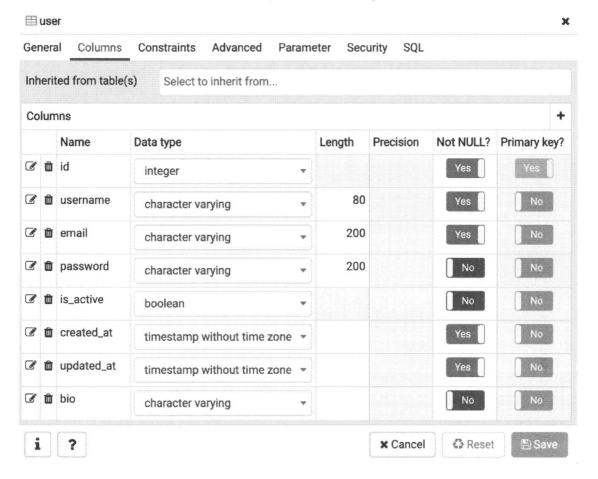

Figure 3.20: Checking whether the new field has been created in the database

Run the **downgrade** command to remove the new field:

```
flask db downgrade
```

This command will invoke **downgrade()** to downgrade the database:

```
INFO  [alembic.runtime.migration] Context impl PostgresqlImpl.
INFO  [alembic.runtime.migration] Will assume transactional DDL.
INFO  [alembic.runtime.migration] Running downgrade 6971bd62ec60 ->
a6d248ab7b23, empty message
```

Check whether the field has been removed. Go to **smilecook → Schemas → Tables → user → Properties to verify**:

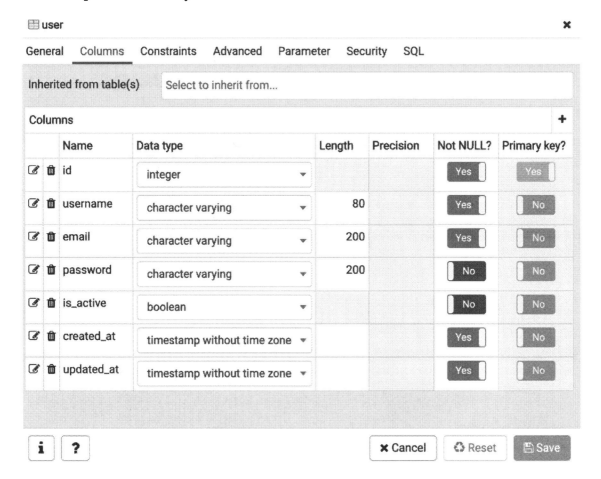

Figure 3.21: Checking whether the field has been removed from the database

Chapter 04: Authenticated Services and Security with JWTs

Activity 7: Implementing Access Control on the publish/unpublish Recipe Function

Solution

1. Modify the **put** method in **RecipePublishResource** to restrict access to only authenticated users. In **resources/token.py**, add the **@jwt_required** decorator on top of the **RecipePublishResource.put** method. Use the **get_jwt_identity()** function to identify whether the authenticated user is the owner of the recipe:

```python
@jwt_required
def put(self, recipe_id):

    recipe = Recipe.get_by_id(recipe_id=recipe_id)

    if recipe is None:
        return {'message': 'Recipe not found'}, HTTPStatus.NOT_FOUND

    current_user = get_jwt_identity()

    if current_user != recipe.user_id:
        return {'message': 'Access is not allowed'}, HTTPStatus.FORBIDDEN

    recipe.is_publish = True
    recipe.save()

    return {}, HTTPStatus.NO_CONTENT
```

This is to publish the recipe. Only users who have logged in can publish their own recipes. The method will perform various checks to make sure the user has published privileges. It will return **204 NO_CONTENT** once the recipe is published.

2. Modify the **delete** method in **RecipePublishResource**. Only an authenticated user can unpublish the recipe:

```
@jwt_required
def delete(self, recipe_id):

        recipe = Recipe.get_by_id(recipe_id=recipe_id)

        if recipe is None:
            return {'message': 'Recipe not found'}, HTTPStatus.NOT_FOUND

        current_user = get_jwt_identity()

        if current_user != recipe.user_id:
            return {'message': 'Access is not allowed'}, HTTPStatus.
FORBIDDEN

        recipe.is_publish = False
        recipe.save()

        return {}, HTTPStatus.NO_CONTENT
```

This unpublishes the recipe. Similar to the previous code, only a user who has logged in can unpublish their own recipe. It will return the **status** code **204 NO_ CONTENT** once the recipe is published.

3. Log in to the user account and get the access token. Select the **POST** token request that we created previously.

4. Check the **raw** radio button and select **JSON (application/json)** from the drop-down menu. Type in the following JSON content in the **Body** field:

```
{
    "email": "james@gmail.com",
    "password": "WkQad19"
}
```

5. Click **Send** to log in to the account. The result is shown in the following screen-shot:

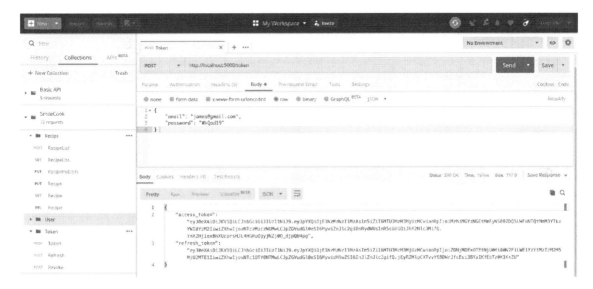

Figure 4.20: Log in to the user account

You will see the HTTP **status** code **200 OK**, meaning the login is successful. And we can see the **access token** and **refresh token** in the response body.

6. Publish the recipe with **id = 3** in the state that the user has logged in. Select **PUT RecipePublish**.

7. Go to the **Headers** tab and put **Authorization** in the KEY field and `Bearer {token}` in the **VALUE** field, where token is the JWT token we got in our previous step.

8. Click **Send** to publish the recipe. The result is shown in the following screenshot:

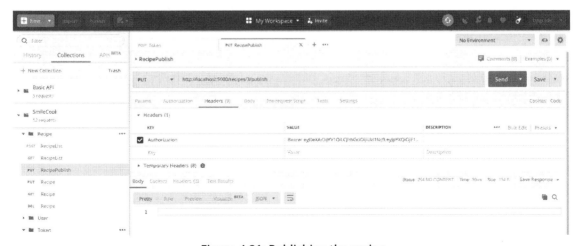

Figure 4.21: Publishing the recipe

You will then see the response, the HTTP **status** code **204** meaning the recipe has been published successfully.

Finally, try to get all published recipes. Select **GET RecipeList** request, then click **Send** to get all published recipe details. The result is shown in the following screenshot:

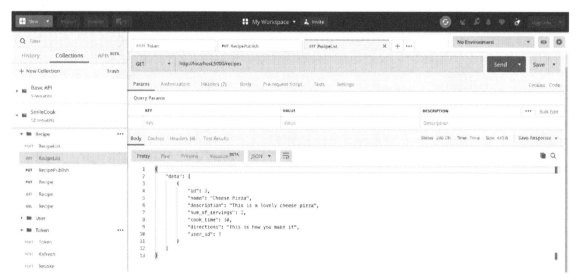

Figure 4.22: Retrieving all published recipes

You will then see the response, the HTTP **status** code **200** meaning the request is successfully, and you can see there is one published recipe that we created is returned.

9. Unpublish the recipe with **id = 3** in the state that the user has logged in. Create a new request under the **Recipe** folder, and name it **RecipePublish**, and then save it.

10. Click on the **RecipePublish** request that we just created (the one with the HTTP method set to **GET**).

11. Select **DELETE** as the HTTP method in the dropdown list and type in **http://localhost:5000/recipes/3/publish** in the request URL.

12. Go to the **Headers** tab and put **Authorization** in the KEY field and **Bearer {token}** in the **VALUE** field, where token is the JWT token we got in *step 5*.

13. **Save** and **Send** the request to unpublish. The result is shown in the following screenshot:

Figure 4.23: Unpublishing the recipe

Chapter 05: Validating APIs Using marshmallow

Activity 8: Serializing the recipe Object Using marshmallow

Solution

1. Modify the recipe schema to include all attributes except for **email**. In **schemas/ recipe.py**, modify **only=['id', 'username']** to **exclude=('email',)**. This way, we will be showing everything except for the user's email address. Besides, if we have a new attribute for the **recipe** object in the future (for example, a **user avatar** URL), we won't need to modify the schema again because it will show everything:

    ```
    author = fields.Nested(UserSchema, attribute='user', dump_only=True,
    exclude=('email', ))
    ```

2. Modify the **get** method in **RecipeResource** to serialize the **recipe** object into JSON format using the recipe schema:

    ```
    return recipe_schema.dump(recipe).data, HTTPStatus.OK
    ```

    This is mainly to modify the code to use **recipe_schema.dump(recipe).data** to return the recipe details by using the recipe schema.

3. Right-click on it to run the application. Flask will then be started up and run on the localhost (**127.0.0.1**) at port **5000**:

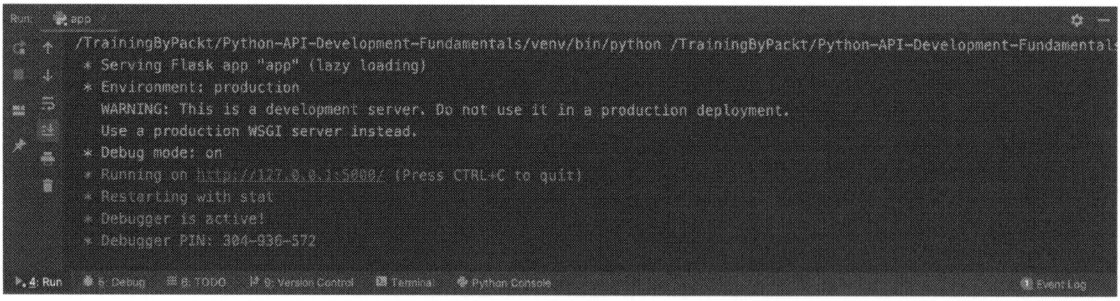

Figure 5.18: Run Flask on the localhost

4. Test the implementation by getting one specific published recipe in Postman. Select the **GET Recipe** request. Enter **http://localhost:5000/recipes/4** in **Enter request URL**. Click **Send** to get specific recipe details. The result is shown in the following screenshot:

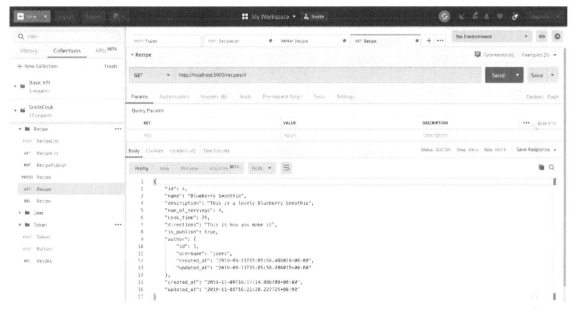

Figure 5.19: Select the GET Recipe request and send the request

You will then see the return response. The HTTP status code **200 OK** here indicates that the request has succeeded. In the response body, we can get the recipe details with ID 4, and as you can see, you can also see the user's registration time, which is **created_at**.

Chapter 06: Email Confirmations

Activity 9: Testing the Complete User Registration and Activation Workflow

Solution

1. We will first register a new user through Postman. Click on the **Collections** tab and choose the **POST UserList** request.

2. Select the **Body** tab and then select the **raw** radio button and choose **JSON (application/json)** from the drop-down list.

3. Put in the following user details (in JSON format) in the **Body** field. Change the username and password to the appropriate one:

```
{
    "username": "john",
    "email": "smilecook.api@gmail.com",
    "password": "Kwq2z5"
}
```

4. Send the request. You should see the following output:

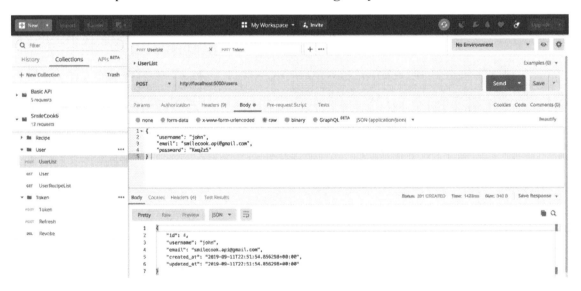

Figure 6.10: Registering a user through Postman

You should see the new user details (**ID = 4**) in the response, with **HTTP status 201 OK**. That means the new user was created successfully in the backend.

5. Log in through the API and click on the **Collections** tab. Then, select the **POST Token** request we created before.

6. Now, click on the **Body** tab. Check the **raw** radio button and select **JSON(application/json)** from the drop-down menu.

7. Type in the following JSON content (email and password) in the **Body** field:

```
{
    "email": "smilecook.api@gmail.com",
    "password": "Kwq2z5"
}
```

8. Send the request. You should see the following output:

Figure 6.11: Sending the request using JSON

You should get a message saying the user account is not activated yet, with **HTTP status 403 Forbidden**. This is expected behavior because our application would require the user to activate the account first.

9. Please check your mailbox for the activation email. There should be a link there for you to activate the user's account. Click on that link to activate the account. It should look as follows:

Figure 6.12: Activation mail

10. Log in again after the account is activated. Click on the **Collections** tab.

11. Select the **POST Token** request that we created earlier and send the request. You'll see the following:

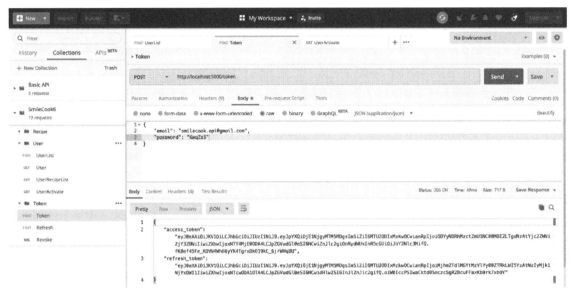

Figure 6.13: After activating the account, select the POST Token request

You should see the access token and the refresh token in the response, with HTTP status **200 OK**. That means the login was successful.

Activity 10: Creating the HTML Format User Account Activation Email

Solution

1. Click **Sending** >> **Overview** on the `Mailgun` dashboard, then add the email of our new user to the authorized recipient list on the right. `Mailgun` will then send a confirmation email to that email address:

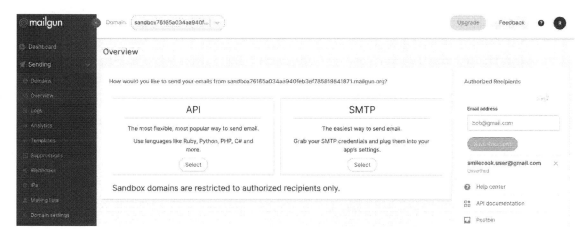

Figure 6.14: Sending a confirmation email to our new user

> **Note**
>
> Since we are using the sandbox version of **Mailgun**, there is a limitation on sending out emails to external email addresses. These emails have to be added to the authorized recipient list first.

2. Check the mailbox of the new user, and click **I Agree**. This will be as shown in the following screenshot:

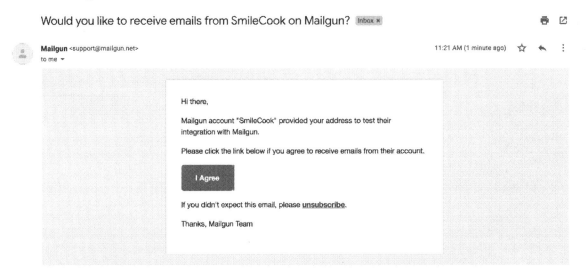

Figure 6.15: The mailbox of a new user with an email from Mailgun

3. On the confirmation page, click **yes** to activate the account. The screen will appear as follows:

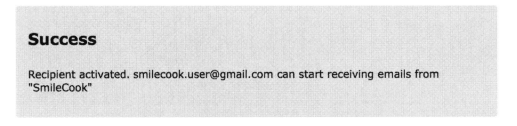

Figure 6.16: Activation complete message

4. HTML template code is provided by `Mailgun` out of the box. We can find it under **Sending > Templates**. There, click **Create Message Template** and select **Action template**. We will find a template for a confirmation email and preview it:

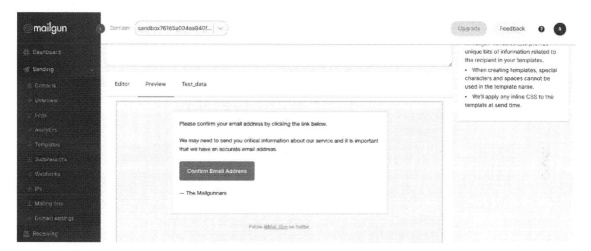

Figure 6.17: Previewing the confirm email address template

5. Then, create a **templates** folder under our project. We will put all the HTML templates in this folder going forward. Inside the **templates** folder, create a subfolder, **email**, for email-related HTML templates.

6. Now, create a template file, **confirmation.html**, and paste the sample HTML code from **Mailgun** in *step* 4. Take a look at the sample HTML code from **Mailgun** that follows:

Figure 6.18: Sample HTML code from Mailgun

> **Note**
>
> Please note that we need to change the http://www.mailgun.com link to **{{link}}**. This placeholder will be replaced programmatically with the account activation link.

7. Import the **render_template** function from Flask by entering the following line of code in **resources/user.py**:

```
from flask import request, url_for, render_template
```

8. In the **POST** method under **UserListResource**, we will pass in the HTML code as a parameter to the **send_mail** method. The HTML code can be rendered using the **render_template** function. You can see that the **link = link** parameter here is to replace the **{{link}}** placeholder in the HTML template with the actual account validation link:

```
mailgun.send_email(to=user.email,
                          subject=subject,
                          text=text,
                          html=render_template('email/confirmation.
html', link=link))
```

9. Register a new account using Postman:

```
{
    "username": "emily",
    "email": "smilecook.user@gmail.com",
    "password": "Wqb6g2"
}
```

> **Note**
>
> Please note that the email address was validated in **Mailgun** beforehand.

The output will be as follows:

Figure 6.19: Registering a new account using Postman

10. The account activation email will then be received in HTML format. The output is shown in the following screenshot:

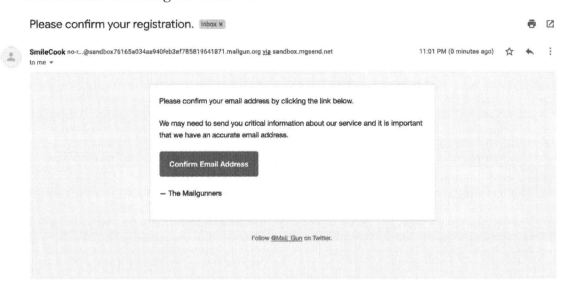

Figure 6.20: Account confirmation email

Chapter 07: Working with Images

Activity 11: Implementing the Recipe Cover Image Upload Function

Solution

1. Add the **cover_image** attribute to the User model in **models/recipe.py**:

    ```
    cover_image = db.Column(db.String(100), default=None)
    ```

    The **cover_image** attribute will contain the image filename as a string, with a maximum length of 100 characters.

2. Use the flask db migrate command to generate a database table update script:

    ```
    flask db migrate
    ```

    You will see that a new column, **'recipe.cover_image'**, has been detected:

    ```
    INFO  [alembic.runtime.migration] Context impl PostgresqlImpl.
    INFO  [alembic.runtime.migration] Will assume transactional DDL.
    INFO  [alembic.autogenerate.compare] Detected added column 'recipe.cover_
    image'
      Generating /TrainingByPackt/Python-API-Development-Fundamentals/
    Lesson07/smilecook/migrations/versions/91c7dc71b826_.py ... done
    ```

3. Check the script at **/migrations/versions/xxxxxxxxxx_.py**:

    ```
    """"empty message

    Revision ID: 91c7dc71b826
    Revises: 7aafe51af016
    Create Date: 2019-09-22 12:06:36.061632

    """
    from alembic import op
    import sqlalchemy as sa
    ```

```
# revision identifiers, used by Alembic.
revision = '91c7dc71b826'
down_revision = '7aafe51af016'
branch_labels = None
depends_on = None


def upgrade():
    # ### commands auto generated by Alembic - please adjust! ###
    op.add_column('recipe', sa.Column('cover_image',
sa.String(length=100), nullable=True))
    # ### end Alembic commands ###


def downgrade():
    # ### commands auto generated by Alembic - please adjust! ###
    op.drop_column('recipe', 'cover_image')
    # ### end Alembic commands ###
```

From its content, we can see that two functions have been generated in the script. The **upgrade** function is used to add the new **cover_image** column to the database table, while the **downgrade** function is used to remove the **cover_image** column so that it goes back to its original state.

4. Run the **flask db upgrade** command to update the database and reflect the change in the **User** model:

```
flask db upgrade
```

After running the preceding command, we should see the following output:

```
INFO  [alembic.runtime.migration] Context impl PostgresqlImpl.
INFO  [alembic.runtime.migration] Will assume transactional DDL.
INFO  [alembic.runtime.migration] Running upgrade 7aafe51af016 ->
91c7dc71b826, empty message
```

5. Check the new **cover_image** column in pgAdmin:

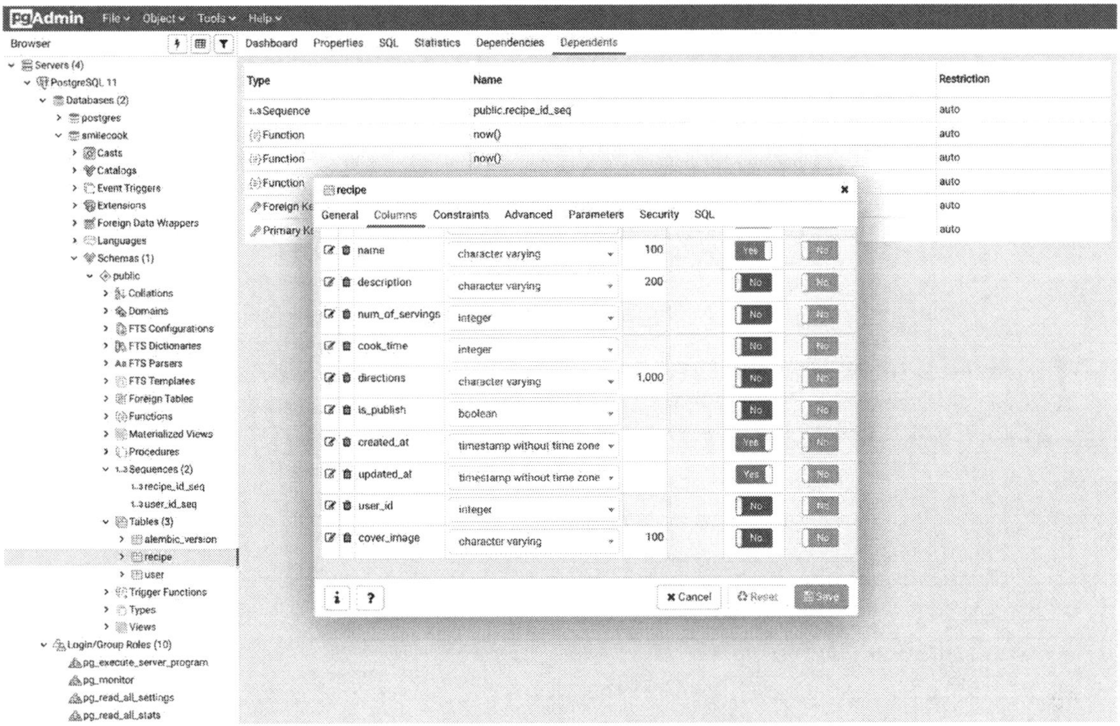

Figure 7.10: The cover_image column in pgAdmin

This confirms that the new **cover_image** column has been added to the recipe table.

6. In **schemas/recipe.py**, import the **url_for** package and add the **cover_url** attribute and the **dump_cover_url** method:

```
from flask import url_for


cover_url = fields.Method(serialize='dump_cover_url')


def dump_cover_url(self, recipe):
    if recipe.cover_image:
        return url_for('static', filename='images/recipes/{}'.
format(recipe.cover_image), _external=True)
    else:
        return url_for('static', filename='images/assets/default-
recipe-cover.jpg', _external=True)
```

Add the **default-recipe-cover.jpg** image to **static/images**:

Figure 7.11: Folder structure after adding default-recipe-cover.jpg

7. In **resources/recipe.py**, add the import **os**, **image_set**, and **save_image** functions:

```
import os

from extensions import image_set

from utils import save_image
In resources/recipe.py, add recipe_cover_schema, which just shows the
cover_url column:
recipe_cover_schema = RecipeSchema(only=('cover_url', ))
```

8. In **resources/recipe.py**, add the **RecipeCoverUpload** resource to upload the recipe cover to the recipes folder:

```
class RecipeCoverUploadResource(Resource):

    @jwt_required
    def put(self, recipe_id):

        file = request.files.get('cover')

        if not file:
            return {'message': 'Not a valid image'}, HTTPStatus.BAD_
REQUEST

        if not image_set.file_allowed(file, file.filename):
            return {'message': 'File type not allowed'}, HTTPStatus.
BAD_REQUEST
```

The **@jwt_required** decorator before the **PUT** method states that the method can only be called after the user logs in. In the **PUT** method, we are trying to get the cover image file in **request.files**. Then, we are trying to verify whether it exists and whether the file extension is permitted.

9. After that, we retrieved the recipe object using **recipe_id**. First, we check whether a user has the right to modify the recipe. If the user has the right to, we will go ahead and modify the cover image of the recipe:

```
recipe = Recipe.get_by_id(recipe_id=recipe_id)

if recipe is None:
    return {'message': 'Recipe not found'}, HTTPStatus.NOT_
FOUND

current_user = get_jwt_identity()

if current_user != recipe.user_id:
    return {'message': 'Access is not allowed'}, HTTPStatus.
FORBIDDEN

if recipe.cover_image:
    cover_path = image_set.path(folder='recipes',
filename=recipe.cover_image)
    if os.path.exists(cover_path):
        os.remove(cover_path)
```

10. Then, we use the **save_image** function to save the uploaded image and set the **recipe.cover_image = filename**. Finally, we save the recipe using **recipe.save()** and return the image URL with an HTTP status code of **200**:

```
filename = save_image(image=file, folder='recipes')

recipe.cover_image = filename
recipe.save()

return recipe_cover_schema.dump(recipe).data, HTTPStatus.OK
```

11. In **app.py**, import RecipeCoverUploadResource:

```
from resources.recipe import RecipeListResource, RecipeResource,
RecipePublishResource, RecipeCoverUploadResource
```

12. In **app.py**, link **RecipeCoverUploadResource** to the route, that is, **/recipes/<int:recipe_id>/cover**:

```
api.add_resource(RecipeCoverUploadResource, '/recipes/<int:recipe_id>/
cover')
```

Now, we have created the function for uploading the recipe cover image. Let's move on and test it.

Activity 12: Testing the Image Upload Function

Solution

1. Log in to the user account using Postman. Click on the **Collections** tab and select the **POST Token** request. Then, click the **Send** button. The result can be seen in the following screenshot:

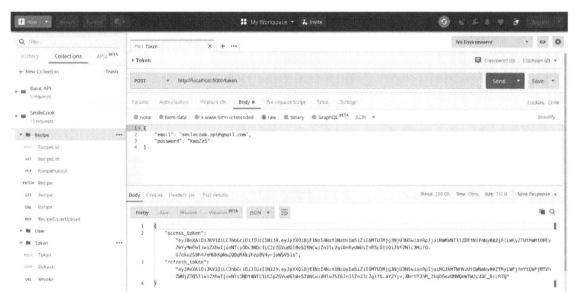

Figure 7.12: Sending a POST Token request

2. Send a client request to our API to create a recipe and click on the **Collections** tab.

3. Select the **POST RecipeList** request and put `Authorization` in the **KEY** field and `Bearer {token}` in the **VALUE** field, where the token is the access token we retrieved in the previous step. Then, click the **Send** button. The result can be seen in the following screenshot:

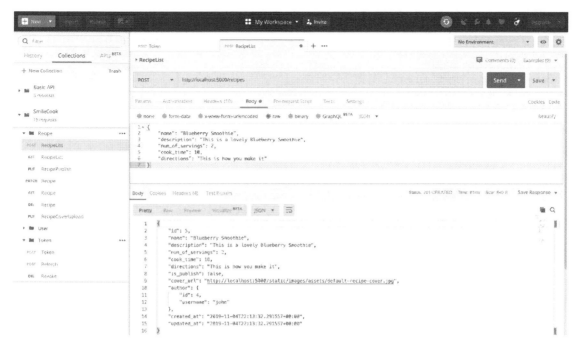

Figure 7.13: Sending a client request to our API to create a recipe

4. Upload the recipe images. Click on the **Collections** tab and right-click on **...** next to the `Recipe` folder to create a new request.

5. Set the **Request Name** to `RecipeCoverUpload` and save it in the `Recipe` folder.

6. Select **PUT** as the HTTP method and type in `http://localhost:5000/recipes/<recipe_id>/cover` as the request URL (replace `<recipe_id>` with the recipe ID we got from the previous step).

7. Select the **Headers** tab and put `Authorization` in the **KEY** field and `Bearer {token}` in the **VALUE** field, where the token is the access token we retrieved in the previous step.

8. Select the **Body** tab. Then, select the form-data radio button and type cover into **KEY**.

9. Choose **File** in the drop-down menu next to **KEY** and select the image file to upload.

10. Click the **Save** button and then the **Send** button. The result can be seen in the following screenshot:

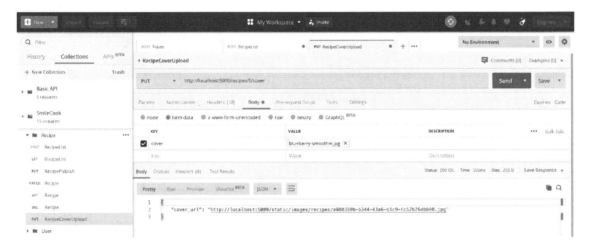

Figure 7.14: Uploading a recipe image

11. Check whether the image has been compressed in PyCharm. We can see from the application log in PyCharm that the file size has been reduced by **97%**:

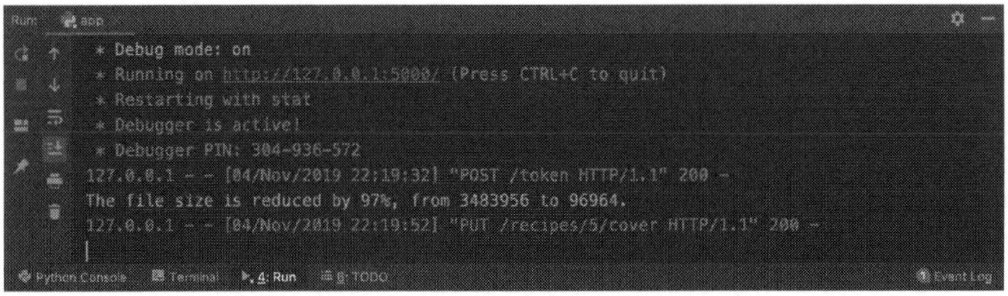

Figure 7.15: Checking whether the images are compressed in PyCharm

12. Check the uploaded image in **static/images/recipes**:

Figure 7.16: Checking the uploaded image in the path

13. Get the recipe back and confirm that the **cover_url** attribute is populated. Now, click on the **Collections** tab and select the **GET Recipe** request. Then, type **http://localhost:5000/recipes/5** into the **URL** field. You may replace the recipe ID, that is, 5, with any ID that is appropriate. Then, click the **Send** button. The result can be seen in the following screenshot:

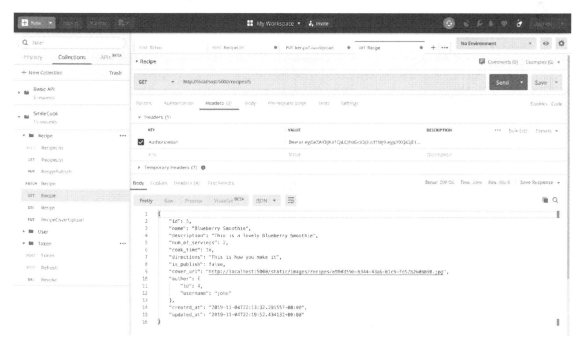

Figure 7.17: Getting the recipe back and confirming that the cover_url attribute is populated

Congratulations! We have tested the recipe cover image upload function. It works great!

Chapter 08: Pagination, Searching, and Ordering

Activity 13: Implementing Pagination on the User-Specific Recipe Retrieval API

Solution

1. Modify the code in the **get_all_by_user** method under **models/recipe.py**, as follows:

    ```
    @classmethod
    def get_all_by_user(cls, user_id, page, per_page,
    visibility='public'):

        query = cls.query.filter_by(user_id=user_id)

        if visibility == 'public':
            query = cls.query.filter_by(user_id=user_id, is_publish=True)
        elif visibility == 'private':
            query = cls.query.filter_by(user_id=user_id, is_publish=False)

        return query.order_by(desc(cls.created_at)).paginate(page=page,
    per_page=per_page)
    ```

2. Import **RecipePaginationSchema** into **resources/user.py**:

    ```
    from schemas.recipe import RecipeSchema, RecipePaginationSchema
    ```

3. Declare the **recipe_pagination_schema** attribute in **resources/user.py**:

    ```
    recipe_pagination_schema = RecipePaginationSchema()
    ```

4. Here, we've added the **@user_kwargs** decorator to **UserRecipeListResource.get**. It takes a few parameters, including **page**, **per_page**, and **visibility**:

    ```
    class UserRecipeListResource(Resource):

        @jwt_optional
        @use_kwargs({'page': fields.Int(missing=1),
                     'per_page': fields.Int(missing=10),
                     'visibility': fields.Str(missing='public')})
    ```

5. Modify the **UserRecipeListResource.get** method in **resources/user.py**:

```python
def get(self, username, page, per_page, visibility):

    user = User.get_by_username(username=username)

    if user is None:
        return {'message': 'User not found'}, HTTPStatus.NOT_FOUND

    current_user = get_jwt_identity()

    if current_user == user.id and visibility in ['all', 'private']:
        pass
    else:
        visibility = 'public'

    paginated_recipes = Recipe.get_all_by_user(user_id=user.id,
page=page, per_page=per_page, visibility=visibility)

    return recipe_pagination_schema.dump(paginated_recipes).data,
HTTPStatus.OK
```

The **Recipe.get_all_by_user** method gets the paginated recipes by a particular author, and then lets **recipe_pagination_schema** serialize the paginated object and return it.

Activity 14: Testing Pagination on the User-Specific Recipe Retrieval API

Solution

1. Get all the recipes under John using Postman, page by page, with a page size of two. First, click on the **UserRecipeList** request.

2. Type **http://localhost:5000/{username}/recipes** into the **Request** URL. The **{username}** here should be the same as the one we inserted in the previous exercise. In our case, it will be **john**.

3. Select the **Params** tab and put in the key-value pair (**per_page**, **2**).

4. Send the request. The result is shown in the following screenshot:

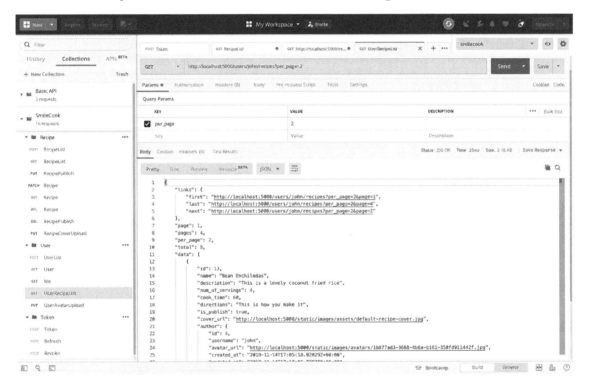

Figure 8.9: Getting all the recipes under John using Postman

In the details of the recipe, we can see that there are links with the URLs of the **first**, **last**, and **next** pages. We can't see the **prev** page here because we are on the first page. There is a total of four pages, and we have two records per page. We can also see the sorted recipe details in the HTTP response.

5. Click the next URL in links to query for the next two records in Postman with the request URL populated (**http://localhost:5000/users/john/recipes?per_page=2&page=2**). Then, we just need to click on **Send** to send the request. The result is shown in the following screenshot:

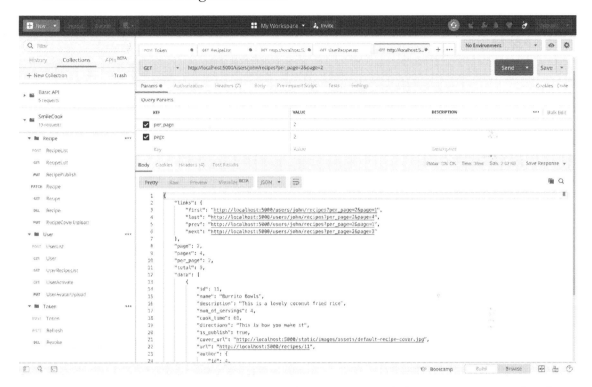

Figure 8.10: Querying for the next two records in Postman with the request URL populated

From the result, we can see that there are links to the **first**, **last**, **next**, and **prev** pages. We can also see that we are currently on page two. All the recipe data is there as well.

Activity 15: Searching for Recipes with Specific Ingredients

Solution

1. First, in **models/recipe.py**, add the **ingredients** attribute to the **Recipe** model:

   ```
   ingredients = db.Column(db.String(1000))
   ```

2. Run the following command to generate a database migration script:

   ```
   flask db migrate
   ```

   You will see that a new column called **recipe.ingredients** has been detected:

   ```
   INFO  [alembic.autogenerate.compare] Detected added column 'recipe.
   ingredients'
     Generating /TrainingByPackt/Python-API-Development-Fundamentals/
   smilecook/migrations/versions/0876058ed87e_.py ... done
   ```

3. Check the content in **/migrations/versions/0876058ed87e_.py**, which is the database migration script that was generated in the previous step:

   ```
   """empty message

   Revision ID: 0876058ed87e
   Revises: 91c7dc71b826
   Create Date: 2019-10-24 15:05:10.936752

   """
   from alembic import op
   import sqlalchemy as sa

   # revision identifiers, used by Alembic.
   revision = '0876058ed87e'
   down_revision = '91c7dc71b826'
   branch_labels = None
   depends_on = None

   def upgrade():
       # ### commands auto generated by Alembic - please adjust! ###
       op.add_column('recipe', sa.Column('ingredients',
   sa.String(length=1000), nullable=True))
       # ### end Alembic commands ###
   ```

```
def downgrade():
    # ### commands auto-generated by Alembic - please adjust! ###
    op.drop_column('recipe', 'ingredients')
    # ### end Alembic commands ###
```

Here, we can see that two functions have been generated in the script. The **upgrade** function is used to add the new column, **ingredients**, to the recipe table, whereas the **downgrade** function is used to remove the **ingredients** column so that it goes back to its original state.

4. Run the following **flask db upgrade** command to update the database schema:

```
flask db upgrade
```

You will see the following output:

```
INFO  [alembic.runtime.migration] Context impl PostgresqlImpl.
INFO  [alembic.runtime.migration] Will assume transactional DDL.
INFO  [alembic.runtime.migration] Running upgrade 91c7dc71b826 ->
0876058ed87e, empty message
```

5. In **schemas/recipe.py**, add the **ingredients** attribute to **RecipeSchema**:

```
ingredients = fields.String(validate=[validate.Length(max=1000)])
```

6. Modify the **RecipeResource.patch** method in **resources/recipe.py** to be able to update **ingredients**:

```
recipe.ingredients = data.get('ingredients') or recipe.ingredients
```

7. Modify the **Recipe.get_all_published** method in **models/recipe.py** so that it gets all the published recipes that it can through the ingredients:

```
return cls.query.filter(or_(cls.name.ilike(keyword),
                cls.description.ilike(keyword),
                cls.ingredients.ilike(keyword)),
            cls.is_publish.is_(True)).\
    order_by(sort_logic).paginate(page=page, per_page=per_page)
```

8. **Right-click** on it to run the application. Flask will then start up and run on **local-host (127.0.0.1)** at port **5000**:

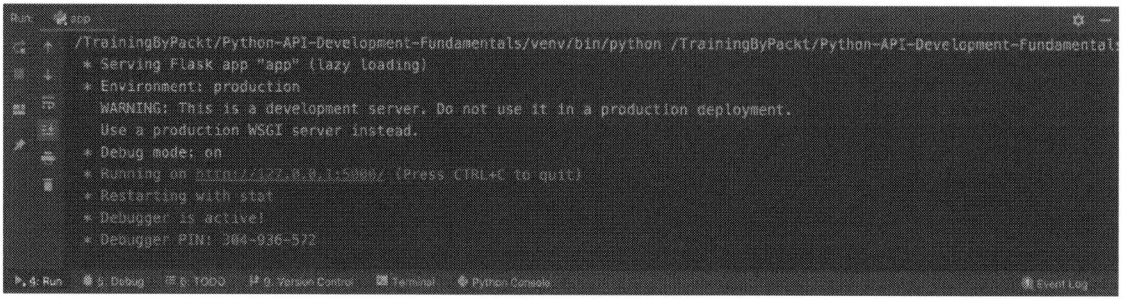

Figure 8.11: Running Flask on the localhost

9. Log in to a user account and create two recipes by running the following **httpie** command in the PyCharm console. The **{token}** placeholder should be replaced with the access token:

```
http POST localhost:5000/recipes "Authorization: Bearer {token}"
name="Sweet Potato Casserole" description="This is a lovely Sweet Potato
Casserole" num_of_servings=12 cook_time=60 ingredients="4 cups sweet
potato, 1/2 cup white sugar, 2 eggs, 1/2 cup milk" directions="This is how
you make it"

http POST localhost:5000/recipes "Authorization: Bearer {token}"
name="Pesto Pizza" description="This is a lovely Pesto Pizza" num_of_
servings=6 cook_time=20 ingredients="1 pre-baked pizza crust, 1/2 cup
pesto, 1 ripe tomato" directions="This is how you make it"
```

10. Publish these two recipes by using the following **httpie** command:

```
http PUT localhost:5000/recipes/14/publish "Authorization: Bearer {token}"
http PUT localhost:5000/recipes/15/publish "Authorization: Bearer {token}"
```

11. Search for recipes that contain the **eggs** string in the name, description, or ingredients. Click on the **RecipeList** request and select the **Params** tab. Then, insert the first key-value pair (**q**, **eggs**) and send the request. The result is shown in the following screenshot:

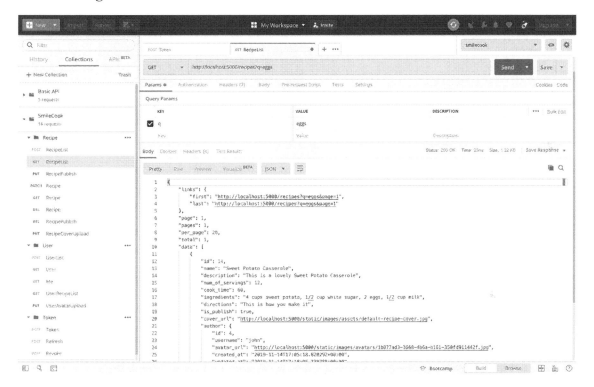

Figure 8.12: Searching for the eggs ingredient by sending a request

From the preceding search result, we can see that there is a recipe with eggs in the ingredients.

Chapter 09: Building More Features

Activity 16: Getting Cache Data after Updating Recipe Details

Solution

1. Get all the recipe data back, click on **RecipeList** and send the request. The result is shown in the following screenshot:

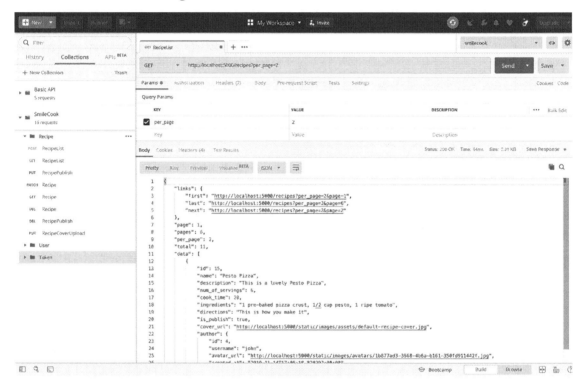

Figure 9.15: Get the recipe data back and send the request

2. Log in to your account, click on the **Collections** tab and select the **POST Token** request. Then, send the request. The result is shown in the following screenshot:

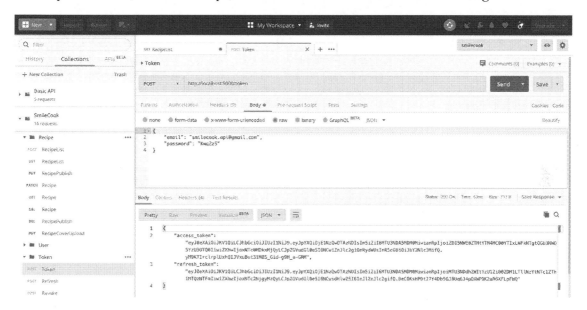

Figure 9.16: Select the POST Token request and send it

3. Modify a recipe record using the **PATCH** method. First, select the **PATCH Recipe** request.

4. Now select the **Headers** tab and modify **Bearer {token}**; the token should be the access token.

5. Select the **Body** tab and modify **num_of_servings** to **5**, and **cook_time** to **50**:

```
{
    "num_of_servings": 5,
    "cook_time": 50
}
```

6. Send the request. The result is shown in the following screenshot:

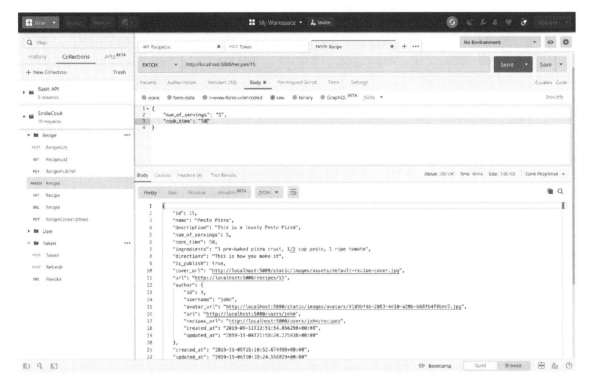

Figure 9.17: Modifying a recipe record using the PATCH method

7. Get all the recipe data back again, click on **RecipeList**.

8. Send the request. The result is shown in the following screenshot:

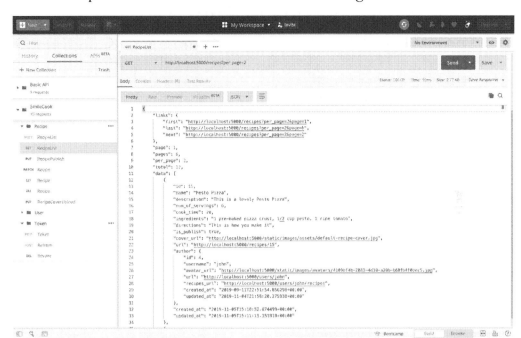

Figure 9.18: Get all the recipe data back again

We can see that when we get all the recipe details again, the details are not updated, which will cause the user to see the wrong information.

Activity 17: Adding Multiple Rate-Limit Restrictions

Solution

1. In **resources/user.py**, import **limiter** from **extensions**:

   ```
   from extensions import image_set, limiter
   ```

2. In **UserRecipeListResource**, put the **limiter.limit** function in the **decorators** attribute:

   ```
   class UserRecipeListResource (Resource):
       decorators = [limiter.limit('3/minute;30/hour;300/day',
   methods=['GET'], error_message='Too Many Requests')]
   ```

3. Comment out the whitelist in **app.py**:

   ```
   #  @limiter.request_filter
   #  def ip_whitelist():
   #      return request.remote_addr == '127.0.0.1'
   ```

In PyCharm, to comment out a line of code, if you are using Mac, you can use *Command + /*, and if you are using Windows, you can use *Ctrl + /*.

4. When we are done, click **Run** to start the Flask application; then, we are ready to test it:

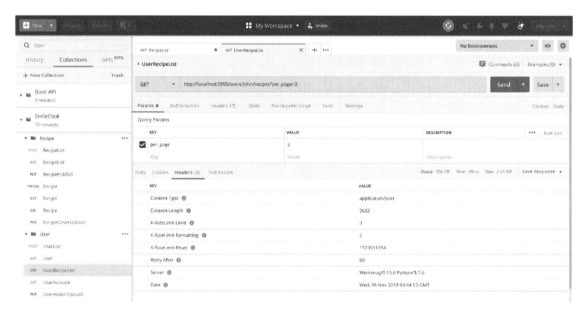

Figure 9.19: Starting the Flask application

5. Get all the recipes for a user and check the rate limit information in the response header. First, click on `UserRecipeList` and send the request.

6. Then, select the **Header** tab in **Response**. The result is shown in the following screenshot:

Figure 9.20: Checking the rate limit information in the response header

In the HTTP response, we can see that the rate limit for this endpoint is three, while we only have two remaining request quotas. The limit is going to be reset in 60 seconds.

Chapter 10: Deployment

Activity 18: Changing access_token to a Variable in Postman

Solution

1. Perform user login and get the access token. Use the **POST Token** request to get the access token. You should see the following output:

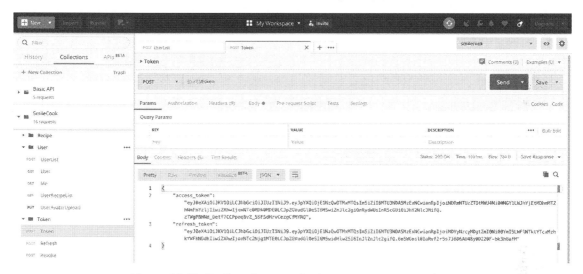

Figure 10.29: Performing user login to get an access token

2. Click **Manage environments** in the top right-hand corner in Postman. Create the **access_token** variable. The value is the access token we obtained in the previous step. Then, click **Update**:

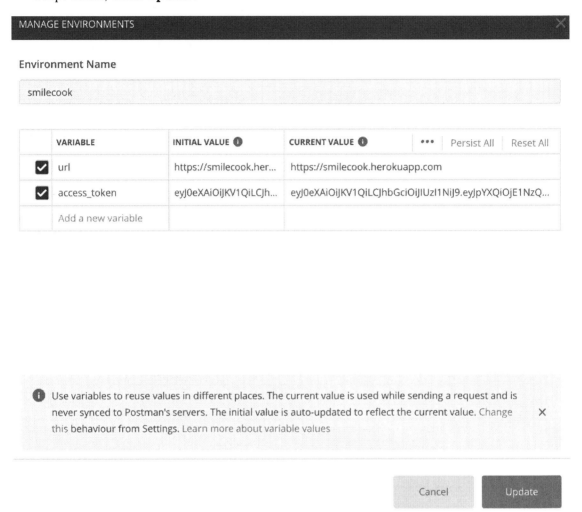

Figure 10.30: Adding more environment variables in Postman

3. Select the **GET User** request. In the **Headers** tab, change the **Authorization** value to `Bearer {{access_token}}`, which is the environment variable we added in the previous step, and then send the request. You should see the following output:

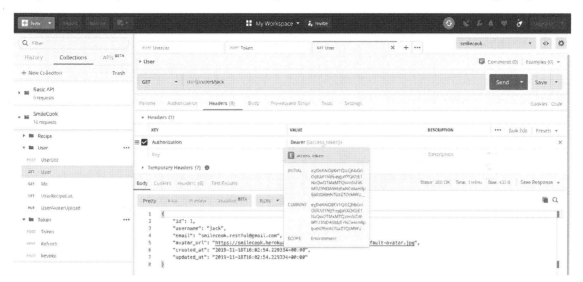

Figure 10.31: Using more environment variables in Postman

Index

Made in the USA
Coppell, TX
03 June 2021